Teaching the New English

Published in association with the English :
Director: Ben Knights

Teaching the New English is an innovative
English degree in universities in the UK and elsewhere. The series add
developing areas of the curriculum as well as more traditional areas that are reforming
in new contexts. Although the Series is grounded in intellectual and theoretical concepts of the curriculum, it is concerned with the practicalities of classroom teaching.
The volumes will be invaluable for new and more experienced teachers alike.

Titles include:

Gail Ashton and Louise Sylvester (*editors*)
TEACHING CHAUCER

Heather Beck (*editor*)
TEACHING CREATIVE WRITING

Richard Bradford (*editor*)
TEACHING THEORY

Charles Butler (*editor*)
TEACHING CHILDREN'S FICTION

Ailsa Cox (*editor*)
TEACHING THE SHORT STORY

Robert Eaglestone and Barry Langford (*editors*)
TEACHING HOLOCAUST LITERATURE AND FILM

Michael Hanrahan and Deborah L. Madsen (*editors*)
TEACHING, TECHNOLOGY, TEXTUALITY
Approaches to New Media and the New English

David Higgins and Sharon Ruston (*editors*)
TEACHING ROMANTICISM

Andrew Hiscock and Lisa Hopkins (*editors*)
TEACHING SHAKESPEARE AND EARLY MODERN DRAMATISTS

Lesley Jeffries and Dan McIntyre (*editors*)
TEACHING STYLISTICS

Andrew Maunder and Jennifer Phegley (*editors*)
TEACHING NINETEENTH-CENTURY FICTION

Peter Middleton and Nicky Marsh (*editors*)
TEACHING MODERNIST POETRY

Anna Powell and Andrew Smith (*editors*)
TEACHING THE GOTHIC

Andy Sawyer and Peter Wright (*editors*)
TEACHING SCIENCE FICTION

Fiona Tolan and Alice Ferrebe (*editors*)
TEACHING GENDER

Gina Wisker (*editor*)
TEACHING AFRICAN AMERICAN WOMEN'S WRITING

Teaching the New English
Series Standing Order ISBN 978–1–403–94441–2 Hardback
978–1–403–94442–9 Paperback
(*outside North America only*)

You can receive future titles in this series as they are published by placing a stand-ing order. Please contact your bookseller or, in case of difficulty, write to us at the address below with your name and address, the title of the series and the ISBN quoted above.

Customer Services Department, Macmillan Distribution Ltd, Houndmills, Basingstoke, Hampshire RG21 6XS, England

Teaching Creative Writing

Edited by

Heather Beck
Senior Lecturer in Creative Writing,
Manchester Metropolitan University, UK

First published 2012 by
PALGRAVE MACMILLAN

Palgrave Macmillan in the UK is an imprint of Macmillan Publishers Limited,
registered in England, company number 785998, of Houndmills, Basingstoke,
Hampshire RG21 6XS.

Palgrave Macmillan in the US is a division of St Martin's Press LLC,
175 Fifth Avenue, New York, NY 10010.

Palgrave Macmillan is the global academic imprint of the above companies
and has companies and representatives throughout the world.

Palgrave® and Macmillan® are registered trademarks in the United States,
the United Kingdom, Europe and other countries.

ISBN 978–0–230–24007–0   hardback
ISBN 978–0–230–24008–7   paperback

This book is printed on paper suitable for recycling and made from fully
managed and sustained forest sources. Logging, pulping and manufacturing
processes are expected to conform to the environmental regulations of the
country of origin.

A catalogue record for this book is available from the British Library.

A catalog record for this book is available from the Library of Congress.

10 9 8 7 6 5 4 3 2 1
21 20 19 18 17 16 15 14 13 12

Printed and bound in Great Britain by
CPI Antony Rowe, Chippenham and Eastbourne

Contents

Series Editor's Preface

One of many exciting achievements of the early years of the English Subject Centre was the agreement with Palgrave Macmillan to initiate the series 'Teaching the New English'. The intention of the then Director, Professor Philip Martin, was to create a series of short and accessible books which would take widely-taught curriculum fields (or, as in the case of learning technologies, approaches to the whole curriculum) and articulate the connections between scholarly knowledge and the demands of teaching.

Since its inception, 'English' has been committed to what we know by the portmanteau phrase 'learning and teaching'. Yet, by and large, university teachers of English – in Britain at all events – find it hard to make their tacit pedagogic knowledge conscious, or to raise it to a level where it might be critiqued, shared or developed. In the experience of the English Subject Centre, colleagues find it relatively easy to talk about curriculum and resources, but far harder to talk about the success or failure of seminars, how to vary forms of assessment, or to make imaginative use of Virtual Learning Environments. Too often this reticence means falling back on received assumptions about student learning, about teaching, or about forms of assessment. At the same time, colleagues are often suspicious of the insights and methods arising from generic educational research. The challenge for the English group of disciplines is therefore to articulate ways in which our own subject knowledge and ways of talking might themselves refresh debates about pedagogy. The implicit invitation of this series is to take fields of knowledge and survey them through a pedagogic lens. Research and scholarship, and teaching and learning are part of the same process, not two separate domains.

'Teachers', people used to say, 'are born not made'. There may, after all, be some tenuous truth in this: there may be generosities of spirit (or, alternatively, drives for didactic control) laid down in earliest childhood.

But why should we assume that even 'born' teachers (or novelists, or nurses or veterinary surgeons) do not need to learn the skills of their trade? Amateurishness about teaching has far more to do with university claims to status, than with evidence about how people learn. There is a craft to shaping and promoting learning. This series of books is dedicated to the development of the craft of teaching within English Studies.

Ben Knights
Teaching the New English series editor
Director, English Subject Centre,
Higher Education Academy

The English Subject Centre

Founded in 2000, the English Subject Centre (which is based at Royal Holloway, University of London) is part of the subject network of the Higher Education Academy. Its purpose is to develop learning and teaching across the English disciplines in UK Higher Education. To this end it engages in research and publication (web and print), hosts events and conferences, sponsors projects, and engages in day-to-day dialogue with its subject communities. www.english.heacademy.ac.uk.

Notes on Contributors

Heather Beck is Senior Lecturer at Manchester Metropolitan University's Writing School where she established an online MA in Creative Writing in 2001. Her main writing interests are short stories and novels, including *Home is Where* (2003).

Rachel Blau DuPlessis is a poet-critic and Professor at Temple University in Philadelphia. Her poetry, *Drafts*, started in 1986, is collected in *Torques: Drafts 58–76* (2007) and in other instalments from Wesleyan and Salt. She has written *Blue Studios: Poetry and Its Cultural Work* (2006) and *The Pink Guitar: Writing as Feminist Practice* (2006) and *Genders, Races, and Religious Cultures in Modern American Poetry, 1908–1934* (2001). Her work can be accessed on PENNSound, and her website is wings.buffalo.edu/epc/authors/duplessis.

Mary Cantrell is an Associate Professor of English at Tulsa Community College and a long-time fiction editor for *Nimrod Literary Journal*. Her creative work has been published in *Mochilla Review, Iowa Women* and *Big Muddy*. She has published several articles on Creative Writing pedagogy including, 'Teaching and Evaluation: Why Bother?' (*The Authority Project: Power and Identity in the Creative Writing Classroom*, 2005) and with Anna Leahy and Mary Swandor, 'Theories of Creativity and Creative Writing Pedagogy' (*The Creative Writing Handbook*, 2007).

Jon Cook teaches at the University of East Anglia where he is Professor of Literature, Dean of Faculty for Arts and Humanities and Director of the Centre for Creative and Performing Arts. He was convenor of the MA in Creative Writing at the University of East Anglia from 1986 to 1996. His recent publications include *Poetry in Theory* (2004) and *Hazlitt in Love* (2005). He is a member of the AHRC Peer Review College and a Literature Advisor to the British Council.

Tony Curtis is Professor of Poetry at the University of Glamorgan where he leads the M.Phil. in Writing. He has published over thirty books of poetry, criticism, anthologies and art commentary. His most recent collection was *Crossing Over* (2007) He is a Fellow of the Royal Society of Literature.

Steven Earnshaw is Professor and Head of English at Sheffield Hallam University. A former course leader of Hallam's MA in Writing, he is the editor of *The Handbook of Creative Writing* (2007) which includes his essay, 'The Writer as Artist'. Other publications include *Beginning Realism* (forthcoming) and *Existentialism: a Guide for the Perplexed* (2006). He is also founder of the arts and literature e-zine, *Proof*.

Maureen Freely is a Senior Lecturer at the University of Warwick. She is a writer, journalist and translator and a member of English PEN. She has also taught Creative Writing at the University of Florida, the University of Texas and at Oxford since 1984. Her freelance work appears in major newspapers such as the *Guardian*, the *Observer*, the *Daily Telegraph*, and the *Independent on Sunday*. She has published several novels: *Mother's Helper* (1979), *The Life of the Party* (1985), *The Stork Club* (1991), *Under the Vulcania* (1994), *The Other Rebecca* (1996) and *Enlightenment* (2007).

Katharine Haake is Professor and Chair of the Creative Writing programme at California State University, Northridge. She has published novels and short stories and her fiction is recognized by Pushcart Prize nominations, distinguished story recognitions from Best American Short Story and Best of the West. She is author of the Creative Writing pedagogy book, *What Our Speech Disrupts: Feminism and Creative Writing* (2000) and she edited with Hans Ostrom and Wendy Bishop, the pedagogy book *Metro: Journeys in Creative Writing* (2001).

Graeme Harper is Professor of Creative Writing and Director of Research (College of Arts and Humanities) at Bangor University, Wales. He is a member of the AHRC Peer Panel, AHRC Peer College and AHRC National Steering Committee of Practice-led Research. He is Editor-in-Chief of the journal, *New Writing: the International Journal for the Practice and Theory of Creative Writing*. He has edited several Creative Writing pedagogy books, including *Teaching Creative Writing* (2006), *The Creative Writing Guidebook* (2008), and with Jeri Kroll, *Creative Writing Studies: Research, Practice and Pedagogy* (2008). He publishes fiction under the name of Brooke Biaz.

Gary Hawkins is Director of the Undergraduate Writing Program and Director of First-Year Seminars at Warren Wilson College, Asheville, North Carolina. He is a poet and essayist. His work – poems, criticism, pedagogy – has appeared in the *Virginia Quarterly Review*, the *Emily Dickinson Journal*, *American Book Review*, the *Hardy Review*, and *Encountering* Disgrace: *Reading and Teaching Coetzee's Novel*. A collaborator on *Artefact*, a recurrent letter-press anthology of poetry and beauty, he lives in Black Mountain, North Carolina with his poet-artist wife.

Robin Hemley is Director of the Nonfiction Writing Program at The University of Iowa. He has published seven books of nonfiction and fiction and with Michael Martone co-edited the anthology, *Extreme Fiction: Fabulists and Formalists* (2004). His fiction awards include the Nelsen Algren Award from *The Chicago Tribune*, the George Garrett Award for Fiction from *Willowsprings*, the Hugh J. Luke Award from *Prairie Schooner* and two Pushcart Prizes. He was Editor-in-Chief of *Bellingham Review* for five years.

DeWitt Henry is Professor of Writing, Literature and Publishing at Emerson College in Boston. He is the author of *Safe Suicide*, and *The Marriage of Anna Maye Potts* (winner of the inaugural Peter Taylor Prize for the Novel). The founding editor of *Ploughshares*, he has also edited several anthologies, including, *Sorrow's Company: Writers on Loss and Grief*.

Kim Lasky recently completed a Ph.D. in Creative and Critical Writing at Sussex University, considering the relationship between poetry and critical theory. She has taught on both undergraduate and postgraduate Creative Writing programmes, and her poems have been published in magazines such as *Agenda*, *Seam* and *The Frogmore Papers*, and the pamphlet, 'What it Means to Fall' (2006). She is currently working on a collection of poems inspired by science, informed in part by a residency in the Physics and Astronomy Department at Sussex.

Anna Leahy teaches on the BFA and MFA programs at Chapman University, California. Her poetry collection, *Constituents of Matter* (2007) won the Wick Poetry Prize, and she has published two chapbooks. She edited *Power and Identity in the Creative Writing Classroom* (2007), and her essays on Creative Writing pedagogy appear in *The Handbook of Creative Writing* (2007) and *Can It Really Be Taught?* (2007).

Steve May is Head of Department, Creative Studies, at Bath Spa University and Vice Chair of the National Association of Writers in Higher Education Committee. He has won awards for drama, poetry and fiction. His fiftieth play for radio, *Horizon*, was broadcast on BBC Radio 4 in 2008, and his book for students, *Doing Creative Writing*, was published in 2007.

Graham Mort is a Senior Lecturer in Creative Writing at Lancaster University. He has published *Visibility: New & Selected Poems* (2007), and a book of short fiction, *Touch* (2010). He directs Lancaster's Centre for Transcultural Writing and Research and designs literature projects for the British Council in Africa. His research includes emergent African writing, Creative Writing pedagogy and original work in poetry, short fiction and radio.

Joseph Moxley is Professor of English at the University of South Florida. He has published numerous books, including *Creative Writing in America: Theory and Pedagogy* (1989). He developed *College Writing Online*, an interactive writing environment designed to serve the needs of most university level writing classes, and this has received the 2004 Computers and Composition Distinguished Book Award, which is the highest honour for a book in the field of Computers and Writing. He has received approximately $500,000 in research funding to support learning communities and new media scholarship.

David G. Myers teaches English at Texas A&M University. He is author of *The Elephants Teach: Creative Writing Since 1880* (2006). He has published essays and reviews in *Philosophy and Literature, Journal of the History of Ideas, Commentary, New Criterion, AWP Chronicle* and the *Sewanee Review*. With Paul Hedeen he co-edited the anthology *Unrelenting Readers: the New Post-Critics* (2003).

John A. Nieves teaches at the University of South Florida. His interests include online composition and wikis.

Stephen O'Connor teaches in the MFA programs of Columbia University and Sarah Lawrence. He is the author of *Rescue: Will My Name Be Shouted Out?* (2008) and *Orphan Train* (2008). His fiction and poetry have been published in *Poetry, Conjunctions, TriQuarterly, Threepenny Review, New England Review, The Missouri Review, The Quarterly* and the *Partisan Review*. His essays and journalism have appeared in *The New York Times, DoubleTake, The Nation, AGNI, The Chicago Tribune* and *The Boston Globe*.

Jena Osman is Associate Professor of English at Temple University, where she teaches in the graduate Creative Writing program. Her books of poetry include *The Character* (2009), *An Essay in Asterisks* (2009) and *The Network* (2009). She was a 2006 Pew Fellow in the Arts and has received grants from the National Endowment for the Arts, the New York Foundation for the Arts, and the Pennsylvania Council on the Arts.

Hans Ostrom is Dolliver NEH Professor of English at the University of Puget Sound. He is author of *The Coast Starlight: Collected Poems 1976–2006* (2006) and many other books. His Creative Writing pedagogy books edited with Wendy Bishop include *Rethinking Creative Writing and Pedagogy* (2002), *Colors of a Different Horse* (2004), *Genres and Writing: Issues Arguments and Alternatives* (2007), *The Subject is the Story* (2009), and with Wendy Bishop and Katharine Haake he has edited *Metro: Journeys in Writing Creatively* (2010). He is a member of the PEN/American Center.

Rob Pope is Professor of English at Oxford Brookes University where he is Director of Research Student Development and National Teaching Fellow. His publications include *Textual Intervention: Critical and Creative Strategies for Literary Studies* (1995), *The English Studies Book* (2002) and *Creativity: Theory, History and Practice* (2006). He is a regular keynote speaker and workshop programme organizer for the British Council.

Robert Sheppard is Professor of Poetry and Poetics at Edge Hill University, where he tutors the MA in Creative Writing. As a poet, he recently published *Complete Twentieth Century Blues* (2007), and *Warrant Error* (2008), and as a critic, *Iain Sinclair* (2010). He is the co-editor of the *Journal of British and Irish Innovative Poetry* and *Pages* at www.robertsheppard.blogspot.com.

Michael Symmons Roberts is Professor at Manchester Metropolitan's Writing School. His poetry has won the Whitbread Poetry Award and has been shortlisted for the Griffin International Poetry Prize, the Forward Prize, and twice for the T.S. Eliot Prize. His collaboration with composer James MacMillan has led to several productions. He also produces broadcast work and has published two novels.

Stephanie Vanderslice is an Associate Professor of Writing at the University of Central Arkansas. Her essays have been included in such books and journals as *Creative Writing Studies, Teaching Creative Writing* (2007) and *The Creative Writing Handbook* (2009). With Dr Kelly Ritter she edited *Can It Really Be Taught?: Resisting Lore in the Teaching of Creative Writing* (2010) and wrote *Teaching Creative Writing to Undergraduates: A Resource and Guide* (2010).

Michelene Wandor teaches at the University of Lancaster. She is an award-winning dramatist, poet and fiction writer, as well as a broadcaster, reviewer and critic. Her poetry collection, *Musica Transalpina* was a Poetry Book Society Recommendation for 2006. She has held a Royal Literary Fund Fellowship since 2004 and has published a Creative Writing pedagogy book, *The Author is Not Dead, Merely Somewhere Else: Creative Writing Reconceived* (Palgrave Macmillan, 2008).

Introduction

Heather Beck

Intended readership

This book is for those who would like to find out more about how Creative Writing is taught in Higher Education. This includes students learning more about Creative Writing pedagogy, as well as seasoned practitioners. This book is also for those not directly involved in learning and teaching Creative Writing but who are curious about the subject and wish to obtain a quick overview.

Rise of creative writing

As readers will see in the history chapters of this volume, Creative Writing has a long history in the USA, but it is still relatively new in the UK. The MA at the University of East Anglia was founded in 1970 with the prestige of Malcolm Bradbury. Creative Writing in Adult and Continuing Education was popular in the late 1970s (see O'Rourke, 2005).[1] Nonetheless Creative Writing was slow to expand into BA programmes. David Craig taught writing at Lancaster in the early 1970s. Sheffield Hallam taught modules from 1982 (see Monteith and Miles).[2] It was only in the mid to late 1990s, boosted by writing fellowships and writer-in-residence schemes that Creative Writing really took off in the UK (see Knights and Thurgar-Dawson).[3]

Scope and why this book is important

Creative Writing is now taught in some form or other at most institutions of Higher Education in the UK and USA as well as in the rest of the world, and there has been a long ongoing dialogue between countries as this process has unfolded. This is especially so between the UK and USA as is evident from pedagogy publications and international conferences. (See list of Further Readings at the end of this book for further examples.) In three main countries, national organizations have arisen to help Creative Writers working in Higher Education. These are the National Association of Writers in Education (NAWE) in the UK, the Association of Writers and Writing Programs in the USA (AWP) and the Australian Association of Writing Programmes (AAWP).[4] Recently in 2008, NAWE published a Creative Writing Benchmark that helps clarify why the discipline is important as well as what it entails. The discipline is important for numerous reasons including the following: it encourages divergent forms of thinking wherein the notion of being 'correct' gives ways to broader issues of value. That is, most importantly, Creative Writing encourages the capacity to see the world from different perspectives and the study of Creative Writing thus involves a commitment to improve the quality of one's own and others' cultural experiences (see NAWE Creative Writing Benchmark).

While ideally, this book could include chapters from all over the world, given space limitations, as well as an interest in the ongoing dialogue between the UK and USA in Creative Writing, the book limits itself to the scope of these two countries. Where possible, in each of its parts chapters are divided equally between the UK and USA. The book itself is important in contributing to an ongoing dialogue between the UK and USA for the following three reasons:

1. it furthers knowledge and understanding of creative writing;
2. it supports good practice in teaching and learning at all levels in higher education;
3. it also encourages discussion of teaching and learning methods.

How the book is organized: a conceptual map

This book contributes to the long tradition of dialogue primarily between the UK and USA concerning Creative Writing pedagogy in Higher Education. It amalgamates views from two dozen writers teaching in Higher Education from these two countries. The book is organized into eight sections to give a conceptual map of how Creative Writing is organized in Higher Education. These eight sections are arranged as follows: histories, workshops, undergraduate, postgraduate, reflective activities, assessment, critical theory and uses of information technology.

The book begins with histories to give readers a grounding in how Creative Writing began in the UK and USA. Next it considers workshops since this is the central concept in teaching Creative Writing in Higher Education. After that the book proceeds from undergraduate to postgraduate sections to give an idea of how progression from beginning levels to postgraduate work proceeds. Reflective activities follow these sections to give an in depth map explaining how such activities that reflect on the process of writing are required at all levels of undergraduate and postgraduate teaching. The assessment section follows as it entails issues raised in all the earlier sections.

After this, since Creative Writing can be a discipline in its own right as well as something taught alongside English Studies, there a section on Critical Theory which gives an in depth view of how Creative Writing addresses topics related to the academic study of literature. The book concludes with a section on Information Technology to give a sense of how this impacts on teaching possibilities both now and looking towards the future.

The book can be read in order sequentially or it can be 'dipped into' according to readers' different interests. For this reason there is some repetition allowed between chapters, especially concerning the shared histories of the subject area.

Summary of contents

Graeme Harper opens the *Histories* section by taking as problematic the view that Creative Writing is a relatively recent American invention; instead he traces informal courses into the early histories of Oxford and Cambridge. DeWitt Henry then explores how informal and formal courses in the USA were linked to the legitimacy of contemporary literature as an academic discipline. D.G. Myers closes the histories section by considering reforms in Creative Writing as well as its different organizational relationships to English Departments.

Rachel Blau DuPlessis and Jena Osman open the *Workshops* section by clarifying assumptions, and arguing that primarily writers need an audience. Next, Gary Hawkins questions assumptions that focus only on teaching and critiquing craft. Michelene Wandor closes the workshop section by clarifying tacit assumptions and different influences on the workshop model.

The *Undergraduate* section begins with Steve May's national UK survey results focusing on origins of undergraduate teaching, institutional justifications for teaching and students' reasons for learning. In the USA, Anna Leahy draws on national statistics to consider Creative Writing's impact in Higher Education and then to consider three topics of writerly reading, craft and creativity. Also from the USA, Hans Ostrom considers how power, self and knowledge play out in workshops using two case studies. Maureen Freely closes the undergraduate section by comparing her USA and UK teaching experiences.

Opening the *Postgraduate* section, from the UK, Steven Earnshaw's research argues that programmes need to provide 'complete environments', including chances for students to present and publish their work. From the UK, Jon Cook describes how Creative Writing Ph.D.s are structured. From the USA, Robin Hemley argues for a low-residency model as this is more like how professional writers work with editors and colleagues.

The *Reflective Activities* section opens with Robert Sheppard's UK surveys and interviews to consider assumptions made in setting and assessing reflective activities. From the USA Stephanie Vanderslice then argues how developing reflective abilities goes hand in hand with students' developments as writers. Tony Curtis closes the section with a personal reflection on his experiences from Wales to Vermont in the UK and USA.

The *Assessment* section opens with Michael Symmons Roberts exploring ways in which poetry can and cannot be assessed in UK Higher Education. From the USA, Mary Cantrell argues how assessment empowers students by ensuring they understand elements of craft. Stephen O'Connor, writing from the USA, closes the section by taking a firm line arguing against assessment due to its assumptions of objectivity.

The *Critical Theory* section begins with Katharine Haake in the USA arguing how critical theory can empower students. From the UK, Rob Pope argues against separating critical from Creative Writing. Also from the UK, Kim Lasky uses her Ph.D. as a case study to explore tensions between critical and Creative Writing.

In *Uses of Information Technology* John Nieves and Joseph Moxley introduce a range of technical tools to enhance quality in their teaching in the USA. Graham Mort in the UK closes the section by relating how IT structures a distance learning MA as well as a mentoring scheme with eight African countries.

Contribution to intellectual infrastructure

While the 'roots' of Creative Writing as a distinctive subject may extend deeply at least informally in Higher Education, it is nonetheless a relatively new or developing subject in this context insofar as only recently has it become the focus of formalization across so many institutions worldwide. Not long ago much pedagogic research focused on such questions as, 'What is Creative Writing and can it even be taught or assessed?'

As this volume indicates, most Higher Education institutions now teach Creative Writing in some form or another, and good practice guides and benchmarks exist and are still emerging. There are international organizations, conferences and several peer reviewed journals and websites focusing on the theory, practice, research and pedagogy of Creative Writing. However, these sorts of fundamental developments indicate that Creative Writing in Higher Education is still very much building and developing its intellectual infrastructures. The main outcome of this volume is a contribution to the intellectual infrastructure of Creative Writing as an emerging discipline within the context of Higher Education.

I hope this account, with its wide range of lively and often conflicting viewpoints, will encourage readers to reflect on their own viewpoints as well as to consider new ways of teaching Creative Writing in Higher Education.

Notes

1. Rebecca O'Rourke, *Creative Writing: Culture, Education, and Community* (Leicester: National Institute of Adult Continuing Education, 2005).
2. Moira Monteith and Robert Miles (eds), *Teaching Creative Writing: Theory and Practice* (Buckingham: The Open University Press, 1992).
3. Ben Knights and Chris Thurgar-Dawson, *Active Reading* (London: Continuum, 2006).
4. NAWE (National Association of Writers in Education) website is www.nawe.co.uk; AWP (Association of Writers and Writing Programs) website is www.awpwriter.org; AAWP (Australian Association of Writing Programs) website is www.aawp.org.au (all sites accessed on 24 March 2012).

Part I
History

David Fenza argues that many writers in Higher Education do not know the long history of their profession as teachers of Creative Writing. As a result, they may find it challenging to explain, advance and defend their work against scholars, theorists and commentators.[1] As such, this volume begins with a histories section. There is some repetition between papers as each is intended to stand individually as well as in a group for this section. Papers in this section use scholarly written accounts as their research methods as well as reflections on their own personal experiences.

Graeme Harper takes as problematic the view that Creative Writing is a relatively recent American invention and instead traces informal courses in the early histories of Oxford and Cambridge. Following this, he discusses twentieth-century developments in UK Higher Education, arguing that the founding of polytechnics and adult education programmes in the 1960s and 70s helped establish a formalized pattern of Creative Writing in the 1980s and 90s at undergraduate as well as postgraduate levels.

DeWitt Henry draws on published histories of Creative Writing to trace informal and then formal courses in USA Higher Education, arguing that these later developments were linked to the legitimacy of contemporary literature as an academic discipline. He then considers the emergence of the Associated Writing Programs (AWP) and its role in developing curricular standards before considering how Creative Writing Programmes have moved into the role of developing manuscripts into publishable documents, which was formerly occupied by editors in the publishing industry. Henry concludes by explaining his involvement with the history of Creative Writing at Emerson where he works.

D.G. Myers considers reforms in Creative Writing as well as its differing organizational relationships to English Departments. In relating his research to Paul Dawson's findings in *Creative Writing and the New Humanities*, Myers argues that Creative Writing is unlikely to reform in ways Dawson suggests since it is fundamentally defined by free expression. In making this case, Myers draws on his earlier book, *The Elephants Teach*. His research outcome is that Creative Writing may not be able to reform itself from within since it lacks a value system that moves beyond the subjective needs of individual expression.

Note

1. David Fenza, 'Creative Writing and Its Discontents,' *The Writers' Chronicle*, www.awpwriter.org/magazine/writers/fenza01.htm, Mar/April 2000, accessed 22 Dec. 2011.

1
A Short History of Creative Writing in British Universities

Graeme Harper

Writing about the history of Creative Writing in British universities means at least indirectly considering the nature of the relationship between higher learning and the activities of a university; in that way better grounding the relationship between creative writers and British academe in historical and pedagogic or andragogic (meaning relating to the teaching of adults) contexts. A discussion focused on Creative Writing teaching and learning in British universities is not the same as one focused on university classes labelled as 'Creative Writing.' The former begins from the point of view that the university is a place of potential formal and informal learning, and the discussion therefore covers the history of British university education in a synthetic fashion. The latter, which has been far too common an approach, only notes the university's ability to formalize teaching and learning into disciplines and subject areas.

Scholastic thought in the medieval universities of Europe formalized higher learning into disciplines, linked to the *trivium* and the *quadrivium*, the *trivium* being the principle undergraduate degree, consisting of grammar, rhetoric and logic, and the *quadrivium*, being the principle postgraduate course, consisting of arithmetic, geometry, music and astronomy. Ancient British universities, such as Oxford, adopted this process of formalization of higher learning; and this has continued to this day in Britain and elsewhere. Marshalling sites of knowledge into categories and subject areas, disciplines and courses of study is a holistic practice; but teaching and learning is also individualist in method, being about individual people and their modes of considering, understanding and formulating ideas, and of creating. If holistic formalization were all there was to teaching and learning then most of Britain's oldest universities, as well as its newest ones for that matter, would have badly failed their Creative Writing students. However, Creative Writing teaching and learning in British universities has been both holistic and individualistic in approach.

Published originally in 1690–2 Anthony Wood's *Athenae Oxonienses: an Exact History of all the Writers and Bishops who have had their Education in the University of Oxford from 1500 to 1690*, offers some insight into the early period of Creative Writing in British higher education – with one proviso. That proviso is simply that Wood's seventeenth-century notion of the 'writer' is quite naturally a little different to that we encounter here in the twenty-first century, due not least to changes in the modes and methods by which writing is undertaken and distributed. Wood's intention in compiling his *Athenae Oxonienses* is also a little different from the intention here; Woods was an antiquary, and that is the starting point for his interest. Extracts from typical entries in Wood's *Athenae Oxonienses* include:

> JASPER HEYWOOD, a quaint poet in his younger days, son of Jo. Heywood the famous epigrammatist of his time, was in born in London, sent to university at 12 years of age, an. 1547, educated in grammar, as well as in logic, there, took a degree in arts in 1553; and forthwith was elected probationer-fellow of Merton coll. . . .[1]
>
> THOMAS CAREW, one of the famed poets of his time for the charming sweetness his lyric odes and amorous sonnets. . . . had his academical education in Corp. Ch. Coll. as those that knew him have informed me, yet occurs not matriculated as a member of that house, or that he took a scholastical degree Afterwards improving his parts by travelling and conversation with ingenious men in the metropolis, he became reckon'd among the chiefest of his time for delicacy of wit and poetic fancy.[2]

These entries do not suggest that Heywood or Carew attended classes with titles anything like 'Creative Writing' or 'Writing Poetry'; however, each of Wood's entries notes how a particular writer was influenced, educated and developed at university and went on further to this to work as a creative writer, or in Creative Writing *and* another field (as was, and is, common among creative writers and, even more so, entirely typical of the careers of poets). For example, 'Samuel Daniel, the most noted poet and historian of all time [*sic*]' enters 'Magdalen Hall', improves himself 'much in academical learning by the benefit of an excellent tutor', and leaves the university to exercise his learning 'much in English history and poetry, of which he then gave several ingenious specimens'.[3] Wood's *Athenae* fills two hefty volumes.

When talking about Creative Writing in British universities prior to the commercialization of the British book market in the eighteenth century and to the changes wrought in the nature of Creative Writing by the emergence of such things as copyright law, commercial printing and modern notions of authorship, how we talk needs to be matched by how we think about books, publishing/performing and the role of the writer. It is not until the late eighteenth century that the notion of the modern, individual author actually emerges, directly connected with the Romantic movement, and with the concept of individual genius generated by that movement. Prior to the

Romantics, the notion of writing and publishing was more collaborative and collective, and far less focused on authorial individuality. Creative Writing was undertaken, to return to the period of Wood's *Athenae*, more for what it could *do*, than what it *was*.

When Creative Writing first entered British universities it came not with the expectation of commercial worth. Nor was it touted as an off-shoot of the study of literature in English (the first Chairs of English in Britain were appointed, Colin Evans notes, 'first in London, 1828, 1835; then in Scotland, 1862, 1865, 1893; and then, symbolically, in Oxford'[4]). Rather than being attached to the subject of English, then, from the outset the learning of Creative Writing in British universities attached itself more broadly to the universities' role as purveyors of cultural ideals and cultural history.

Naturally subject to historical change, Creative Writing in and around British universities has certainly had many dimensions. The very common anecdotal suggestion that it owes its existence to the influence of post-WWII American hegemony is just one of them. Malcolm Bradbury, well known for his work in developing Creative Writing courses in the UK, used to note that many people thought of Creative Writing in universities as an American thing, 'like the hoola-hoop' he would say. In some key ways, the strength of that 'new world' myth has been the key problem for relating the earlier history of Creative Writing in British universities.

Beyond the 'ancient universities' (that is, those established prior to the nineteenth century) the 'red brick' civic universities founded on Victorian industrialism considered their concentration was on the kinds of practical knowledge associated with industrial development – the subject of Engineering being an obvious example. Such universities have listed, and continue to list, those students who studied at them and founded their creative writing careers, either during or soon after their study. Detailed history of this Creative Writing learning process is scarce, but far from impossible to surmise from minimal recorded evidence. Take for example the emergence from the 'red brick' University of Birmingham (founded 1900) of poets and novelists Francis Brett Young, Walter Allen and Henry Treece; and from the University of Leeds (founded 1904, with historical links back to the 1830s) of prolific novelist and critic (Margaret) Storm Jameson.

Between the 'ancient universities' – writers including Ben Jonson studying at St John's College, Cambridge, Laurence Sterne at Jesus College, Cambridge (BA, 1776), J.M. Barrie receiving his MA from the University of Edinburgh in 1882 – between these ancients and the red bricks, by the time British university education entered the twentieth century the pattern of British universities providing a platform for the learning undertaken by creative writers was at least clear. Clear enough that even one oft-quoted example – Lewis Carroll's career as Lecturer in Mathematics at Christ Church College, Oxford (1855–1881) and as author of *Alice in Wonderland* (1865) and *Through the Looking-Glass* (1872) – determines that there can be little real argument with the idea that British universities were home to Creative Writing education well prior to the twentieth Century.

At the opening of the twentieth century, an increased emphasis in British higher education on ensuring industrial success met with the greater emphasis in the tenets of British Modernism and Imperialism on a style of education applicable to Western progress. Here, the 1895 Bryce Commission report on British education announced the further involvement of the State in the work of universities. Here T.H. Huxley's poignant defence to the Cowper Commission of 1892 that 'the primary business of universities is with *pure* knowledge and pure art – independent of all application to practice; with progress in culture, not with wealth'.[5] What today is seen by some as a tension between 'vocationalism' and a less directly 'economic' notion of higher learning manifested itself in British higher education in the early twentieth century in the changing relationship between learning and the market for learning. Even though State subsidized universities remained (and remain) the norm in Britain, UK universities were destined to be impacted upon more discernibly by economic forces.

It is easy, in light of the considerable vibrancy of the *fin de siècle*, to get the history of Creative Writing in academe at that time wrong. For example, referring to Creative Writing in American universities, D.G. Myers in his book *The Elephants Teach: Creative Writing since 1880* writes:

> Originally the teaching of writing in American universities ('creative' or otherwise) was an experiment in education. Creative Writing as such emerged out of this experiment, gradually taking shape over the six decades from 1880 to the Second World War.[6]

But Myers' comment is conflating several shifts linked to Modernism and Imperialism, along with hegemonic shifts in world power relations, economic forces playing a key, if not the only, part. The history of Creative Writing in US higher education certainly exhibited much change in the early twentieth century; but it is as important with regard to the US, as it is with regard to Britain, to recognize that an earlier history existed, and that formalization and declaration of formalized courses is not the beginning of Creative Writing in universities in any country.

How general changes in the management of British academe impacted upon the Creative Writing life of universities around the turn of the century has not been widely investigated; but such changes certainly reflected the forward-marching tenets of a style of education focused on economic progress. Developments in the first half of the century included the formation of the Committee of Vice Chancellors and Principals (1930) 'for the purposes of mutual consultation' and, indeed, greater concern with educational marketability associated with promoting 'Britishness' and its links with a history of quality higher education.

From the end of the Second World War, the impact of Local Education Authorities (LEAs) paying student fees combined with the later 1962 Education Act, a national Mandatory Award giving students on full-time courses LEA maintenance grants, to decade by decade widen access to higher education. In 1963, the Robbins Committee Report on Higher Education recommended, among other things, that Colleges of Advanced Technology should be given the status of universities. Mid-century developments, thus, placed a greater emphasis on British universities as places of modern discovery for a wider range of the population, while the general atmosphere of British education in this period saw an increased concern, quite naturally perhaps, with curriculum development. This was a situation British philosopher of Education R.S. Peters pointed out in 1965 was 'a novel feature' involving not only practical evolution but 'debate and theoretical speculation'.[7]

Not unsurprisingly, given the economic emphasis inherent in government policy, the 1960s in Britain were the high point for the founding of polytechnics, the 'polys'. The intention of the polys was to provide professional and vocational post-secondary education. Indeed, the strength, or perceived lack of strength, of poly students with regard to such 'university' subjects such as English fed the growth of Creative Writing, and drew on notions of what a productive polytechnic education might entail, and how it might be differentiated from a university education.

A 1967 speech by critic F.R. Leavis adds weight to the suggestion that in some quarters of British academe the prestige of formal Creative Writing classes as 'higher learning' was not well recognized. In his speech, later published in *English Literature in Our Time and the University: The Clark Lectures 1967*, Leavis states: 'I don't at all think that candidates for Honours should be encouraged to believe that by submitting original poems, novels or plays they may improve their claim to a good class'.[8] Leavis' comments were also a refraction, if not a direct reflection, of the relative bemusement of British writers of the period who visited Creative Writing workshops in the USA and saw a notable difference in andragogic ideals produced by differences in the history of university education in the USA to that in Great Britain. Yet, back in Britain, the 'ancients' and the 'red bricks' continued to offer opportunities for informal learning of Creative Writing in a way they had always done, while the polytechnics were providing new avenues for Creative Writing curriculum development.

Arriving in the 1960s and developing into the 1970s the 'glory days' of British Adult Education also provided Creative Writing with a second Higher Education platform, and one not necessarily connected with the subject of English Literature. Indeed, a parallel history of Creative Writing learning in Great Britain could be written with a focus on 'adult and continuing education'.[9] This would include reference to Creative Writing education as 'personal development' as well as creative education for professional practice, the publishing, media or performance industries. Notably, the discussion about 'institutional learning and 'non-institutional' learning prevails here as with elsewhere. As Roger Fieldhouse suggests in his history of British Adult Education, it is easy to 'over-emphasise[s] formal and institutionalised learning at the expense of the less-well-recorded autodidactic tradition'.[10]

New universities founded in this period included the University of Bradford, the University of East Anglia, the University of Kent, Lancaster University, the University of Stirling, the University of Ulster and the University of York, institutions sometimes called the 'plate glass' universities (named, as were the 'red bricks,' after their prevailing architectural features). These institutions were born out of expansion, and to an extent innovation, prompted by the Robbins Report and the commentary ultimately surrounding it. A number of them would soon show an interest in creating formal courses in Creative Writing.

By the 1970s, the idea that any society had a 'fixed pool of ability' had lost favour in Britain, thus initiating an era in which there was (and is) potentially an unlimited supply of university students. Simultaneously, by the 1970s there were four different British university manifestations of Creative Writing.

Firstly, there was that occurring in the 'ancient universities', based mostly on informal learning. Secondly, there was that in the 'red bricks', largely self-generated because these universities, traditionally, were considered mostly to be concerned with 'real world skills', and the link between Creative Writing and employment in the creative industries had not yet been made.[11] Thirdly, there was that in the polytechnics, where some notion of pragmatism in the approach to subjects such as English Literature in the application of communication skills gave the subject a ground-base. And, finally, there was gradually beginning to emerge in some of the 'plate glass' universities, universities such as East Anglia and Lancaster where, in addition to individual interests of academic staff, which can never be discounted as driving forces in each of these manifestations, the ethos of innovation prevailed, connected with a post-Robbins notion of higher education.

The 1980s expansion of Creative Writing as a formal subject in British higher education developed on the back of this history, with the additional support of visible publication successes around that time, such as that of the future Booker Prize winner, Ian McEwan, graduating out of MA study at the University of East Anglia. Active local moves to expand Creative Writing in British universities and polytechnics in the 1980s also provided an academic counterpoint to the policies of Margaret Thatcher's government. Thatcher, coming into power in May 1979 and remaining there until 1992, did not win great support in British higher education for her economic, social or, indeed, education policies. The 1980s expansion of Creative Writing in British higher education thus owed at least something to an anti-Thatcherite ethos in British universities, highlighting culture over Thatcher's interest in economic 'entrepreneurship'. Paradoxically, however, Creative Writing expansion at Masters level equally owed a great deal to the MA students' vocational aspirations!

As the 1990s commenced, the Further and Higher Education Acts gave the polys the opportunity to become the latest 'new' British universities and, even now with the conversion of a raft of colleges of higher education and institutes to university title in 2004–5, the launch of new universities in the early 1990s remains the most significant evolution in British university education in recent times. From that point until the present there has been a large growth in both MA and Ph.D. programmes in Creative Writing, with the first British Ph.D.s emerging, and paralleling similar growth in Australia (which saw its first doctorates completed also in the early 1990s). MA expansion has likewise continued, further courses being developed across the full range of British universities. The variety of MA approaches has widened. And yet, most MAs draw on the kinds of commercial thrust that helped justify them in the first place. That is, the notion of an MA in Creative Writing as an intensive period to develop a piece of writing specifically for publication or, in the case of dramatic or media writing, for production, remains strong.

There are at present around 80 MA courses in Great Britain and nearly 30 Ph.D. programmes. (See the National Association of Writers in Education website for further details: www.nawe.co.uk.) Postgraduate scholarship support from Britain's primary funder of academic research in the Arts and Humanities, the Arts and Humanities Research Council (AHRC) has grown stronger over the past few years, though still requires some informed further development. Undergraduate expansion in Creative Writing has seemingly built on a number of elements, some of which might be open to debate. Firstly, that traditional Humanities subjects have needed to come up with new ways of attracting students and, for a subject like English in particular, Creative Writing has been a useful bridge from the previous to the current phase of student interest. Some of this is borne on the back of a government push for more vocational university education, some on the back of justifying the existence of universities, some due to the impact of widening access. Secondly, and in a connected way, there has been an expansion of subjects such as Media Studies and Film Studies and degrees in new and digital media, all of which have the potential to offer screen and media writing courses. Finally, success has bred success and it would be naïve to believe that some Creative Writing courses have not been launched in the past ten years simply because one university noticed one of its competitors was doing rather well with such a course.

The history of Creative Writing in British universities is sometimes discussed as if it begins in the 1960s, and as if it is connected with an American influence, like the hoola-hoop. Likewise, it is sometimes discussed as if it is solely 'local history', linked only to one institution or another, but not widely spread. Most worryingly, it is too rarely discussed at all, and this has given the impression that Creative Writing in British higher education has relatively little history. Nothing could be further from the truth.

Notes

1. Anthony Wood, *Athenae Oxonienses: an Exact History of all the Writers and Bishops who have had their Education in the University of Oxford from 1500 to 1690, Vol. II* (Oxford: Ecclesiastical History Society, 1848), p. 663.
2. Anthony Wood, p. 658.
3. Anthony Wood, p. 628.
4. Colin Evans, *English People: the Experience of Teaching and Learning English in British Universities* (Buckingham: Open University Press, 1993), p. 12.
5. A.H. Halsey, 'British Universities and Intellectual Life,' *Universities Quarterly* 12 (1957–8): 148.
6. D.G. Myers, *The Elephants Teach: Creative Writing since 1880* (New Jersey: Prentice Hall, 1996 and 2006), p. 4.
7. R.S. Peters, 'Education as Initiation,' *Theory of Education: Studies of Significant Innovation in Western Educational Thought*, Eds. J. Bowen and P. R. Hobson (Brisbane: John Wiley, 1990), p. 358.
8. F.R. Leavis, *English in Our Time and the University: The Clark Lectures* (Cambridge: Cambridge University Press, 1979), p. 63.
9. For a discussion that begins with an approach to Creative Writing in Adult and Continuing Education see Rebecca O'Rourke, *Creative Writing: Education, Culture and Community* (Leicester: NIACE, 2005).
10. Roger Fieldhouse and Associates, *A History of Modern British Adult Education* (Leicester: NIACE, 1996), pp. vii–viii.
11. The term 'Creative Industries' (meaning that sector of the economy associated with such things as advertising, architecture, the art and antiques market, crafts, design, designer fashion, film and video, interactive leisure software, music, the performing arts, publishing, software and computer games, television and radio) quite obviously, as the list implies, incorporates a number of activities closely associated with Creative Writing. The term Creative Industries, while well used in the UK and Australasia is comparatively less used in the USA. The UK Department of Culture, Media and Sport (www.dcms.gov.uk, accessed 28 February 2012) notes that in Britain the 'Creative Industries accounted for 8.2% of Gross Value Added (GVA) in 2001' and 'grew by an average of 8% per annum between 1997 and 2001'. They continue to grow.

2
A Short History of Creative Writing in America

DeWitt Henry

The teaching of the crafts of fiction, nonfiction and poetry in degree-bearing institutions has its distant antecedent, at least in spirit, in the unofficial atelier or 'school', such as one might regard the Transcendentalists' Brook Farm to be. But just as the combination of shoptalk, mutual editing and critical theory is exemplified by Wordsworth and Coleridge in England, surely the nexus of Hawthorne, Emerson, Fuller, Thoreau and other New England writers of the 1840s exemplifies an American school 'without walls'. Writers talked back to writers about vision and craft. Livelihoods came from second jobs as churchmen, teachers, editors or clerks in customs houses; seldom from publication. Interestingly, as portrayed by Perry Miller in *The Raven and the Whale* (1956), claims for a national literature emanated from such magazines in New York as the *Knickerbocker Magazine*, *The Democratic Review* and Poe's *The Broadway Journal*.[1] Edgar Allan Poe, of course, first in Baltimore, then Philadelphia, then New York, was a central figure; and just as his famous review of Hawthorne, in laying out principles of craft, is often cited as the birth of the American Short Story, so too, it presents the American idiom of *poet and critic*.[2] Like a nineteenth century Aristotle, Poe offers his poetics.[3] Here are works we value. Here are their characteristics. (For a different historical perspective, see D.G. Myers's *Elephants Teach*: 'The search for origins is a historical error.')[4]

Andrew Levy in his book, *The Culture and Commerce of the American Short Story* (1993), points to Poe's essay as the precursor to the writers' handbooks that flourished from the 1890s to 1920s.[5] These were pragmatic 'how to' handbooks, presumably written by the successful. For fiction, the O. Henry snapper formula, a travesty of Poe's earlier insistence on 'unity of effect', prevailed (Levy, 65). Still, the monumental instance of 'how to' is surely *The Art of the Novel: Critical Prefaces* by Henry James (1907);[6] James's emphasis on character and point of view are later followed by Percy Lubbock and E.M. Forster, whose *Aspects of the Novel* remains, for me, the friendliest instance of shoptalk.[7] Ultimately, the handbooks revealed a split between

17

literary culture and writing for markets. As Levy puts it: 'If the critics and scholars of the late nineteenth century labored to construct the "short story" as a genre, the handbook writers . . . worked [to build] a consensus: on the short story, and on what constituted the rules for a national form of expression.'[8]

In the 1920s, such attempts to provide a rhetoric of craft were augmented and countered by the Modernist poet critics, by the expatriate ateliers of Ezra Pound and Gertrude Stein, and by such literary magazines as *The Transatlantic Review Poetry* and *Blast*; and later by critics of contemporary and classical literature on campuses, who were themselves poets. One thinks of the Fugitive group around John Crowe Ransom and *The Kenyon Review*, for instance.

Andrew Levy[9] and George Garrett (in his chapter, 'The Future of Writing Programs', from *Creative Writing in America: Theory and Pedagogy*, edited by Joseph M. Moxley, 1989) also remind us that the study of English was parvenu in the 1880s, with the status of permanence and universality reserved to Greek and Roman classics.[10] Later when the English canon became established, an event marked by the formation of the Modern Language Association in 1884, the study of contemporary literature and writing courses were parvenu. The first creative courses noted by Levy include 'The Art of the Short Story' offered at the University of Chicago in 1896, with similar courses taught at Princeton and at the University of Iowa. As cited in Tom Grimes's *The Workshop: Seven Decades of the Iowa Writers' Workshop* (1999), other histories point to a 'Verse Making' class at Iowa in 1896 that 'led to Edwin Piper's "Poetics" class, which served as a prototype for the workshop. That is, Piper created a class in which students' works were discussed critically. This method mandated a return to the study of classical rhetoric, a belief that literary craft could be learned.'[11] Garrett also points out 'that the somewhat disguised Creative Writing courses, which were offered in American colleges and universities for years before there were any official courses named "Creative Writing," were usually associated with "great books" courses, that is, de facto courses in the classics. Some or all of the students would be allowed to write poems and stories instead of papers . . . Also there were composition courses, of various kinds, that permitted or, indeed, required the students to write poems and stories . . . Long before Iowa, or anywhere else, people in institutions were actively studying the craft of writing fiction and the writing of poetry and getting credit for their efforts'.[12]

The Iowa Writers' Workshop grew from Piper's course, as he convinced the graduate faculty at the University of Iowa to award graduate degree credit for creative work, in 1922. Iowa began to offer a Ph.D. that allowed a creative dissertation in 1931. The writing program, offering the Master of Fine Arts (MFA) degree, was established in 1936 under Walter Schramm. Among its early graduates were Paul Engle, Wallace Stegner and R.V. Cassill-Engle who directed the Iowa program from 1937 to 1965, while Stegner, advocating for regionalism, began the Creative Writing program at Stanford in 1947, and Cassill after teaching at Iowa, founded both the program at Brown in 1966 and the Associated Writing Programs in 1967. Under Engle, the Iowa program grew to 100 students, its present cap, and particularly in the years following World War II and the G.I. bill, made its distinctive mark with such graduates as Flannery O'Connor, John Gardner, Raymond Carver and James Alan McPherson.

Garrett sees the rise of programs in Creative Writing as linked to the growing legitimacy of contemporary literature as an academic field, particularly in the 1950s. Working writers were hired as faculty. 'Prior to World War II', writes Garrett, 'there had been on campus a few, only a few, distinguished and mostly decorative part-time people, most notably Robert Frost.'[13] By the mid 1960s, 'everybody had a poet or two, and maybe a fiction writer also, on the staff', and the colleges had become the primary patrons of writers' careers.[14] Where the promise of the paperback revolution had been lost to the rise of television, the founding of the National Endowment for the Arts (NEA) in 1965 promised additional patronage through its Literature Program, granting funds to writers, to literary publishers, to audience development projects and to hosts for readings and residencies. In any case, Creative Writing programs were taking root at such places as the University of Michigan, the University of Arkansas, Hollins College, Louisiana State University and the University of Montana. In 1967, R.V. Cassill called together the directors of thirteen programs and founded the Associated Writing Programs (AWP), seeking to promote Creative Writing as a field in a way analogous to associations for other disciplines.[15] In addition to members' dues and the shelter of different host colleges, the organization depended heavily on federal grants.

AWP argued for recognition of the MFA degree as a *terminal* degree, equivalent to a Ph.D. in English for purposes of hiring, tenure and promotion. It also sought to establish curricular standards and to distinguish between studio, academic and mixed studio and academic programs. Of course some member programs offered Master of Arts degrees (usually taking one year's study), implying the sequel of a Ph.D. in English; others offered a Ph.D. in English with a creative dissertation. By 1975, out of eighty member programs, twenty-four offered BAs, three BFAs, thirty-two MAs, fifteen MFAs, five Ph.D.s and one a Doctor of Arts (figures quoted from the AWP website cited below). In some cases MA requirements exceeded those for MFA. According to *The AWP Guide to Writing Programs* (2002), there were now 330 college and university member programs. Undergraduate degrees had proliferated to 283 BAs and seventy BFAs; and advanced degrees to 150 MAs, ninety-nine MFAs, forty-two Ph.D.s and one DA. Faculty searches these days tend to present fourth generation MFA degree holders (that is taught by an MFA, who was taught by an MFA, who was taught by an MFA).

David Fenza, the present director of AWP, argued in 2001 that Creative Writing programs now re-invigorate literature programs and 'have become among the most popular classes in the humanities' (www.awpwriter. org/aboutawp/index.htm (accessed 28 February 2012). To this way of thinking, the English curriculum has lost vitality, direction and meaning. 'Many English departments of literature have welcomed writers to join the scholars, critics, and theorists', he writes. '[Students] now see litera-ture animated with a new immediacy, as literature clearly appears a *living* body – growing and evolving . . . In Creative Writing classes, students learn about elements of literature from inside their own work, rather than from an outside text.'

Against this academic progress, there have been various demurs, both from within and from without the Creative Writing field. One, argued by Joseph M. Moxley (op. cit.), is that the pedagogy of Creative Writing has not progressed, if indeed such progress is possible. Workshops remain the primary method, augmented by a study of models for form and for standards of vision. Restive gurus have attempted different pedagogies, such as the process approach of Natalie Goldberg in *Writing Down the Bones*;[16] the exercise approach of Pamela Painter and Anne Bernays in *What If?*;[17] the deep memory approach of Eve Shelnutt (recommended in her chapter of *Creative Writing in America*); or the therapy group approach of Gordon Lish as described by Amy Hempel in her article about his workshop at Yale as 'Captain Fiction'.[18] But a workshop is a workshop, intense in common humility before the art (at best), ready to probe a text's deepest assumptions and to articulate where it is working or not working – all without personal reference to the author. These are like rehearsals of a public performance, a kind of making public of the private dream; yet kinder and more construc-tive in response than the simple yes or no of an editor.

A related complaint concerns standardization. Donald Hall deplores the Macpoem, just as critic John W. Aldridge some years ago complained about 'The New American Assembly-Line Fiction' (*Classics and Contemporaries*, 1992).[19] Workshops supposedly are geared more to produce a well-mannered mediocrity than genius. Both in workshops and in related literature courses, an overemphasis on contemporary models leaves writers poorly read and ignorant of tradition. Then there are the worldly concerns that while MFA degree holders proliferate, academic jobs do not; that for jobs teaching composition, MFAs are in conflict with degree holders in Composition and Composition Theory; and the idea that the MFA degree is attractive to employers outside of academia seems tenuous, though the AWP job list regularly includes jobs in arts administration, public relations, editing and publishing. Lastly, while advocates of Creative Writing programs claim that they are creating *readers* for poetry and fiction, in fact the circulation figures for literary magazines are perhaps one tenth of the number of submissions received, and the sales figures for notable books have remained less than

10,000 throughout the workshop decades (see 'Thinking about Readers,' by William B. Goodman, *Daedalus*, Winter, 1983).[20]

AWP's founder, R.V. Cassill himself, shocked the membership with his address to an annual meeting in Boston in 1982, where he called for the organization to disband (the speech is reprinted by Grimes).[21] After fifteen years, Cassill thought it was time to get writing out of academia and back on the open road: 'we are now at the point where writing programs are poisoning, and in turn are being poisoned by departments and institutions on which we have fastened them'. He saw the institutionalizing of writing ultimately as a sell out. 'Writing will always be funded by writers. By the pawning of their lives, fortunes and sacred honor.'

Contrary to such misgivings, writing programs have continued to flourish and to shape our national literature. New generations of writers have taken hold and found their places as teachers. One thinks back to Debra Spark's *Twenty under Thirty: Best Stories by America's New Young Writers* (Scribners, 1986), featuring Lorrie Moore, David Leavitt and Bret Lott, among other accomplished writers and teachers now nearing fifty.[22]

According to David Fenza (op. cit.), 'AWP has advanced the appreciation of literature as an open and living art – growing and evolving – an art that can be made by anyone with talent who is willing and disciplined enough to devote one's self to its difficult demands.' For writers who teach, as Garrett foresaw, the real challenges today concern technology (from hypertext experiments to desktop publishing to distance learning to printing on demand) and the diversity of students' ethnic, cultural and language backgrounds. Writing teachers need 'to be aware of other traditions and be able to accommodate them', while at the same time preserving 'our own American language and its traditions'. We also need more realism about practical outcomes for our students, in terms of teaching and non-teaching jobs, publication and writing careers. The fact is that for most full-time openings in colleges, in addition to an MFA, the writer also needs a published book. For teaching at the secondary level, the writer probably also needs a degree in education. If, as writers, most of our students will find themselves out in the cold, then we need to give them some survival training, at least in terms of expectations.

Since the conglomeration of the publishing industry, literary editors of the likes of Maxwell Perkins, Edmund Wilson or Theodore Solotaroff have been replaced by lawyers and marketing directors; Jonathan Galassi at Farrar Straus Giroux, who has written about being a 'double agent' for literature, is a rare exception. The writing programs have, in fact, taken over the essential function of helping to develop manuscripts into publishable books and to lead rather than to follow established trends of taste. Of course a literary situation that continues to rely on market driven publishers is culturally bleak. A broad and varied sector of non-profit publishers has emerged, with NEA funded small presses and the university presses publishing books of poetry and fiction on merit, often under the aegis of one juried award or another.

Emerson College, where I teach, offered Bachelor of Fine Arts (BFA) and MA degrees in Creative Writing before it received accreditation for the MFA degree twenty years ago. James Randall, the program's founder, reconfigured the English Department into a department of Writing, Publishing and Literature in 1980. For the publishing component he took over a fledgling Professional Writing program that Emerson had begun in imitation of the program at the University of Southern California. I was hired initially, as the editor of *Ploughshares* literary magazine, a fiction writer and a Ph.D. in English, to direct the Professional Writing program and to bolster the MFA application. Later for five years I chaired this hybrid department, while also directing the MFA. By 1990, Emerson had acquired *Ploughshares*, we had 400 undergraduate majors, 120 MFA and fifty MA in Professional Writing students. Thanks to our Boston location and the prestige of *Ploughshares*, I was able to hire in addition to talented full timers, an array of remarkable part-time instructors and writers in residence. We suffered growing pains, pushed by the college to admit more graduate students than we could serve. Tension grew between the belletristic and professional directions of the program, and also from non-MFA literature faculty pursuing canon revision, literary theory and cultural criticism. Under successive, gifted chairs – in particular Theodore Weesner, John Skoyles and now Daniel Tobin – we established a rapport between our disciplines and integrated our curriculum, moving away from the idea of 'professional writing', and towards a concentration on publishing courses in editing, design and marketing. We also developed a course in 'Teaching Freshman English', that prepared graduate students to be composition teachers. Our students continue to challenge and impress me. We are ranked by *U.S. World and News Report* as one of the top twenty graduate writing programs of our kind.

I subscribe to Tolstoy's theory of history, as the integral of individual actions. In these twenty years, I have been privileged to see our very first MFA graduate, Don Lee, succeed me as editor of *Ploughshares* and establish himself as a writer with the publication of his stories *Yellow* and his novel *Country of Origin*. Though I regularly advise our former students to concentrate on their writing and not to start literary magazines, Rusty Barnes and Rod Siino have established *Night Train*; John Rubins publishes an online magazine *Tatlin's Tower* 'for curiously strong fiction'; and Jennifer Cande is six issues deep so far with *Quick Fiction*. Visiting our department library, I was daunted to count some two thousand hard bound MFA theses (roughly 100 for each year), including film scripts and plays, memoirs and books of non-fiction, academic studies, and children's books: along with a preponderance of novels, collections of stories and poems. Some have been published as books: non-fiction by Pamela Gordon and Beth Leibson Hawkins; memoir by Carmit Delman; children's books by Christopher Lynch, Lisa Jahn-Clough and Kim Ablon Whitney; criticism by Kathleen Rooney;

poetry by Denise Duhamel; and fiction by Janet Tashjian, Risa Miller, Lee (Harrington) Forgotson, among some thirty titles listed on our department website. Many others have won grants and awards, published in magazines, and will have books. Many students have gone on to teach. I think of Michael Henry and Andrea Dupree, who founded the center Lighthouse Writers in Denver. Some have dedicated themselves to careers as scriptwriters in Hollywood. Some work in magazine publishing. My name appears as chair or reader on my share of these theses, along with the names of my colleagues, past and present. Proud company, indeed.

As a writer, teacher and editor, I have believed in some notion of justice. Literature is that which I will not willingly let die, whether it is Shakespeare's plays, Eudora Welty's fiction, a story by an unknown in a literary magazine or a workshop story in manuscript. When writing is good, I want to recognize it, reader to writer, and to share it with others. Initially my sharing took the form of *Ploughshares*. Since then it has resulted in my editing various anthologies, including *Breaking Into Print* and *Sorrow's Company*. Most recently I have mounted a website, featuring students experimenting with post-modern forms. I have no claim to being a Poe, or a George Garrett, a Wallace Stegner, an Oakley Hall or a Frank Conroy, but I have helped to make something tenuous authentic, and I hope that our literature is better for this integer of effort.

Notes

1. Perry Miller, *The Raven and The Whale* (New York: Harcourt, Brace, and World, 1956).
2. Edgar Allen Poe, 'Review of Hawthorne – Twice Told Tales,' *Grahams Magazine* (May 1842): 298–300.
3. Edgar Allen Poe, 'The Philosophy of Composition,' *Grahams Magazine* (April 1846) 163–7.
4. D.G. Myers, *Elephants Teach: Creative Writing Since 1880* (New York: Prentice Hall, 1995).
5. Andrew Levy, *The Culture and Commerce of the American Short Story* (Cambridge, MA: Cambridge University Press, 1993).
6. Henry James, *The Art of the Novel: Critical Prefaces* (New York: Scribners, 1934).
7. E.M. Forster, *Aspects of the Novel* (New York: Harcourt, Brace & Company, 1956).
8. Andrew Levy, *The Culture and Commerce of the American Short Story*.
9. Ibid.
10. George Garrett, 'The Future of Writing Programs,' *Creative Writing in America: Theory and Pedagogy*, Joseph M. Moxley, Ed. (Urbana, IL: National Council of Teachers of English, 1989).
11. Tom Grimes, Ed., *The Workshop: Seven Decades of the Iowa Writers' Workshop* (New York: Hyperion, 1999).
12. George Garrett, 'The Future of Writing Programs.'
13. Ibid.
14. Ibid.

15. *The AWP Guide to Writing Programs* (Paradise, CA: Associated Writing Programs, Dustbooks, Annual, 2008).
16. Natalie Goldberg, *Writing Down the Bones* (Boston: Shambhala, 1996).
17. Anne Bernays and Pamela Painter, Eds., *What If?* (New York: Harper Resource, 1991).
18. Amy Hempel, 'Captain Fiction,' *Vanity Fair* (December, 1984), 90–3, 126–8.
19. John W. Aldridge, *Classics and Contemporaries* (Minneapolis: Augsburg Fortress Publishers, 1992).
20. William Goodman, 'Thinking About Readers,' *Daedalus* (Winter, 1983), 65–84.
21. Tom Grimes, Ed., *The Workshop*.
22. Debra Spark, Ed., *Twenty under Thirty: Best Stories by America's New Young Writers* (New York: Scribners, 1986).

3
On the Reform of Creative Writing

David G. Myers

Creative Writing was no sooner established than reformers set out to change it. First came those who wanted to do away with it altogether. In a famous broadside published in *Poetry* magazine in 1986, Greg Kuzma called it a catastrophe, demanding its abolition.[1] But Kuzma was trying to take away the bone after the dog had already buried it. By 1980 the number of writing programs in the US had climbed to over a hundred, and by the end of the decade more than a thousand degrees in Creative Writing were being awarded annually. Creative Writing was not about to disappear. Next came those who granted its existence, but not without an improvement in its habits. 'The question today', concluded the poet Christopher Beach ten years after Kuzma wrote, 'is not whether such programs should exist, but how and where they can and should exist within the academic structure of the English department and the university as a whole.'[2] By the mid-nineties, in short, the question was bureaucratic.

And so, with its existence assured, the debate moved on to Creative Writing's organizational relationship to the rest of the English department. The arguments ranged from those, like David Radavich in the MLA's trade journal *Profession*, who urged creative writers to abandon their pretensions of autonomy and become more fully integrated into the department ('writers in the academy should earn traditional Ph.D.s and become more like scholars'), to those like D.W. Fenza, executive director of the Associated Writing Programs, who insisted that Creative Writing should continue to stand apart, providing institutional resistance to literary theorists' efforts to demote authors to 'mere unwitting conduits through which society, markets, religion, politics, and prejudices of all kinds – the real authorities – manufacture literary texts'.[3] Calls for integration or resistance, however, took for granted not only Creative Writing's place in the English department, but its unique and irreplaceable contribution to English studies. And for some there was a prior question that clamoured for an answer: 'What, after all, *is* the discipline of Creative Writing? If we taught it, what would we be teaching?'[4] The uncertainty about the organization's ultimate purpose, as distinct from more immediate organizational goals, was an unmistakable symptom of Creative Writing's bureaucratization. No one was sure any more that Creative Writing even was a discipline. On the one hand, the novelist Francine Prose quips that the writing workshop is 'not an academic discipline, it's fraternity hazing'; on the other, Paul Dawson argues that, to merit its place in the curriculum, Creative Writing must first become a discipline ('a body of knowledge and a set of educational techniques for imparting this knowledge').[5]

Dawson's *Creative Writing and the New Humanities* (2005) is the first book-length attempt to propose a root-and-branch reform of the subject and not just a bureaucratic reshuffling. Two things must be done if Creative Writing might become a discipline of knowledge. First, the workshop ethos of free expression, the common opinion of Creative Writing teachers and students that poems and stories are individual utterances of deeply personal experience, needs to be discarded and replaced by a 'sociological poetics', the view that literature is the 'conscious artistic dramatization' of the clash between 'living discourses in society' (p. 209). And secondly, then, Creative Writing must undertake a social purpose. 'The responsibility of writers lies not in whom they address or speak for', Dawson says, 'but in recognizing how literature functions in society' (p. 204). And it functions, to repeat, not by expressing the autonomous artist, but by dramatizing the clash of social viewpoints. The purpose of the writers' workshop, then, can never be to serve the individual development of literary artists, but 'to act as a medium between the academy and the public sphere . . .' (p. 203).

Although there is much to admire in his account, Creative Writing is unlikely to reform itself along any such lines. Dawson badly underestimates the degree to which the ethos of free expression fundamentally *defines* Creative Writing, thwarting its reformation as a discipline of knowledge. To show how will require a brief excursion into its history.

In my book *The Elephants Teach*, I located the first use of the phrase *Creative Writing* in Emerson's 1837 Phi Beta Kappa address on 'The American Scholar'.[6] Dawson disputes my account, objecting that 'there is no sense of naming here, there is no *thing* being labelled . . .' He traces Creative Writing's name instead to Wordsworth, who is the first to speak of 'Creative Art' in an 1815 sonnet. Again, in *The Elephants Teach* I claimed that the academic and not the literary use of the name has historic priority; but Dawson disputes this claim, observing that in *Rousseau and Romanticism* (published in 1919, the year before Hughes Mearns inaugurated the subject at the Lincoln School) the critic Irving Babbitt had spoken of an ethical imagination that 'gives high seriousness to Creative Writing . . .' Wordsworth named, then, a 'certain type of writing' and Babbitt uses the phrase to describe 'high' literature (pp. 33–4). The point is more than *pilpul*, because Dawson wishes to finger a certain theory of literature – the magisterial claims of high seriousness – as the source of the discipline's problems, which must be junked if Creative Writing is to be reformed.

There is, however, no *thing* being labelled in Babbitt either. He is not using the phrase as a synonym for 'high literature', because Creative Writing has never denoted that. Quite the opposite. As a literary classification, the phrase refers to fiction in the old sense – any writing, prose or poetry, that is make-believe – before it has been canonized as literature. Babbitt's use of the phrase is an accident of style in the service of a more important distinction between the ethical imagination and 'idle sing[ing] of an empty day'.[7] Why does he stumble into the phrase? Simple. The term *creative* was being used promiscuously in the first decades of the twentieth century.[8] In literary criticism, the term had some currency thanks to Joel E. Spingarn's book *Creative Criticism*, first published in 1917. Spingarn was influential in introducing the aesthetic thought of the Italian philosopher Benedetto Croce to American readers. So pervasive was the influence, in fact, that H.L. Mencken saw the need to attack it in *Prejudices*, denouncing it as the 'Croce–Spingarn–Carlyle–Goethe theory' of literature (Spingarn quoted remarks by Carlyle and Goethe to reinforce his argument). More than two decades later, after he had considered the epithet creative more fully, Babbitt also reviled Spingarn's conception.[9] Even so, he contributed to the currency of the term. He uses the phrase *Creative Writing* as Spingarn, not as Wordsworth, might.

Spingarn's 'creative criticism' sounds like a restatement of Emerson's 'creative reading'. For Emerson the point is to recover 'the sacredness of the act of creation, the act of thought', which literary scholarship transfers to the record, treating it like a holy relic. Spingarn says the same thing somewhat differently. A work of literary art seeks only to express itself – not the clash of living discourses in society – and criticism is only the study of expression; that is, an inquiry into whether and how a literary text has expressed itself. Spingarn explains:

> [T]he poet's aim must be judged at the moment of the creative act, that is to say, by the art of the poem itself, and not by the vague ambitions which he imagines to be his real intentions before or after the creative act is achieved.

Not only does Spingarn here strikingly anticipate Wimsatt and Beardsley's 'intentional fallacy', but what is more, he lays the predicate for an intrinsic criticism, a method of reading a literary text that is concerned solely with the 'laws of its own being' rather than 'laws formulated by others'.[10] This intrinsic criticism would become known somewhat later as the workshop method. The Emerson–Spingarn phrases *creative reading* and *creative criticism* not only prepare the ground for the genre of Creative Writing (that is, not-yet-canonized fiction). Moreover, they rotate the axis of literary study away from passive reception and appreciation toward active production and participation. Creative Writing is the unavoidable outcome of creative reading or criticism. Sugar caramelizes when it is burnt.

The turn from reception to production creates a new disciplinary conception of literary study (if *study* is the right word), but it also inserts the splinter that remains in Creative Writing's foot. To be absorbed wholly with the demands of one's own literary text, with the 'laws of its own being' rather than 'laws formulated by others', is to risk self-absorption. *Il n'y a pas de hors-le-moi* – that might be Creative Writing's motto. Too many students of Creative Writing conform to 'the heuristic model of Writing the Self,' as a distinguished essayist and novelist confided to me after teaching the subject for the first time. When asked to describe the most unusual event in their lives, 'the majority of them came up with one or another variation on getting stoned'.[11] Is it any surprise that the overriding concern with the intrinsic requirements of their work can lead them to confuse experience with psychic states? Students take it as a betrayal of their métier to be asked to do basic research or to handle abstract ideas. As one investigator found after interviewing forty of them at various universities, students of the subject uniformly associate Creative Writing with the personal, especially with private experience:

> The general assumption . . . is that, in contrast to essay writing, Creative Writing provides a writing opportunity which permits students to tap into a much more private, personal and emotional reality for their ideas and material. It is characterized by freedom from the non-personal, external demands of facts and other people's ideas, comments and forms. For the most part it is concerned with original, creative, personal experiences and feelings that can be discovered by the self and which provide the basis for their material.

What is most striking, however, is not merely the radical nature of such subjectivism, but its 'general and widespread acceptance' in writers' workshops.[12] It is more than a commonplace. The social enterprise of Creative Writing – large numbers of unrelated people engaging in noticeably similar practices at various spots around the globe – depends upon the shared allegiance to subjectivist expressionism. But there is also a logical distinction between writing that pursues the laws of its own being and writing that recognizes other people's laws, even if the distinction proves to be false in the fullness of time. Creative Writing postulates the very distinction. And what goes on in its name at universities around the world is the collective effort, the organized attempt, to follow that postulate to its logical conclusion. Writing becomes 'creative' in a process much like that by which some American schools, established to train children in literacy, penmanship, arithmetic and good manners, exchanged their original civic function to become 'child-centred', acknowledging individual strengths and different learning styles, fostering self-discovery and experimentation, providing a positive educational environment, and distinguished not by shared knowledge or disciplinary conceptions but by an identifiable brand of classroom teaching.

The reason for the universal triumph of subjectivist expressionism becomes evident when turning from the history of criticism to the history of education. Although it was founded and championed on the university level by cultural conservatives like Norman Foerster and the southern New Critics, Creative Writing has never shaken off the dust of its origins on the secondary level, where it was put in motion nearly nine decades ago by a progressive educator. It is no accident that the term I used in *The Elephants Teach* for the original idea behind Creative Writing – what I called constructivism – is also the name that is now used in education schools for what was once known as progressive education. As the historian of education Diane Ravitch explains:

> Associated with this [educational] philosophy are such approaches as whole language, fuzzy math, and invented spelling, as well as a disdain for phonics and grammar, an insistence that there are no right answers (just different ways to solve problems), and an emphasis on students' self-esteem. Constructivists dislike any kind of ability grouping or special classes for gifted children. By diminishing the authority of the teacher, constructivist methods often create discipline problems.[13]

The vulgarization of Emerson's creative reading or Spingarn's creative criticism into the radical subjectivism of today's Creative Writing pedagogy can be accounted for by the collapse of literary constructivism into educational constructivism. Pedagogically, Creative Writing has been reduced almost exclusively to the workshop method.

The phrase *Creative Writing* may have been coined by Emerson and given currency by Spingarn's creative criticism, then, but the meaning that the phrase came to have in the philosophy of education – freedom from external demands and other people's laws – is its primary meaning. Creative Writing is what goes on in certain classroom assignments and discussions. Dawson says that such a view 'cannot be sustained' (p. 34). For him Creative Writing's fundamental defect is that it remains wedded to what others have taken to calling the magisterial tradition, the widely discredited view that literature is a fixed and restrictive canon of select masterpieces. Creative Writing is simply behindhand in not discrediting the view. The problem, however, lies not primarily in Creative Writing's conception of literature, but in its theory of education, which prevents any other idea of literature from rising to notice. Having poured a subjectivist/expressionist ethos as its foundation, Creative Writing can offer no objective criteria for the production and evaluation of new work. Small wonder that the workshops have largely abandoned traditional genres and other literary conventions like poetic meter and rhyme. According to the workshop ethos, there are as many genres and conventions as there are individual writers.[14] And yet Creative Writing students desperately need other people's laws. As Arthur Saltzman observes after teaching the subject for several years, 'students tend to be passionate according to formula'. They rarely 'risk reactions along any but established paths'. In order 'to make them consider values that lie beyond face value', the Creative Writing teacher 'need[s] to expose the evaluative criteria that they invariably bring to the discussion'.[15]

Just here is the dilemma. Since the writers' workshop presupposes the rejection of any but intrinsic criteria – the judgement whether a literary text stands or falls according to the laws of its own being – how are the Creative Writing teacher's own criteria to survive public exposure? Even the most rigorous attempts to uncover the shared disciplinary conceptions of Creative Writing, reflecting writers' collective literary ambitions and methods, are doomed to end in a restatement of subjectivist expressionism.[16] The best writers are well aware of the dilemma. In her novel *Blue Angel* (2000), Francise Prose shows that the bind in which the Creative Writing teacher finds himself would be tragic if it were not so funny.

Prose is a veteran of the workshop system. She teaches Creative Writing at Bard College, where she joined the faculty after several visiting stints at places like Sarah Lawrence, the New School and the Iowa Writers' Workshop and five years with the MFA Program for Writers at Warren Wilson College. Although she is a fully credentialled member of the establishment – she belongs to the Associated Writing Programs – Prose remains ambivalent about it, and about the campus life for a writer.

Blue Angel takes its point of departure from the campus preoccupation with sexual harassment. Prose's hero is not falsely accused of a trivial offence, however; nor is he under any illusion that coitus with a twenty-years-younger woman will somehow regenerate him. A novelist who has not published a new novel in several years, Ted Swenson beds his student Angela Argo because he is seduced by her writing. Swenson is not particularly attracted to her; she is a skinny redhead with streaked hair and half a dozen facial piercings. But she is writing a novel called *Eggs* for his seminar, and Swenson is swept away by it – chapter by chapter, as she hands it in. 'That's what their relationship's really about', he says. 'Sex was just a distraction'.[17] His reaction to her writing is immediate, physical, disorienting; and it doesn't help that Angela seems to be transcribing their affair for her novel. Reading a sex scene, he is reduced to scribbling insipid marginalia in an effort to reassert some control over himself: 'Swenson finds his blue pencil and circles *literally die* and writes "cut 'literally'" in the margin. What in God's name is he doing?' (p. 180). Editorial comments are wildly inappropriate both to the aesthetic and erotic experience of reading Angela's novel. He is so far gone that he prays for 'a purely literary response' (p. 181).

Because he has only an inadequate technical knowledge to offer his students, Swenson is defenceless when one of them produces genuine art. At the start of the novel he does suggest a promising alternative. 'The strongest story', he tells his students, 'makes us see how we could be that [character], how the world looks through that [character]'s eyes.' Even if his students don't become writers, he reassures himself, they have learned 'a way of seeing the world – each fellow human a character to be entered and understood' (pp. 10–11). Although Prose gives no evidence that she is familiar with his views, the philosopher Hilary Putnam says something remarkably similar. The spellbound reader of Céline's *Voyage au bout de la nuit*, for example, does not learn that love does not exist. 'What I learn', Putnam says, 'is to see the world as it looks to someone who is sure that hypothesis is correct. I see what plausibility that hypothesis has; what it would be like if it were true; how someone could possibly think that it is true.' Putnam calls this real knowledge, advancing it as a defence of literature: 'It is knowledge of a possibility. It is conceptual knowledge.'[18]

Swenson does not develop the idea. And in the event, what he discovers is that genuinely original writing causes even the experienced teacher and critic to suffer a reversal, desperately seeking affirmation for literary judgement that is no longer sure of itself. Swenson becomes enthralled with Angela, eventually destroying his marriage and teaching career in a fruitless pursuit of her. He cannot even say what makes her writing so good. His only evaluative criterion is his erotic response, and he cannot begin to explain it.

After a class session in which the workshop is brutal in its criticism, Swenson tries to defend Angela's writing, but he ends by delivering an oration that even he recognizes as 'banal:'

> Sometimes it happens that something new comes along, something fresh and original, unlike what's been written before. Once in a lifetime or once in a generation, there's a Proust or a Joyce or a Virginia Woolf. Almost always, hardly anyone understands what the writer's doing, most people think it's trash, so the writer's life is hell. (p. 202)

When the students giggle, Swenson is reduced to insisting lamely that Angela's writing is 'the real thing'. Even his most loyal student has to snap back: 'That's bullshit, too.' And when one girl in the class declares at his sexual-harassment hearing that the only reason he praised Angela was because he was sleeping with her, Swenson has no argument to offer in reply.

In the end, Swenson gains redemption. Namely: redemption from the hell of teaching Creative Writing. Losing his job is like 'being promoted from the inferno to purgatory' (p. 313). He escapes, that is, from the damnation of teaching a subject in which evaluative criteria are little better than a function of the teacher's experience and classroom authority, which can disappear in a moment of thralldom to genuine art. Swenson finds relief in admitting, 'even for just one moment, how much he will never know' (p. 314). But that is a lesson he cannot take back to the classroom. Imprisoned in the subjectivist/expressionist ethos of Creative Writing, where the only law is the law of one's own being and where even the best teachers must admit how much they do not know, perhaps literary knowledge can be achieved and imparted only by breaking out of the system altogether.

Creative Writing might offer another kind of knowledge, teaching how the strongest stories construct human possibility, but to do so it would have to abandon subjective satisfaction as the sole measure of creative accomplishment and begin to answer to objective facts outside the self, where other people might possibly live. Again, the best writers already know this. When an outstanding novelist who teaches in a front-rank writing program separates herself from the prevailing ethos to affirm values anchored in an ultimate reality, she is less likely to write essays about Creative Writing than to reclaim human civilization by returning to 'the idea that people have souls, and that they have certain obligations to them, and certain pleasures in them', because she is concerned to begin the process of reform at a much more basic level.[19] And that may finally be the problem. Creative Writing may not be able to reform itself from within. A value system that transcends the subjective needs of individual expression may be necessary to produce good writers. In the mean time, though, the workshops will go on if only for the sake of going on.

Notes

1. Greg Kuzma, 'The Catastrophe of Creative Writing,' *Poetry* 148 (1986): 342–54. Kuzma was joined by Bruce Bawer, 'Dave Smith's "Creative Writing,"' *New Criterion* 4 (December 1985): 27–33; Joseph Epstein, 'Who Killed Poetry?' *Commentary* 86 (August 1988): 13–20; David Dooley, 'The Contemporary Workshop Aesthetic,' *Hudson Review* 43 (1990): 259–80; John W. Aldridge, 'The New American Assembly-Line Fiction,' *American Scholar* 59 (1990): 17–38; and R.S. Gwynn, 'No Biz Like Po' Biz,' *Sewanee Review* 100 (1992): 311–23.
2. Christopher Beach, 'Careers in Creativity: The Poetry Academy in the 1990s,' *Western Humanities Review* 50 (Spring 1996): 15.
3. David Radavich, 'Creative Writing in the Academy,' *Profession* 1999: 106–12; D.W. Fenza, 'Creative Writing and Its Discontents,' *Writer's Chronicle* 32 (March–April 2000): 52.
4. Shirley Geok-lin Lim, 'The Strangeness of Creative Writing: An Institutional Query,' *Pedagogy* 3 (Spring 2003): 157.
5. Francine Prose, *Blue Angel* (New York: Harper Collins, 2000), p. 199; Paul Dawson, *Creative Writing and the New Humanities* (London: Routledge, 2005), p. 2. Subsequent references to Dawson's book are inserted between parentheses.
6. D.G. Myers, *The Elephants Teach*, new edn. (Chicago: University of Chicago Press, 2006), pp. 31–3. The book was first published in 1996.

7. Irving Babbitt, *Rousseau and Romanticism* (Austin: University of Texas Press, 1979), p. 271.

8. D.G. Myers, As above, pp. 119–20.

9. Irving Babbitt, 'On Being Creative,' in *On Being Creative and Other Essays* (Boston: Houghton Mifflin, 1932), esp. pp. 25–6.

10. J.E. Spingarn, 'The New Criticism' (1910), in *Creative Criticism and Other Essays*, new and enlarged edn. (New York: Harcourt Brace, 1931), p. 18.

11. Private communication, 26 August, 2005. Name withheld upon request.

12. Geoffrey Light, 'From the Personal to the Public: Conceptions of Creative Writing in Higher Education,' *Higher Education* 43 (March 2002): 265–6.

13. Diane Ravitch, 'Would You Want to Study at a Bloomberg School?' *Wall Street Journal* (12 May, 2005): A16.

14. 'Poets do not really write epics, pastorals, lyrics, however much they may be deceived by these false abstractions', Spingarn says. 'They express themselves, and this expression is their only form. There are not, therefore, only three, or ten, or a hundred literary kinds; there are as many kinds as there are individual poets' (*Creative Criticism*, p. 23).

15. Arthur Saltzman, 'On Not Being Nice: Sentimentality and the Creative Writing Class,' *Midwest Quarterly* 44 (Spring 2003): 324.

16. See Charles Johnson, 'Storytelling and the Alpha Narrative,' *Southern Review* 41 (Winter 2005): 151–9, for an interesting attempt by an interesting novelist to devise a 'fiction-writing curriculum' that is 'highly productive and capacious', requiring large doses of assigned writing, including imitation and copybook exercises that are 'aimed at learning a repertoire of literary strategies', with the ultimate goal's being 'the preparation of journeymen who will one day be able to take on any narrative assignment that comes up in their careers . . .' Even so, when Johnson explains how he teaches a student to develop a story, he circles back to the concept of its intrinsic demands: 'Given *this* character in *this* situation and with *this* specific problem to solve, what might happen next?' he asks (p. 157; his emphasis).

17. Prose, *Blue Angel*, p. 179. Subsequent references are inserted between parentheses.

18. Hilary Putnam, *Meaning and the Moral Sciences* (London: Routledge & Kegan Paul, 1978), p. 90. Emphasis in the original.

19. Marilynne Robinson, *The Death of Adam: Essays on Modern Thought* (New York: Picador, 2005), pp. 8–9. The collection, first published in 1998, was reissued soon after Robinson won the Pulitzer Prize for her brilliant novel, *Gilead*. She teaches at the Iowa Writers' Workshop.

Part II
Workshops

Papers in this section use scholarly written accounts as their research methods as well as reflections on their own personal experiences.

Rachel Blau DuPlessis and Jena Osman's clarification of workshop assumptions begins from the view that instead of advice and evaluation, writers need an audience. They argue how slow reading is key since it 'encourages reflective scrutiny' and they discuss ways they give students a 'shared vocabulary for analytic description'. While in many Creative Writing workshops, students present their own work for feedback, in Blau Du Plessis and Osman's poetry workshops, a student-respondent presents another student's work drawing on a range of analytic strategies from semantic/ etymological, to syntax, to structural organization. Drawing on composition theory they ask students to perform different kinds of response experiments to each other's work, which might even include turning a poem into a different genre. Furthermore, they introduce students to a larger writing culture outside the classroom so that in addition to developing language skills, students learn about larger cultural contexts.

Gary Hawkins begins by questioning assumptions in workshop pedagogy that focus only on teaching and critiquing craft. He sees this situation as deriving in part from pressures in English Departments that still view Creative Writing 'suspiciously as an unrigorous realm of free expression'. However, Hawkins' workshops focus not just on craft but on a poem's ideas. His outcome is to join practical craft with 'irrational aspirations of high art', including its moral claims. Hence, the pedagogy here is 'a combined creative-critical writing' and Hawkins calls for explicit poetics that account for both elements in writing, a poetics that centres on the reciprocal relationship between these two elements.

Michelene Wandor clarifies tacit assumptions by exploring different influences on the Creative Writing Workshop from the academic model centred on training professional writers derived from the University of Iowa to the Postwar emergence of worker-writer groups that encouraged ordinary working people to write. She explores how this results in a confusing and contradictory practice and argues that Creative Writing needs to go beyond current workshop practices to include literary criticism studies, cultural theory and stylistics/linguistics.[1]

Note

1. Editor's note: as indicated by other papers in this collection, many practitioners are already taking these initiatives.

4
Creative Writing and Creative Reading in the Poetry Workshop

Rachel Blau DuPlessis and Jena Osman

> One must be an inventor to read well . . . There is then
> creative reading as well as creative writing.
> > – Ralph Waldo Emerson, 'The American Scholar'

What does Creative Writing teach? Some students who take university-level Creative Writing courses will have the talent, skill, obsession, commitment and urgency (even voracity) to be poets. But the Creative Writing class can not make them so; instead, we see the Creative Writing workshop as a site for learning strategic skills of 'reading'.[1] It is a space for students rigorously to consider the meaning and implications of their writing, and to be responsive to the writing of others in an informed and playful way. We have outlined below a number of strategies (developed in our Creative Writing classes at Temple University) for achieving these goals, all of which encourage methods of analytic description and of 'writing as reading'. These strategies shift the terms of evaluation away from individual mastery, and more toward the concept of writing as an animated conversation with all that is possible in language.

In her methods of close reading, Laura (Riding) Jackson points to 'developing a capacity for minuteness' – the ability to focus on the detail in its implications – 'for seeing all there is to see at a given point and for taking it all with one as one goes along'.[2] Slow reading is key in that it encourages reflective scrutiny. It is also important to have students be fearless when confronting what Peter Middleton has called 'the messiness and temporal incompletion of individual run-ins with the [poetic] text . . . the contingent history of actual sessions of reading'.[3] There is no one ideal and correct response to a work; reading is a process of continuing discovery.

In order to articulate the observations that result from such particulars of reflection, students do need some common language, and we use the topics below as a means to provide them with a shared vocabulary for analytic description. We also assign a number of 'prompts' (found in the second half of this article), which ask students to investigate each other's works performatively. The ultimate goal is to develop the students' capacity for deep, integrative reflection on their own work via creative reading, because – as Peter Elbow and Pat Belanoff have said in their book *A Community of Writers*:

> Evaluation and advice are not what writers need most. What writers need (and fortunately it's what all readers are best at) is an audience: a thoughtful, interested audience rather than evaluators or editors or advice-givers.[4]

The topics that follow – descriptive and performative – can provide a language for responsible and useful responsiveness in graduate and undergraduate poetry workshops.

In a typical three hour workshop we might discuss the works of three students, each presented by a student-respondent. The respondents may be asked to make an initial report by applying up to three of the following terms to the work at hand.

Dictionary: semantic and etymological work

Look up all words in the poem that you do not know, but also look up some words you do know that seem vital to the poem. Figure out what in-depth resonance this knowledge gives to the poem (cf. Susan Howe).[5] Word choice as involved with connotation, implication, cultural suggestiveness.

Structure/organization of statement

Beginning-middle-end. Part/whole relationships. The meaning of the ending. Questions around closure. Dispersive (projective) or 'composition by field' (cf. Charles Olson).[6] Emotional arrangement or trajectory. Controlling the 'sequence of disclosure' (cf. George Oppen).[7] Pacing of materials. Collage, montage, juxtaposition, fragment, 'interruption' – each of these strategies may have multiple justifications and be used for quite different reasons. Discursive structure, argument. Repetition as a tactic. Variation, cutups, recombinings. Seriality.

Form

Fixed (received) form or invented form; uses of, or allusions to existing forms (e.g. sonnet, sestina), including forms from outside the poetic tradition (e.g. primer, diary, index). Form in relation to the page. Choices of 'prose forms' or 'writing'. Invention of any kind of patterned arrangements. Procedural form.

Organization of the line

Line break, rhyme, caesura, space inside the line, the variety of sizes of line segments. What motivates line break in each case? Line in relation to breath and the performing body, to syntax, to the page and material text. Differences in poetics based on differences in line. Metrics and the establishment of line.

Imagery

Nature of imagery. Tendency to metaphor (something described in terms of another) and/or to metonymy (additive list-like juxtapositions). Poetic traditions for imagery (descriptive, allegorical, metaphysical, surrealist, kenning). Development of images through the poem. Arguments proposed by the sequence of images.

Semantic Issues

The themes, materials and conclusions offered by the text. The unrolling of argument. The 'work' done by the text, social, personal, cultural. The assumptions, values and conclusions of the text.

Issues of sound

Sound map. Sound pattern, including rhyme – regular or randomized. Metrics and rhythm as part of sound. Levels and intensities of sound. Sound in relation to semantic issues: Puns, trans-segmental drift (phonemic drift, cf. Garrett Stewart).[8] Crypt words or shadow words (associative, allusive, behind the word). 'The soundscape' (cf. Charles Bernstein).[9]

Linguistic issues

Diction, diction levels, diction ranges, including poetic diction, colloquial diction. Diction, tone and creation of subject position. Key words in a poem and their etymology or historical resonance. Babble, dialect, polyvocality, multilingual strategies, heteroglossia, non-standard uses or mixes. Found language, use of documents and social texts.

Genre

Allusions to or uses of epic, lyric, ballad, elegy, ode, satire, song, fragment, epistle, manifesto, hymn, cento. The language, form, subjectivity typical of any of the genres. Generic mixes; the heterogeneric, hybridity. 'New' genres: such as procedurally derived form, sound or phonemic poetry, non-narrative prose, lists. The discovery and use of any generic inspiration: manifesto, alphabet, 'writing off' or 'through' another poem, homophonic translation.

Tradition

Ancestors of the poem or poetics. Intertextualities and allusions to prior poetic work, dialogues between this work and other works. Dialogues between the poem/poet and other artistic traditions (music, visual art).

Anxieties about influence; influence as productive. Direct allusions to or citations of other poems and practices.

The poetics

The theory of the poem. The method of the poem – method as foregrounded and explored. Its poetic assumptions, its gains, its losses. The philosophical tradition in which the poem (or the poetics) exists. Reasons for writing. Functions of writing. The nature of the poet as defined by the poetics. Claims for the generation of the poem – inspiration, expression, found language, chance, numerological procedures, historical and spiritual imbeddedness and explorations. How is poetic authority assumed and deployed, or avoided?

Syntax

Syntax in its relation to line break, to structure, to semantic issues ('meaning'). Pronouns as identifying speaker, addressee. Nature of syntax (parataxis, hypotaxis, combinations). Unusual features of syntax related to semantics or to line. Nature of nouns (abstract, concrete, simple, complex). Verb tenses and movement.

Subjectivity, 'voice' and/or 'consciousness'

Notions of subjectivity displayed in the work. The kinds of 'I', if any; multiplication of subjectivities. Critique of, or use of narrative, meditative, dramatic or lyric kinds of subjectivity. Other pronouns and their functions and social roles in poems. 'I/you' relations in the poem. The uses of figures of Other or interlocutors or listeners as depicted in the poem. Who or what is the implied 'ear', or listener.

Material text

Page space and its meanings: the arrangement or visual presentation of the poem on the page. White space. Typography – letter size, fonts. Capital letters, and where used (i.e. at the beginning of lines? of sentences? elsewhere?). Deployment of punctuation (regular or a-normative). Letters themselves.

Title and paratext

The 'title to the poem' (Anne Ferry's term).[10] What occupies the title space? Expressive possibilities of titles: introductory? claiming authority? saying something 'about' the poem? being an integral part of the poem? Evasions of titling – implications of no title. Title and authority: entitlement. Issues raised by any ancillary textual material or paratext (dedication, epigraph, gloss, notes, dates, etc.)

Another model for organizing classroom time and for encouraging creative reading practices is to ask students to perform different kinds of response experiments around each other's work. Although Elbow and Belanoff are composition theorists, a number of their 'writing as reading' strategies are quite useful in the Creative Writing workshop.[11] A few of their suggestions for 'responsive' writing, which we've adapted specifically to poetry, include:

Pointing and center of gravity

Which words/phrases stick in the mind and resonate? Seem to be sources of energy? Once the center of gravity is located, write off of that center (another poem, an essayistic musing, etc.).

Reply

How would you reply to the piece at hand? You could write a line in between each line of a poem, or write a line in response to each line, or turn the poem into a dialogue, a letter, etc.

Movies of the reader's mind

Write down everything that comes into your mind as you come into contact with each word/line/idea within the poem at hand.

Ron Padgett also discusses activist response techniques in his book *Creative Reading*, with these suggestions for turning reading procedures into writing procedures.[12]

Changing single words

A line might say that people were carrying a heavy box of provisions. You might change 'provisions' to 'visions'. A corollary procedure would be the *Oulipo* tactic of N+7, where each noun is substituted by the seventh noun that follows it in the dictionary.[13] Padgett defends this by evoking an awakening to the implications of both the original and the substitutions.

Read alternate lines

Leading to fresh combinations of ideas and images.

'Trickle down' reading

cf. Tom Phillips' *A Humument*, Ronald Johnson's *RADI OS*, or Jen Bervin's *Nets*. This method finds the poem within the poem, tracing rivers of words that 'trickle' through the already existing text.

Edge blur

The edges of a page of type are blurred, but the center portion is kept in focus. Or vice versa.

Cut-ups

This method was made popular by Tristan Tzara and William Burroughs. See as examples, T.S. Eliot's *The Waste Land* and Dos Passos' 'Camera Eye' sections of *U.S.A.* Burroughs in fact believed that cut-ups had oracular power. Odier states the following: 'Perhaps events are pre-written and pre-recorded and when you cut the word lines the future leaks out.'[14]

Stencils

Cut out shapes and place the cut paper over the poem. Read or rewrite the poem by moving the stencil in various directions (diagonally, whirlpool pattern, bottom to top, etc.).

Translations

Translate the poem into opposites, or into words that begin with the same letter, or into words that sound like the original words.

Similar experiments for workshops can be adapted from Bernadette Mayer's experiment list (which has been supplemented by Charles Bernstein at www.writing.upenn.edu/pennsound, accessed 28 February 2012).[15] It is important that these experiments not be treated as simple 'recipes' that exist separate from intention. The choice of experiment should be the result of a student's interpretive decisions; something within the original poem should suggest the particular experiment performed. An explanation of why a procedure was chosen, as well as what the procedure revealed about the original, are required as part of the response.

We find that both analytic and performative responses to the works of peers as well as to published poets help students discover what is important to them in their own writing practices. These methods give them the means to investigate and articulate what they find most compelling about language itself – and give them license to seek it, read it and write it in a variety of ways.

In addition to the creative reading practices listed above, we also think it is important to introduce students to a larger sense of writing community – a world outside of the classroom that includes literary magazines, websites (such as epc.buffalo.edu,[16] www.writing.upenn.edu/pennsound,[17] and ubu-web.com[18]) and public readings. Seeing the works of other (aspiring, accomplished, or even somewhat raggedy) practitioners gives students a sense of the broader conversations in which their own work takes part. Local and university sponsored readings by interesting contemporaries move the act of writing out of the sometimes official, distant and museum-like world of anthologies into networks and productions happening in students' real time.

All of these tactics, from the most amusing and playful to the most investigative and analytic, encourage the kinds of endless productive responsiveness and critical engagement that in fact mimics the ways poetic cultures work. These tactics sharpen reading, engage participatory learning, and help create in our students an eye and an ear for language in all its semantic subtlety and cultural resonance. They demand that students become more aware of language in its semantic, social and material aspects, and thus deepen their relationship to their medium. And they encourage a complexity of reading, understanding and assessing language forms that is crucial – not only for the experience of reading and writing poetry, but for the experience of language in any context.

Notes

1. Ron Padgett *Creative Reading* (Urbana, IL: National Council of Teachers of English, 1997).
2. Laura Riding, *The Laura (Riding) Jackson Reader*, Ed. Elizabeth Friedmann (New York: Persea Books, 2005).
3. Peter Middleton, *Distant Reading: Performance, Readership, and Consumption in Contemporary Poetry* (Tuscaloosa, AL: University of Alabama Press, 2005), p. 2.
4. Peter Elbow and Pat Belanoff, *A Community of Writers* (New York: McGraw-Hill, 1995), p. 6.
5. Susan Howe, *My Emily Dickinson (1985)* (New York: New Directions, 2007).
6. Charles Olson, *Collected Prose*, Eds. Donald Allen and Benjamin Friedlander (Berkeley: University of California Press, 1997).
7. George Oppen, 'Statement on Poetics,' *Sagetrieb* 3, 3 (Winter 1984): 25–7.
8. Garrett Stewart, *Reading Voices: Literature and the Phonotext* (Berkeley: University of California Press, 1990).
9. Charles Bernstein, Ed., *Close Listening: Poetry and the Performed Word* (New York: Oxford: Oxford University Press, 1998).
10. Anne Ferry, *A Community of Writers* (New York: McGraw-Hill, 1995).
11. Ron Padgett, as above.
12. Peter Elbow and Pat Belanoff, as above.
13. Warren F. Motte, Ed., *Oulipo: A Primer of Potential Literature* (Lincoln, NE: University of Nebraska Press, 1986).
14. Daniel Odier, *The Job: Interviews with William Burrough* (London: Cape, 1970).
15. Bernadette Mayer and Charles Bernstein, *List of Poetic Experiments*, www.writing.upenn.edu (accessed 28 February 2012).
16. Electronic Poetry Center, epc.buffalo.edu (accessed 28 February 2012).
17. PENNSound at www.writing.upenn.edu/pennsound/ (accessed 28 February 2012).
18. Ubu Web at www.ubuweb.com (accessed 28 February 2012).

5
The Irrational Element in the Undergraduate Poetry Workshop: Beyond Craft

Gary Hawkins

> Poetry must be irrational.
>
> —Wallace Stevens

When I consider the education of the poet, two differing scenes come to mind. The first affirms the unschooled genius of the poet: Keats and Leigh Hunt in long, revelled nights of inspiration at Hunt's cottage, writing sonnets side by side, adorning one another with laurel crowns. The alternate scene proposes an apprenticeship for the poet: novices Plath and Sexton seeking out a master in Lowell, absorbing his skill and advice from the back of his Boston seminar. The workshop, the modern education for poets, often wishes to be more like the former, a creative crucible of contemporaries, but it exists mostly in the latter model, as an ordered craft school of the guild.[1]

Yet my undergraduate students, whether they be serious young poets or young scientists exploring the humanities, arrive at the workshop pressurized with the belief that poetry thrives on inspiration – an irrational faith that will never be completely satisfied by any ordered and rational exercise of craft. In acknowledging their expectation that some portion of poetry has this Romantic source I need not give over the workshop to the myth of the unschooled poet or admit that poetry can not be taught. Still, when I embrace what Stevens terms 'the irrational element in poetry', I allow an element of genius into the classroom, where it arrives not as the final word but rather as an individuality to be cultivated. In truth, the 'irrational element' – what is to Stevens that unpredictable, nearly unaccountable 'individuality of the poet' – ultimately distinguishes poem from mere verse by placing something of consequence at stake.[2] With his individual imagination or idea the poet exceeds the completion of an exercise and presents a work with a moral claim: *this is more than the accomplishment of a sonnet; this is a sonnet which has something to say.*

Strangely, this truth I know as poet I have as teacher too often left at the door. I mean here to examine what has led to this situation in the workshop, and I want to consider some ways that the irrational aspirations of high art might rejoin the teaching of practical craft in the undergraduate workshop to unite two crucial elements of poetic practice.

Our workshop teaching often under-attends the varieties of the irrational for reasons that can be readily understood. Even as we believe poetry can be taught we persist in the Romantic beliefs that the final source of poetry is mysterious and that the poet, if he can reach this source, holds a gift. Stevens gives voice to a common sentiment that 'poets continue to be born not made'.[3] At best, this view treats as given a student's capability of inspiration and moves on to the 'makeable' parts of poetry, its craft. Moreover, this emphasis maintains the considerable virtue of the workshop: it becomes a place of work rather than of therapy. Yet when we also admit, without any cynicism, that our undergraduate courses will yield very few gifted poets, we must ask: what is the purpose of that work when it is absent a more complex engagement with the irrational? What is the fate of the imagination? Of ideas? Such concerns will help us attend both young poets and those who will never claim such a role.[4]

To arrive at an understanding of the workshop as a complex of motives and participants requires us to face a pedagogy that we have left largely unexamined. Instead, Creative Writing classes tend to follow what François Camoin allows is the 'Law of the Workshop', an unvaried format of critique.[5] Such static practice is the focal point of recent critical scholarship, like Hans Ostrom and Wendy Bishop's crucial *Rethinking Creative Writing Theory and Pedagogy*, which reconsiders this protocol. Ostrom finds that 'teachers of Creative Writing . . . may well make up a disproportionate share of those who retreat from theory' as a means of pedagogical self-examination.[6] And Bishop, extending the thinking of Peter Elbow, considers that the inheritance of the 'critical, doubting, winnowing, elite form of the master-teacher workshop' keeps us from liking our students, a prerequisite for a superior writing workshop.[7] Still, the reform that might come from liking student writing seems to represent, admits Elbow, the 'worst kind of subjectivity', and this remains an unlikely shift in pedagogy.[8]

But there may be another reason for our resistance to modifying the workshop. In it we engage in matchless work to remarkable effect. When we welcome students as apprentices, they take positions as novices in the face of language and become awed by its subtleties. When we lead them through the supple form and trope of poetry, they become aware of its rhythmic and structural as well denotative signals. Most significantly, we engage them not as scholars alone but as makers. From this perspective, even the most exquisite and elusive poetic statement – say, the wild surmise of a Keats sonnet at its revealing final turn – is shown to be worked by human hands. And thus the craft of verse comes down to earth a bit.

At times, however, the accessibility of the handiwork of poetry confines the teaching space of the workshop: the work of craft that it does so well becomes the sole thing it aims to do. Taking that pose of a 'craft school' filled primarily with aspiring poets, this kind of teaching fills students with a full repertoire of poetics and forms. The 'individuality of the poet' and its irrational drives are expected to arrive with the young poets themselves. And if their ideas right now are slim, these can simmer and mature on their own while the workshop prepares these poets with tools for their future mastery.

Alternately, a belief in the mysterious source of poetry breeds a set of anxieties to be calmed by craft. So the basic economy of the workshop, a New Critical exchange with the text, stands as a bulwark of objective method against long-standing charges of excessive subjectivity in the humanities. Sometimes this defensiveness responds to pressures in the halls of the English department, which may still view the field of Creative Writing suspiciously as an unrigorous realm of free expression.[9] More impolitic is to admit to a defensive posture forming within the workshop itself. Am I the only teacher whose strict attention toward craft has arisen in part from a weariness at facing the adolescent drives which all too often masquerade as profundities in poems? I suspect I am not. I can even recall myself saying, *I don't care what you write about, so long as it is in the form of a sonnet*, as if by avoiding questions of content I could assure my students – and myself – of pleasure and success.

To break through the calcification of the workshop I look no farther than my students. My greatest successes have come from honouring the initial expressive energy of undergraduates – which cuts through my defences to request a similar generosity of response. Their unschooled sense of poetry as a medium which can allow them a voice they have not known before is poetry at its core. They may not end up as poets, or even aspire to such a lot, but they have something to say, an inspiration, an idea, new and imaginative thoughts. My generous duty is to encourage these irrational impulses and also to offer students some means of refinement. Craft is not absent from this work; it serves to enable students to speak the truth as they see it. But to succeed, craft must set the highest sights.

To assert a combined creative-critical writing pedagogy, which is part of what I aim to do here, does not mark an entirely original plan, and in fact these dual purposes inform many writing programs in America as evidenced by their dual requirements of writing workshops and courses in critical inquiry (including, most commonly, literary studies). However, to combine the creative and the critical across a program's curriculum is not the same thing as making use of both in a workshop.[10] What we need is a poetics that acknowledges the virtue of both elements and aims to keep both consistently in play. Paul Dawson's recent reconfiguration, *Creative Writing and the New Humanities*, attempts to name a 'workshop poetics' to do just this.[11] For Dawson a workshop poetics is 'both criticism, a formalist examination of the methods by which a literary work is made, and a "making," a form of reading which participates in the drafting process'.[12] Ideally this leads to a kind of reciprocity. In learning to 'read like a writer,' a student may recognize her own writerly choice-making as she attends to a model in terms of its choices of craft, and so 'reading like a writer' becomes a creative method in the workshop, producing questions about the choices made in student drafts. With choice comes the potential choice to reject all the advice of the workshop. This seems to allow an opening for a 'irrational' decision that resists the workshop's duty to accomplished craft in order to assert a poem on alternate grounds.

But here Dawson reminds us that such a reading-centered workshop process can lead to a closed system:

> In this critical environment the writer speaks not from the position of an author with a preconceived essence of selfhood that needs to be expressed, a vision of society that must be relayed; the writer is that student who has internalised a set of theoretical principles, thus organising a response according to the same critical strategies adopted to identify exemplary texts.[13]

Rather than follow this situation to that post-structural conclusion in which authorship is a useless fiction, Dawson keeps alive the two historical strands of Creative Writing pedagogy to confirm: 'Creative Writing draws not only on an expressivist view of literature but on a tradition of Anglo-American formalism and structuralist narratology in order to construct a method of teaching.'[14] Thus, following the poetics of this method (founded on 'reading like a writer'), 'authorship exists in the workshop as an implicit assumption, in the sense that an exemplary text is attributed to an agent who has consciously employed techniques of writing'.[15] Such an author is one to whom the workshop can confidently and generously respond. We weigh his conscious choices; we applaud his conscious triumphs; we scold his consciously-played faults. Yet too often our focus on this wholly conscious agent crowds out another author, who may be Romantic and may be a construct, but whom my students still bring to class with them, unreconstructed as they are. And I am searching for ways to acknowledge them as they arrive.

I mean to place the teaching of craft in this dynamic context: knowledge of craft can lead to inspiration, and it will also guide a poem which begins as an idea. This full context will also allow us to break the Law of the Workshop to discuss *what* a poem claims as well as *how* the poem presents it. For those, like me, who were bred on a New Critical craft method like that outlined in John Ciardi's seminal textbook *How a Poem Means* (the bible of my early workshop education), such a proposal seems ill-advised if not pedagogically reckless.[16] Indeed, in releasing from a strict program of craft there is no single approach that can ensure an unchaotic workshop, and

I will not presume mine is an original curriculum. A few ideas will suggest what might be possible.

In his well-known essays, Richard Hugo shows how craft can nurture inspiration. According to Hugo, 'Writing Off the Subject' is a process of diversion in which the immediate field of the poem is merely 'The Triggering Town' leading to more imaginative environs.[17] Stevens describes this oblique pursuit more theoretically as the move away from one's 'true subject' and toward 'the poetry of the subject', an activity which he finds essentially 'unpredictable'.[18] We become better teachers when we, as Hugo advocates, make these tandem pursuits transparent in our teaching. When both aspects of a poem, its craft and its ideas, meet the workshop's scrutiny, students face a high accountability, and, yes, there is an increased opportunity for failure. Finesse in form is insufficient if the poem is vacant morally; and a fine idea is nothing without a precisely executed line. Yet as students confront these consequences, they find value in poetry. As the teacher, I find an encounter with an unruly, searching poem is more rewarding than the scrutiny of well-wrought forms.

To encourage such searching, I often return to the work of Stevens. Stevens is a poet whose imagination is not in free flight but is directed by his continually asserted ideas. Moreover, these ideas are presented not solely in poems (which, as models by themselves, might yield a workshop full of polemics and abstractions) but also in his luminous prose. These fiery but reasoned narrations illustrate the use of a declarative mode to refine the irrational and still imagine an art that exceeds full explanation. Read side-by-side with the poems, this inspired prose is not the more imaginative work (for that I'll choose 'Sunday Morning' over 'The Irrational Element in Poetry' any day). But it does present a model for a critical, personal stake in art, and it shows what can come when inspiration is followed beyond its first spark. Of course, reading this prose is only the first step. When I have asked students to write their own manifestoes, the poems which follow show a drive unlike those birthed by formal exercises alone.

In teaching the practicalities of craft we accept the premise that poetry is something which can be successfully learned and that it is something which can be successfully taught. However, in seeking the full transaction of poetry – one which engages idea, aspires toward beauty and aims to make a meaningful point – craft is only one part. There is no metaphysics of craft alone, and proficiency will not lead to art.

The exigencies of teaching conspire to divert us from this high mark. And some of the highlands of poetry – such as beauty – will always remain gifts arriving unbidden in the arms of the poet. Still, the undergraduate workshop can aspire to create poems which are strongly said in addition to being well wrought. I crave student poems that are – like Randall Jarrell's praise of Elizabeth Bishop's work – inscribed with the affirmation: *I have seen it;*[19] I crave poems that – like Lowell's 'Skunk Hour' – response to Bishop – 'will not scare;' I want poems that defy mere description and take a stand.[20] And my teaching is best – I like my students most – when I create an environment which can fairly expect such creations.

Notes

1. D.G. Myers, *The Elephants Teach: Creative Writing Since 1880* (Englewood Cliffs, NJ: PrenticeHall, 1996 and 2006). Myers corrects the assumption that the workshop is an institutionalized extension of writers working in a community. Rather, he argues that the workshop emerges only as the idea of a humanist education is replaced by an increasingly specialized curriculum for writers.
2. Wallace Stevens, 'The Irrational Element in Poetry' (1939), *Opus Posthumous*, rev. edn (London: Faber and Faber, 1990), p. 224.
3. Wallace Stevens, as above.
4. Wallace Stevens, as above.
5. Camoin, François, 'The Workshop and Its Discontents,' *Rethinking Creative Writing Theory and Pedagogy*, Eds. Hans Ostrom and Wendy Bishop (Urbana, IL: National Council of Teachers of English, 1994), pp. 3–7.
6. Hans Ostrom, 'Undergraduate Creative Writing: The Unexamined Subject,' *Writing on the Edge (WOE)* 1.1 (1989): 56. Addressing all undergraduate students, Ostrom deflects attention from the 'almost pointless' question, 'Can Creative Writing be taught?' to make the more probing query: 'What place does Creative Writing have in the development of young writers and in the undergraduate curriculum?' Also, Ostrom, Hans, 'Of Radishes and Shadows, Theory and Pedagogy,' *Rethinking Creative Writing Theory and Pedagogy*, Eds. Hans Ostrom and Wendy Bishop (Urbana, IL: National Council of Teachers of English, 1994), pp. xi–xxiii.
7. Wendy Bishop, 'Afterword – Colors of a Different Horse: On Learning to Like Teaching Creative Writing,' *Rethinking Creative Writing Theory and Pedagogy*, Eds. Hans Ostrom and Wendy Bishop (Urbana, IL: National Council of Teachers of English, 1994), pp. 280–95.
8. Wendy Bishop, as above.
9. Peter Elbow, 'Ranking, Evaluating, and Liking: Sorting Out Three Forms of Judgment,' *College English* 55.2 (Feb. 1993): 187–206. Eve Shelnutt, 'Notes from a Cell: Creative Writing Programs in Isolation,' *Creative Writing in America: Theory and Pedagogy*, Ed. Joseph M. Moxley (Urbana, IL: National Council of Teachers of English, 1989), pp. 3–24.
10. D.W. Fenza, 'Creative Writing and Its Discontents,' *The Writer's Chronicle* (March/April 2000), www.awpwriter.org/magazine/index.htm (accessed 28 February 2012). In drawing a distinction between Creative Writing in undergraduate studies as compared to graduate writing programs, D.W. Fenza does point to the individual Creative Writing workshop. In noting that, 'teachers of undergraduates are keenly aware that, before a student can even pretend to be a writer, that student must become a talented reader of literature', he assures us that, 'these undergraduate workshops differ from graduate workshops because their primary goal is not to educate artists but to teach students critical reading skills, the elements of fiction and verse, general persuasive writing skills, and an appreciation of literary works of the present and past'. While his insistence that undergraduate classes include a varied curriculum is reassuring, I am not convinced that the goal 'to educate artists' has been – or need be – fully excised.

11. Paul Dawson, *Creative Writing and the New Humanities* (London: Taylor & Francis/ Routledge, 2005). Dawson's work is largely a subtle summation of contemporary practices placed atop their historical origins. In this, he takes us through the kind of rigorous self-reflection that teachers of Creative Writing really need, asking us to reconsider the critical bases of such gospels as 'reading like a writer', 'show don't tell', and 'finding one's voice' as part of his demand that Creative Writing behave like the discipline it is (and needs to claim).
12. Paul Dawson, p. 120.
13. Paul Dawson, p. 115.
14. Paul Dawson, p. 114.
15. Paul Dawson, p. 115.
16. John Ciardi and Miller Williams, Eds., *How a Poem Means* (Boston: Houghton Mifflin Co., 1975): pp. 3, xxiii. *How a Poem Means* purports to desire a similar balance of content and craft, claiming 'Poetry . . . is more than simply "something to say." Nor is it simply an elaborate way of saying something or nothing', but it ultimately remains allegiant to its New Critical *how* and never really dares to move outside of a protected realm of describing 'likeness and differences'.
17. Richard Hugo, *The Triggering Town* (New York: W.W. Norton & Co., 1979).
18. Wallace Stevens, 'Adagia,' *Opus Posthumous*, rev. edn (London: Faber and Faber, 1990), p. 227.
19. Randall Jarrell, *Poetry & the Age* (New York: The Ecco Press, 1953), p. 235.
20. Robert Lowell, 'Skunk Hour,' *Life Studies* (1959): *Collected Poems* (New York: Farrar, Straus and Giroux, 2003), p. 192.

6
The Creative Writing Workshop: a Survival Kit

Michelene Wandor

The Creative Writing workshop (undergraduate and graduate) exists in two senses: the Workshop, which characterizes the distinctiveness of Creative Writing as an academic discipline, and the workshop – the subject and methodology of Creative Writing pedagogy. The nouns have spawned a verb. Student writing is 'workshopped' in a fashion special to the teaching of Creative Writing. In *Creative Writing: a Good Practice Guide*, Dr Siobhan Holland commented that Creative Writing 'is best understood as a practice-based rather than a vocational or service-based discipline', and that 'The Creative Writing workshop provides the most common form of delivery for Creative Writing programmes at undergraduate and MA level.'[1]

In this context, then, the process of 'workshopping' is offered as a pedagogical methodology, as a result of which students are assumed to be able to gain an understanding of what is involved in imaginative writing (my preferred term to the ubiquitous 'creative'), and to be able to engage more fully in its practice. I am deliberately avoiding the widespread conclusion that Creative Writing workshops 'produce' professional writers, since this is a vexed and inadequately explored assumption. In the course of analysing the history and practices of the 'workshop' itself, some further light will, I hope, be cast on why this assumption is so problematic; explicitly and/or implicitly it underlies the ideology of Creative Writing. In traditional academic terms, the workshop is a version of the seminar, small-group teaching which aims to maximize student participation. However, as we shall see, the origins of the W/workshop are more than academic, and more than directly educational, stemming from a variety of historical, cultural, educational and ideological origins.

Iowa

The most specific historical precedent for Creative Writing in higher education is that of the University of Iowa, whose Writers' Workshop became the founding model for (initially) postgraduate Creative Writing study. Iowa's first taught course in 'Verse Making' in the spring of 1897 paved the way for 'creative' work to be submitted as part of the requirements of postgraduate Masters [*sic*] degrees in the 1920s.[2] Norman Foerster, director of the Iowa School of Letters (1930–44) succeeded in getting the creative dissertation accepted for the Ph.D. degree in the early 1930s, and in 1939, the title 'Writers' Workshops' was officially used for the first time. In 1949 the teaching of Creative Writing spread downwards, as it were, to the undergraduate programme, and in the same year the Iowa English Department incorporated Creative Writing into its offerings for an English Major. Iowa had a double remit: the first was to encourage the production of a new, regional literature, and the second (directly related) was to formalize some of the processes already being undertaken by writers' groups, on and off campus.

The consolidation of Iowa's achievements in the 1940s and 1950s, led to the Iowa Writers' Workshop becoming the prototype for Creative Writing courses in the US during the 1960s, with its methodology as the dominant model. Consciously following Iowa's example, novelists and critics, Malcolm Bradbury and Angus Wilson, set up a postgraduate MA in Creative Writing in 1970 at the University of East Anglia (UEA) in the United Kingdom.

Education and democracy

Jon Cook, who was a postgraduate student at UEA in 1970, has pointed out another source for the concept of the workshop, which derived from manual work, rather than educational structures: 'nineteenth-century uses of the word were concerned with a world of industrial or artisan labour and the activity of shaping materials by technological means into artefacts or commodities'.[3]

This nineteenth-century association had political, democratizing links and ideals. The Co-operative Movement, for example, 'conceived a new order in workshop life as the result of the management of industry by working men themselves'.[4] Such notions of industrial self-government were also applied to educational campaigns, particularly in the adult education movement of the nineteenth century. The 'tutorial class', developed by the University Extension movement, took its teaching models from the oldest-established universities of Oxford and Cambridge, making a distinction between mass lectures and the small group:

> There is frankly not much to be said for lecturing as the normal means of instruction for ordinary adult groups engaged in some branch of liberal study . . . ever since the first university tutorial classes were established, stress has been laid upon the importance of discussion as a method of adult education.[5]

Postwar culture

It is salutary to recall events in postwar Britain, which helped pave the way for Creative Writing in the UK. The oral history movement of the 1950s and 1960s, and the grassroots cultural movements of the 1960s and 1970s, when worker-writer groups formed the Federation of Worker Writers and Community Publishers (FWWCP) in 1976, also infused new content and approaches to writing. The worker-writer groups encouraged ordinary people to write memoirs, stories and poems, and much of this material was self-published. These movements consciously highlighted the voices (recorded and written) of working men and women, and people from immigrant/ethnic, other cultural, communities; in historian Sheila Rowbotham's evocative phrase, voices once 'hidden from history' were heard and celebrated.[6]

These are brief accounts of the ideologically disparate influences which feed into the apparently discrete phenomenon of the Creative Writing workshop. It is important to understand the complexity of this history, because its variety is partly responsible for the principles and values informing workshop practice in a contradictory and/or confusing way.

Contradictions

At the centre of Creative Writing ideology is a fundamental contradiction which challenges the assumed directness and specialness of workshop practice and its informing principles. Jon Cook's articulation of this has a slightly cautious tone:

> The ideal of democratic participation, of entitlement to imaginative creativity, can brush up against the ideal of the masterclass, the workshop as the place where a new generation of significant writers finds its voice.[7]

In terms of pedagogy, this can also be articulated as a division between Creative Writing's promise to train professional (and, by implication, successful) writers, and the wider claims of 'creativity' and self-expression, represented by late twentieth-century cultural politics. The dichotomy is revealed and played out in some of the accounts of what actually happens in the workshop.

Workshop practice

Today's dominant workshop principles and practices belong very largely to the 'production of (great) writers' school, which harks back to Iowa's legacy.

Whatever occasional ancillary reading might be included (and this applies generally in both under- and postgraduate courses), most class time is allocated to reading and discussing incomplete pieces of their own writing, brought in by students. This is given an attractive pedagogic gloss, when it is likened to professional literary practices.

In 1961 Paul Engle wrote to Stephen Wilbers, comparing 'the teaching that can be done in a workshop to the function of an editor like Maxwell Perkins, who shaped and pared into presentable form the massive manuscripts of Thomas Wolfe'.[8] This is echoed by Robert Miles: 'In effect, the seminar reduplicates, in miniature, publishing.'[9]

For the FWWCP, there was a similar approach: 'the workshop group . . . a commitment to using the group as the first readership or audience for work, and as the body that decides about editing, shaping, public reading or publication'.[10] More democratic in its participatory aims, but the same method. Both ends of the Creative Writing spectrum thus treat the workshop as if it is, in fact, a vocational literary training, which is the inspiration for a particular kind of pedagogy.

Underlying the professional (editorial) paradigm lies the assumption that criticism of a very particular kind is at the heart of workshop practice. This is summarized by Danny Broderick. In the 'seminar/workshop . . . students' own work in progress is reviewed and revised through critical discussion . . . This cooperative critiquing of work by peers . . . places emphasis on the analysis of the text as literary artefact . . . Students are asked to make value judgements on their own and each others' texts as part of the process of arriving at the artefact.'[11]

Creative Writing literature, conferences and journals explore what this special criticism consists of, and how it is undertaken. Sometimes it is seen as analogous to 'peer assessment', a process which is part of wider educational philosophies seeking to encourage collaborative discussion. Often the distinction is made between encouraging students with 'constructive criticism' (i.e., saying nice things first, pointing out what you 'like', is 'good'), before or alongside saying the opposite – 'negative criticism', pointing out what is 'wrong' or what does not 'work'. My rash of inverted commas is deliberate; the use of such terms, whatever textual evidence is adduced, is pretty well without reference to any kind of explicit literary value system, or even quasi-theoretical approach which makes the criteria clear.

However, even with the best of intentions, the 'criticism' offered is nothing like that in the publisher/writer relationship. The Creative Writing student is not submitting finished work, and the Creative Writing teacher is not in a position to offer publication. Publishers' editors offer their responses based on a mixture of literary and market-based comments and value judgements, in which the primary outcome is either to publish or not to publish. Of course, that rare phenomenon (these days), the excellent, sensitive publisher's editor, can contribute to the writer's improved sense of his/her own writing, but the editor's function is to make the text 'publishable', not to 'teach' the writer.

What is at stake in the Creative Writing classroom is *not* publication, but pedagogy, the process of teaching and learning. Workshops offer value judgements on unfinished work; these value judgements are largely based on un- (or under) studied empirical responses, made (or offered) by fellow students, with degrees of refereeing by teachers. While this may be a perfectly interesting and rewarding way of running an informal writers' group, it is questionable whether it amounts to a viable pedagogical procedure in higher education.

One of the most popular justifications of this approach is embedded in the phrase 'reading as a writer', as if this is a training which can largely be gleaned by students reading fragments of each others' texts, along with some selected examples from (generally contemporary) published writers. In one apparently neat phrase, the whole of literary history and critical training through the acquisition of literary history, criticism and theory, seems to be dismissed.

This 'reading as a writer' is offered as, in itself, a training in 'criticism'. The difficulty (to compress a very complex argument) is that literary criticism (sometimes called formalist criticism) evolved over a period of decades as both description and evaluation of complete works in the public domain. In Creative Writing methodology this is transformed (using selected bits and pieces from the critical terminology) into prescriptive advice. Dependent on the individual knowledge and understanding of the teacher, it is rarely (if ever) conveyed via a discussion of its history, theory or cultural assumptions. This is ironic, in view of the fact that Creative Writing claims so strongly to produce new 'literature'.

Hard-cop, soft-cop: therapy

As all teachers know, the atmosphere, dynamic and precise procedures of any class/seminar can be difficult to convey or describe. But we do have some interesting observations on workshop practice. Robert Graham, who visited the Iowa Workshop, wrote in 2001 about Frank Conroy's class. Conroy's comments on the workshop included: 'We . . . spend 95% of our time finding out what is wrong.' A student noted that 'Conroy believes he isn't doing his job unless the occasional student bursts into tears or faints.' Another teacher described his own classroom role as 'traffic cop. I make sure things aren't getting out of control.'[12]

The hard-cop approach represented by this cruel version of critical vigour is balanced at the opposite end by a soft cop response to the 'vulnerability' of the student. Siobhan Holland's report refers to 'The need for robust support structures to students who may well draw on traumatic experiences in the processes of reading and writing.'[13]

In Creative Writing literature, this takes the form of eliding the workshop with the function of a therapy group. To suggest that the teacher must also be a therapist (something widely implied in the literature) is breathtakingly problematic, not just because it suggests that the teacher needs to be trained as an ersatz therapist, but because it so casually co-opts another set of principles and practices into an unsuitable context.

Resistance

Among students there can be a cautious groundswell of anecdotal/gossipy criticism of the workshop. They may often think a teaching method is questionable, but the majority of students will have no experience with which to compare it, and, after all, they will be dependent on their teacher for final grading of assignments. In a rare venture into the risky business of challenging hallowed principles, Rob Mimpriss has raised some cautious reservations: 'I have been moving towards the conclusion that the workshop has little to offer the writer, and may at times do harm.'[14] I suspect this is only the tip of the critical iceberg.

While I would hesitate to generalize on tactics of student resistance to the difficulties of the workshop, there are certain defensive approaches which I have observed myself, or heard about from other teachers. Students will bring to the workshop pieces of writing which are not particularly important to them, and which they may not even be interested in continuing. This way, 'negative' comments, or 'constructive' suggestions are less likely to hurt their feelings or influence them, much less teach them anything much. Students may bring in extracts from already finished pieces of writing, or which they have already taken to other workshops or groups. The problem here is not student behaviour, but a pedagogic practice which lends itself so easily to counter-productive defensiveness, rather than real learning.

Alternatives

What, then, might be a more genuine and productive way to approach the pedagogy of Creative Writing, with alternatives to the ossified workshop? First, what it is not, and cannot be. It cannot be about training Creative Writing teachers to be ersatz therapists. It cannot be about training students to become professional writers, though this may be the ambition of many and the outcome of a very few. After all, the literary world has functioned perfectly well (whatever its problems) for centuries without Creative Writing being a necessary spur. The polarization of approaches to Creative Writing as either an outreach activity for Romantic genius or of writing-as-therapy does teachers, students and the extraordinary world of fiction writing no favours. The real remit of Creative Writing is, and must be, educational.

In this context, the arrival of Creative Writing in UK higher education is one of the most exciting developments of recent decades. It offers the potential of augmenting literary history, critical and theoretical learning with a writerly understanding and execution of imaginative writing. My reservations about the workshop do not come from the belief that Creative Writing can not/should not be taught. On the contrary, I am absolutely certain that Creative Writing *can* be taught, that it can be rewarding, rigorous, informative and skill-enhancing to teach and learn. But in order to be all of these, it needs to be reconceived, freed from the straitjacket of the workshop, which involves teachers abandoning the hard-cop, soft-cop routine, and developing other approaches.

In every sense, and from every point of view, the structural position of Creative Writing is entirely bound up with literary studies, cultural theory and stylistics/linguistics. This is not a novel idea, though it is not at all widely accepted by Creative Writing teachers, even where Creative Writing is lodged in English Departments. Poet and teacher Anne Cluysenaar was already arguing for, and building courses with a combination of Creative Writing, linguistics and stylistics at Lancaster University in the late 1960s.[15] However, since those pioneering days, Creative Writing has tended to see itself as a subject 'in its own right', dismissive of the heritage (if sometimes vexed) of literary studies.

This will have no easy solutions. While it is absolutely right that Creative Writing should be taught by practising (if not always fully professional or widely published) writers, not all of these teachers will be steeped in literary history, criticism or theory. While it is absolutely admirable that postgraduate Creative Writing students are admitted to MAs and/or Ph.D.s on the basis of submitted portfolios of writing, the concomitant difficulties that they may know little or nothing about literary history, etcetera need to be addressed.

The extent to which the 'teaching' of imaginative writing can be effective in the classroom will depend not only on what the teacher brings and makes explicit, but also on the student's knowledge. Not all Creative Writing students have studied literature or cultural theory; few will be studying stylistics or linguistics. All are essential for anyone seeking to undertake the practice-based study of literature. This makes the course content crucial – and difficult to reconcile with the workshop model.

Writing, not re-writing: imaginative modes of thought

Methodology apart, the underlying pedagogic drive of the Creative Writing workshop is based on the practice of piecemeal, symptomatically prescriptive adjustments to fragments of writing. This means that the procedure is driven by *re-writing*, not *writing* and certainly not *criticism*, although both those activities are marginally entailed as well.

The real task of Creative Writing is to address the fact that as a 'subject' it engages with imaginative modes of thought, realized in the production of literary forms and genres (contested as these have been in recent decades in literary theory. The 'materials' for this, as it were, are contained within language uses, the conventions of these literary forms, and their various and varied histories.

It has taken me a long time to develop the thinking which lies behind this chapter, and which has evolved from a mixture of my own experience as a writer-teacher, like all others, making it up as I went along, and then reading and thinking.

I never subscribed to the punitive workshop method, but have rather evolved ways of teaching prose fiction, poetry and drama, based on student writing in class, which is then subject to linguistic analytical scrutiny and always discussed (to use a shorthand) in terms of their literary/stylistic features. Through this, each student produces completed, or nearly completed pieces of writing in class by the end of each course.

This allows students to begin to see how they already use language, how they think and imagine, and see possibilities for ways in which they might use language imaginatively in the future. All this is possible – with the right critical equipment in the teacher – from the student texts. I would never claim that this can be a complete process. In any given class (under- or postgraduate), students never have a shared background in literary study or critical discussion, and this makes even the simplest descriptive task really quite laborious and complex. Add this to the serious crisis in literacy, of which the whole of higher education is aware, and Creative Writing is made even more difficult to teach. When undergraduates are often unclear about what a noun/verb is, or the difference between and adverb and an adjective, it often seems a complete waste of time trying to make serious inroads on their understanding of imaginative uses of language.

From the student writing produced in class, I draw out the distinctive features of whichever genre is relevant: prose fiction, poetry or drama. Where necessary and useful, I make forays into aspects of theory, but this too is hamstrung by limited time and knowledge.

However, value judgements, and the expression of evaluative terminology is always and absolutely ruled out. The Creative Writing classroom/seminar is the place where, as in all other subjects, a learning process takes place, on the basis of which students can hopefully develop a responsibility for their independently worked assignments, which are then marked and graded by the teacher.[16]

I do not at all underestimate the complexity of the implications of this: Creative Writing teachers may well be challenged to look seriously at their own methods, to expand their reading and to approach class work differently. It is not enough for teachers to bemoan the fact that students do not read (a common cry), if they, as teachers, do not demand serious reading from their students. For students, there will, of course, be moments of insight on any Creative Writing course, and having dedicated time to devote to forms of imaginative writing in itself provides opportunities for thought and development. But this is not enough. At the heart of Creative Writing courses is the potential for genuine, searching, difficult and rewarding learning experiences. This the workshop cannot provide.

Notes

1. Siobhan Holland, *Creative Writing: a Good Practice Guide*, English Subject Centre, Report Series No. 6, February 2003, www.english.heacademy.ac.uk/explore/resources/creative/guide.php (accessed 28 February 2012).
2. Stephen Wilbers, 'The Iowa Writers' Workshop,' *Seven Decades of the Iowa Workshop*, Ed. Tom Grimes (New York: Hyperion, New York, 1999).
3. Jon Cook, 'A Brief History of Workshops,' *The Creative Writing Coursebook*, Eds. Julia Bell and Paul Magrs (New York: Macmillan, 2001), p. 296.
4. Albert Mansbridge, *The Trodden Road* (London: Dent, 1940), p. 50.
5. Robert Peers, *Adult Education* (New York: Routledge, 1959, 1972).
6. Sheila Rowbotham, *Hidden from History: 300 Years of Women's Oppression and the Fight Against It* (London: Pluto Press, 1977).
7. Jon Cook, as above, p. 299.
8. Wilbers, as above, p. 84.
9. Robert Miles, 'Creative Writing, Contemporary Theory and the English Curriculum', *Teaching Creative Writing: Theory and Practice*, Eds. Moira Monteith and Robert Miles (Buckingham: Open University Press, 1992), p. 41.
10. Dave Morley and Ken Worpole, Eds., *The Republic of Letters* (London: Minority Press, Group Series No. 6, 1982), p. 5
11. Danny Broderick, NAWE Website, Members' Archives, 1999, www.nawe.co.uk (accessed 28 February 2012).
12. Robert Graham, The Iowa Writers' Workshop, February 2002, www.nawe.co.uk (accessed 28 February 2012).
13. Holland, as above, p. 6.
14. Rob Mimpress, 'Rewriting the Individual: a Critical Study of the Creative Writing Workshop,' *Writing in Education*, NAWE Members' Archives, www.nawe.co.uk (No. 26, 2002), (accessed 28 February 2012).
15. Personal interview with author, July, 2004.
16. Michelene Wandor, *The Author is not Dead, Merely Somewhere Else: Creative Writing Reconceived* (Basingstoke: Palgrave Macmillan, 2008).

Part III
Undergraduate Creative Writing

How is Creative Writing taught at undergraduate levels? In the UK, Steve May draws on national surveys and interviews to research three points:

1. origins of undergraduate teaching,
2. institutional justifications for teaching,
3. and students' reasons for learning.

May concludes that Creative Writing in Higher Education originated quite often through individual staff innovations. Once established, institutional initiatives for undergraduate courses derived from student popularity and the ability to generate income. Students' motivations for learning ranged from wanting to be professional writers and/or teachers to a minority who saw it as a 'soft' option.

May's research indicates both diversity and tension with Creative Writing commonly being taught as part of another main degree subject such as English; less commonly it is taught as a degree subject itself. May's research also reveals tensions in assessment of Creative Writing between 'pure aesthetic worth' to 'mass marketability'. He says that this plays out at times between 'academic-tutors' and 'professional writer-tutors'.

In the USA, Anna Leahy draws on national statistics from the Association of Writers and Writing Programmes (AWP) and the Association of Departments of English (ADE) to consider the popularity and large impact Creative Writing has in Higher Education. Leahy then details qualities of Creative Writing Undergraduate Programmes at Knox College, Oberlin College, and Sarah Lawrence College as examples of good practice with small workshop sizes, committed teachers, and numerous extracurricular opportunities.

Next, Leahy explains that regardless of the institution or resources, undergraduate programmes share three common teaching and learning goals: (1) writerly reading, (2) craft and (3) creativity.

Writerly reading centres on close readings of texts, not merely for plot or theme, but for how the texts achieve effects based on decisions writers make. Leahy then considers craft as a 'toolbox' of techniques such as metaphor, image and point of view. These are in part observable and measurable and therefore best meet formal aspects of delineation required for assessment by institutions. Concerning creativity, Leahy begins by referring to criticism of Creative Writing workshops insofar as they might result in homogenous work. By contrast, Leahy gives numerous examples, as to why creativity flourishes in undergraduate workshops, especially insofar as these encourage an open exchange of ideas. Leahy concludes with a case study from her own teaching that illustrates these three teaching and learning goals in practice.

Hans Ostrom begins by responding to criticisms that Creative Writing should neither be considered education, nor should it try to compete with other undergraduate degrees such as Literature and Language. In contrast, Ostrom cites the following purposes of teaching and learning Creative Writing: literacy, imitation, craft, and experiencing literature as a writing reader (as per Leahy's 'reading as a writer').

Ostrom then explores a further hidden purpose to Creative Writing insofar as it encourages students to occupy the space Foucault locates among power, self and knowledge. Ostrom's first step in exploring power considers how emotions and 'emoting' are banned or at least avoided in academia, including Creative Writing, for example, by focusing on the 'alleged unemotional study of craft'.

Ostrom's second step focuses on self and self expression in two case studies from his own teaching in which students radically reconfigure how they view themselves as writers through workshops and one-to-one tutorial discussions. Ostrom's third step examines how we may underestimate the extent to which Creative Writing is a way of knowing and making knowledge. Ostrom concludes that Creative Writing is uniquely positioned in undergraduate studies to allow students to assimilate everything and anything they have learned.

Maureen Freely begins from the principle that good writers make better readers and vice versa. She explores why Creative Writing teachers need to move freely between academic and literary cultures as university regulations may stifle the imagination. Freely then reflects on her own teaching experiences in the UK and USA to consider the benefits and constraints of Creative Writing in Higher Education. Benefits include teachers' roles as editors and the safe environments universities create for young writers insofar as these are not subject to mass media laws of the publishing market. Such benefits encourage students to take risks instead of focusing just on what might make a best seller list. They also realize that they don't have to 'dumb down' their writing to make it sell. Further benefits include opportunities for students to run their own writing groups set up magazines, publishing houses and community arts programmes.

Constraints include having to design courses to 'factory-like specifications' and being under resourced for staff and time to spend reading and giving weekly feedback to young writers. A further constraint centres on having to conform to assessment standards that were designed for a very different kind of teaching than the close one to one weekly feedback required in Creative Writing.

7

Undergraduate Creative Writing Provision in the UK: Origins, Trends and Student Views

Steve May

Recent surveys and statistics confirm that the provision of Creative Writing at undergraduate level is expanding in UK Higher Education Institutions (HEIs). However, to regard Creative Writing as a single, coherent subject is perhaps premature, given the diversity of its origins, forms and purposes across the Higher Education sector. [1] This chapter aims to do the following:

1. outline various origins of undergraduate Creative Writing provision in UK HEIs, and to indicate current trends;
2. establish institutional justifications for Creative Writing provision; and
3. touch on the issues of purpose from a student perspective.

The origins of undergraduate creative writing in UK HEIs

Some institutions started off with MA provision (for example, the Universities of East Anglia and Winchester), subsequently adding undergraduate options; others (like Bath Spa University, Warwick and Glamorgan) did it the other way round.[2] In some cases, as at Sheffield Hallam, Creative Writing was built in to an English degree programme from the start for pedagogical (and political) reasons. It was purpose-built in the late 70s as an alternative to conventional English degree programmes. It was conceived as tripartite, with straight English flanked by New Theory and Creative Writing ('challenging the students to decide whether as authors they were dead or not'). Alongside the underlying radical political inspiration a practical 'skill' orientation was built in from the start.[3] However, this kind of planning is the exception rather than the rule:

> Historically a trend is clear: in the 80s and earlier most Creative Writing in HE was developed in the form of single modules within existing courses by individuals motivated by political, social, or personal principles.[4]

Those 'existing courses' were extremely various. For example at Bretton Hall and Bath Spa, Creative Writing started as an optional element in a B.Ed. programme. At Glamorgan Creative Writing was born independently in English, and (for scriptwriting) in Drama and Media. At Norwich it began in the School of Art and Design. At many institutions (such as Bretton Hall and Gloucestershire) there also existed Creative Writing options run by Continuing Education departments. At Gloucestershire these were later absorbed into the undergraduate programme; at Bristol, writing (along with all continuing education provision) was moved into Departments (for writing, into English and Drama), but remained separate from degree programmes in administration and staffing.

Creative Writing also started 'invisibly' in many institutions, where individual staff experimented with small 'taster' elements of writing within established courses. Nick Everett of Leicester University describes

> the overwhelmingly positive response of students on my final-year optional course on form in modern poetry to my first, tentative suggestion that writing poetic exercises might give them a more direct sense of the formal and stylistic features we were examining.[5]

Once born in a small way, Creative Writing tends to grow, as the Gloucestershire example attests. In 2001 there were two modules available (in the Field of English Studies and Creative & Contemporary Writing, in the School of Humanities: one at Level One, one at Level Three), with the opportunity also to submit creative work for project modules. At the time of writing there is a full programme, comprising seventeen dedicated Creative Writing modules, plus other acceptable modules from various fields including Journalism and Film Studies.[6]

Some institutions, like Warwick, while offering a comprehensive writing programme, retain the 'mother-subject' orientation:

> The aims of the Warwick Writing Programme are to encourage good reading as well as writing, to develop sound expository skills, to bridge 'academic' and 'creative' approaches to literature in a fully integrated range of activities.
> The BA in English Literature and Creative Writing 'puts the practice of writing in different genres on an equal footing with critical and cultural-historical approaches to literature'.[7]

While some institutions retain this 'mother-subject' orientation, other Creative Writing programmes have been variously located in their relatively short histories. At Buckinghamshire New University (formerly Buckinghamshire Chilterns University College):

> Creative Writing sits within the Faculty of Applied Social Sciences and Humanities. Previously it was placed in the Field Group of English Studies,

Visual Arts and Creative Writing. It was subsequently moved to the Field Group of Video Production, Drama Production and Creative Writing. After further reorganisation in 2001 Creative Writing now stands alone with its own Field Chair.[8]

This odyssey is perhaps emblematic of Creative Writing's search for identity once detached from its mother subject.

Key here seems to be the connected questions of purpose and assessment. When writing is an isolated element servicing another subject, outcomes and assessments will be geared towards the main subject, and questions of 'level of study' and progression in the writing elements themselves need not arise.[9] As the provision becomes more extensive, and writing itself becomes the object of assessment, then the issues of level, progression and assessment criteria for that writing become unavoidable.

When writing itself is considered without reference to a 'mother-subject', assessment criteria can be divided into two broad categories, which are not mutually exclusive, but betray differences in emphasis and values. One set of criteria might be termed the 'aesthetic absolute'. Work is judged on its innate worth without reference to sordid questions of market (although one senses that awkward questions regarding the basis of assumptions of worth may be avoided). The other refers to industry standards, including 'publishability'. Work is judged by how far it is fit for purpose in (some restricted version of) the 'real world'. This paragraph from a Bath Spa MA handbook (dealing with the qualities required to merit a distinction) sums up the tension between these criteria:

It must be recognised that not all students who earn the award will reach publishable standard; nor will all the work that does reach this standard in the judgement of the examiners be successful in finding a publisher. Some work will be of the highest quality in intellectual and artistic terms but not appealing to commercial publishers. Some will simply be unlucky in the market place. A distinction mark certainly means that the course team believes that the work deserves to be published.[10]

A course which deals with what 'ought' to be published can be taught by non-writers (or unpublished writers). A course that claims to deal with what can be and is published begins to need industry professionals (whether they be writers or editors or other persons of relevant experience) to give it credibility.

A common solution to this staffing dilemma is to employ writers on an hourly paid basis, which complicates the question of purpose, and the formal lines of communication:

The Field of Creative Writing is currently staffed principally by one full-time member of the Department's staff, with some contribution from another full-time staff member, as well as teaching input from two Part Time Visiting Lecturers who are professional writers. Given the demands of professional work on the Part Time Visiting Lecturers it is not easy to hold regular formal course team meetings.[11]

This situation is quite common: regular academic staff administering courses actually taught by part time writer-tutors who are paid only to teach, not to contribute to course development.[12]

Here a glance at some statistics may be in order. Creative Writing is one of the least common compulsory courses in English departments, but one of the most common optional courses. It is one of the most popular with students, but is perceived by academics to have a very low importance. It is also the fastest growing element in English.[13]

What do these indicators suggest? I offer the following tentative interpretation. Creative Writing is popular with students. Therefore, at institutional level there is pressure to offer it as an engine for recruitment. However, the majority of English academics do not see it as important, and this attitude is reflected in the fact that it is rarely compulsory.[14]

Institutional justifications for creative writing provision

Institutions broadly use two strategies in their recruitment literature.[15] Particularly when the provision is not extensive, the typical Prospectus will emphasize Creative Writing as something exciting, different, new, adding spice to the main subject:

> English at X is a diverse, progressive and innovative programme, designed to appeal to a wide range of students with a love of literature, pushing at the boundaries of the discipline and giving opportunities to enjoy a thought-provoking mix of traditional and non-traditional material . . . Whether you like new or old literature, Creative Writing or creative thinking, Shakespeare or Queer Theory, there will be something that will stimulate your interest.

Where writing is the whole or largest part of a degree programme some (but by no means all) institutional literature assumes that prospective students want to be writers: 'clearly . . . the majority of students involved on the course will have as an ultimate aim the publication of their own writing'.

This assumption or implication of 'vocationality' raises several important issues. Firstly, judged by their success in producing published, professional writers, most if not all undergraduate Creative Writing programmes are abysmal failures. A hairdressing college or chef school with the same level of success rates would soon be closed down.[16]

So, instead of naked vocationality, most prospectuses emphasize worthy transferable skills and a more general possibility of employment in 'the Creative Industries':

> Creative and Professional Writing students develop a range of key transferable skills which are valued by employers, including effective communication skills (both written and oral), problem solving, working with others, self-awareness, time management and achieving targets. Editing, publishing, writing including journalism, teaching, advertising, public relations, civil service and broadcasting, are obvious and popular career routes but graduates may go on to work in any number of other areas where these key skills are valued.

The question remains, why are students choosing the subject in increasing numbers?

Undergraduate creative writing: student perspectives

Surveys at my own institution suggest that around 35–40 per cent of those doing Creative Writing want to be professional writers: 'I would like the course to be taught on the assumption that everyone in the room wants to be published.'[17] A similar proportion want to do English but in a new, different, perhaps more 'personal' way:

> I chose Creative Writing because I've done English Literature and I was fed up with 'isn't Jane Austen great,' you know, 'oh, let's do Shakespeare again,' because to me it all felt like it was dead white people and it had all been done before. I wanted to do something myself.[18]

A large minority are would-be teachers, taking Creative Writing to enhance their teaching. Many mature students are doing it with no practical end in view, because they have come to a point in their lives where they feel they want to do something 'for themselves':

> I didn't have any career intended at the end of it, I'd dropped my career, and I just wanted three years for me, enjoying it, so I just picked a course that seemed most suitable.

A small minority are what might be termed time-wasters, or free loaders, who think that Creative Writing will be a soft option:

> If the truth be known I started the course as a bet and to reduce my workload.

Interestingly, and perhaps reassuringly for prospectus writers, over 60 per cent expect the course to teach them 'skills valued in the market place'.

In my own institution this variety is complicated by the modular scheme. For example, in a second year poetry group not only is there diversity of ability and motivation, there is wide divergence in the amount of Creative Writing in each individual's degree. Sitting next to the dedicated would-be writer doing single honours (hence six modules per year) may be History students taking Creative Writing as a minor element of their degree (two modules per year). One of these students (we can not be sure which one) may have done a first year poetry module, and the other not. And they may be taught by a tutor who (being part time hourly paid) has no personal knowledge or experience of 'Level One' or 'Level Three' poetry modules.

Conclusions

Creative Writing is expanding in UK HEIs. While most Creative Writing provision began as the result of innovation on the part of individual committed staff, the main drivers now would appear to be popularity with students, leading to institutional initiatives. Courses range in their aims from those where writing services another subject, to those where writing becomes the chief focus of study. There are tensions in terms of the competing criteria of 'absolute aesthetic worth' and marketability, which are reflected to some degree in the dichotomy between academic tutors and writer-tutors. At the moment administrative structures tend to leave course development to the academics, and isolate writer-tutors in purely teaching roles. Meanwhile, students are choosing to do Creative Writing for a wide variety of reasons, which only partially match with staff motivation or institutional justifications. It is the challenge for all of us involved in the teaching of Creative Writing, while respecting and preserving the differences between different kinds of provision, to make our subject both clear and coherent for those choosing to take it.

Notes

1. English Subject Centre, *Survey of the English Curriculum and Teaching in UK Higher Education* (2003), www.english.heacademy.ac.uk (accessed 28 February 2012). For another even longer view of the history of Creative Writing see Carl Tighe, 'Creative Writing?' *Writing in Education* 40 (2006): 51–7. In the Higher Education Statistics Agency statistics (www.hesa.ac.uk) 'Imaginative Writing' first appears as a subject in its own right in 2002/3 with 775 full time undergraduate students. This rises to 2250 in the most recent (2005/6) figures (accessed 28 February 2012). It is a feature of Creative Writing provision to be somewhat difficult to find and define, so it would be interesting to know which courses feature in these statistics.
2. The question of articulation (or lack of it) between undergraduate and postgraduate Creative Writing provision is an interesting one, which I have not space to consider here.

3. Steve May, *Doing Creative Writing* (London: Routledge, 2007), pp. 24–40.
4. University of Gloucestershire website, www.glos.ac.uk (accessed 28 February 2012).
5. Nick Everett, 'Creative Writing and English,' *Cambridge Quarterly* 35, 4 (2005): 231–42.
6. Steve May, p. 80.
7. Steve May, pp. 24–5. David Morley, who built the Warwick programme with Jeremy Treglown, told me in an interview in March 2002: 'We're trying to create a generation of good thinkers and good readers . . . Writing and reading share an interdependent orbit around language. You cannot have one without the other. If the student does not turn into a great writer (and there are lots of those around already), then they may turn into a great reader, which is far rarer species.'
8. Subsequently Creative Writing has migrated twice more: first it joined a cluster of subjects, including English, in a Department of Arts and Media, but now sits in the Faculty of Creativity and Culture. This department also offers options in Professional Writing. See the Buckinghamshire New University website at bucks.ac.uk (accessed 28 February 2012). The story at Gloucestershire is similar.
9. See Everett (2005), p. 237.
10. Bath Spa University, MA in Creative Writing Handbook 2004, p. 11. Compare this extract from the Bath Spa University, Creative Studies in English Student Handbook, p. 16, under the heading of Assessment Criteria: '*Originality:* This is important, and will often be an important quality of writing that receives very high marks. Yet a piece of writing that very effectively satisfies the demands of its genre, and market niche, may not necessarily be original. In fact, originality may even be a problem in such a context.'
11. This paragraph comes from a validation document. It would be a breach of trust for me to reward such honesty with identification.
12. Other institutions (like my own) also employ writers on fractional contracts. This mitigates, but does not entirely solve problems of purpose, course design, administration and communication.
13. English Subject Centre *Survey of the English Curriculum and Teaching in UK Higher Education* (2003), www.english.heacademy.ac.uk (accessed 28 February 2012).
14. For the tensions in the Academy between English and Creative Writing see the following: Andrew Cowan, 'Questions, Questions,' *Writing in Education* 41 (2007): 56–61; Graeme Harper, Ed., *Teaching Creative Writing* (London: Continuum, 2006); Lauri Ramey, 'Creative Writing and English Studies: Two Approaches to Literature,' www.english.heacademy.ac.uk/find/search (accessed 28 February 2012).
15. Again, I am loathe to attribute these prospectus entries, for fear of singling out individual institutions for praise or blame: when it comes to 'prospectus-ese', for good or ill, we all do it.
16. Even if every student who studied undergraduate Creative Writing became a Nobel Prize winning author, this in itself would not satisfy the Quality Assurance Agency for Higher Education (QAA) requirements for a degree programme. Those requirements can be summarized as demanding that graduates do not only learn how to *do* something, but gain a 'systematic understanding' of their field of study. They should be able to 'apply the methods and techniques that they have learned to review, consolidate, extend and apply their knowledge and understanding, and to initiate and carry out projects'. Now, it is quite possible – common, in fact – for a writer to produce publishable work without having any understanding of the 'field of study', nor any understanding of how they did it, or more important, how to do it again (hence perhaps the common phenomenon of 'second

novel syndrome'). If one of our students is talented or lucky enough to achieve publication, that will be of course a source of satisfaction for all concerned, but it will not necessarily be sufficient to earn a degree. To get the degree, the student must also reflect on the process. See 'The framework for higher education qualifications in England, Wales and Northern Ireland', January 2001, www. qaa.ac.uk (accessed 28 February 2012). There's an interesting discussion of these and other related issues in Richard Kerridge, 'Creative Writing and Academic Accountability,' *New Writing* 1, 0 (2004): 3–5.

17. Each year around 180 students take the Bath Spa compulsory first year General Writing Workshop module. We give them a questionnaire to fill out in week two. The figures quoted here refer to the last two years' results. In both cases seventy-six students completed the questionnaires. There are interesting trends in terms of age and gender, which I have not space to discuss here. Quotes are from third year students at Bath Spa, two of many gathered as part of research for my book for would-be Creative Writing students; Steve May, *Doing Creative Writing* (London: Routledge, 2007).

18. Steve May, *Teaching Creative Writing at Undergraduate Level: Why, how and does it work?* Report on English Subject Centre sponsored research project, 2003, available at www.english.heacademy.ac.uk/explore/projects/archive/creative/creative3.php (accessed 28 February 2012).

8
Undergraduate Creative Writing in the United States: Buying In Isn't Selling Out

Anna Leahy

The Association of Writers and Writing Programs (AWP) director, David Fenza, asserts, 'Creative Writing classes have become among the most popular classes in the humanities' and member undergraduate programs jumped from 155 in 1984 to 318 just twenty years later.[1] The AWP Official Guide to Writing Programs now lists 421 undergraduate programs.[2] In addition, a recent report on 'The Undergraduate English Major' by the Association of Departments of English (ADE) mentions the addition of Creative Writing as one way that English departments have addressed the drop in percentage of English majors since the 1970s. This report claims, 'there is at least anecdotal evidence to suggest that when Creative Writing is an option or track within English, it often contributes significantly to the success of the English major'.[3] In ADE's study, 'Nearly half (49.3%) the chairs [. . .] identified Creative Writing as second only to literature as the focus chosen by English majors.'[4] We are now established as a discipline in universities and colleges and, to some extent, valued. The fear is that, in buying into the academy, we might sell out our art or craft.

The ADE report notes, 'A key strength of English as a centerpiece of liberal education has surely been its breadth and depth'.[5] Because of this variety, it is difficult to make generalizations about English programs, 'the specificity of one department's contingent context not applying to another's'.[6] The rural state university branch has different goals and a different student population than the highly selective private college. The large research university has the resources to offer numerous tracks in the major, whereas the liberal arts college may have a single creative writer cover all genres. That said, there exist some common characteristics of undergraduate Creative Writing.

I earned my own BA at Knox College, where Creative Writing is one of the most popular majors on campus (but where no major or group of majors dominates). Knox, Oberlin College and Sarah Lawrence College were featured in *Poets & Writers* as schools that have worked 'to make these [Creative Writing] degrees a hallmark of their respective institutions'.[7] What is claimed about Knox's program is probably representative of most ambitious baccalaureate programs: 'Knox challenges its undergraduate writers to value creativity as a means of enhancing self-expression, developing the ability to solve problems, and to value imagination'.[8]

Common attributes exist in these three programs. Small class size is common: Oberlin offers 'introductory classes of 25, smaller workshops of 12, and one-on-one independent work for advanced students'.[9] Sarah Lawrence requires seminars of 12–15 students.[10] Extra-curricular opportunities abound: Knox boasts an award-winning literary journal entitled *Catch*, and students at Sarah Lawrence created an exhibit for the Dodge Poetry Festival and attend symposia at other institutions.[11] Good teachers are key: 'Undergraduate Creative Writing programs, which take students from wet-behind-the-ears late teens into early adulthood, are intense, requiring gifted teachers willing to spend lots of time with each student.'[12] The field as a whole can look to extraordinarily successful undergraduate programs to find characteristics that encourage excellence, but each Creative Writing program also develops in its own ways in its institutional context.

Regardless of institution type or resources available, however, Creative Writing programs buy into some basic goals: 'students can attain lifelong skills of critical thinking, empathy for others, and an understanding of the creative process, the key to all innovation'.[13] These goals for students are supported by AWP's 'Hallmarks of Undergraduate Programs' in The AWP Director's Handbook: accomplished faculty, a rigorous and diverse curriculum, excellent support for students, and other complementary assets and infrastructure.[14] I now will focus on three aspects I see in these goals and hallmarks: writerly reading, craft and creativity.[15] AWP states the need to promote what I call writerly reading among our students, the need to go beyond memorization of facts and to synthesize and apply what he or she knows:

Because a writer must first become a voracious and expert reader before he or she can master a difficult art, a strong undergraduate program emphasizes a wide range of study in literature and other disciplines to provide students with the foundation they need to become resourceful writers – resourceful in techniques, styles, models, ideas and subject matter. The goal of an undergraduate program is to teach students how to read critically as writers and to give students the practice of writing frequently so that, by creating their own works, they may apply what they have learned about the elements of literature.[16]

Likewise, Francine Prose, in her recent book *Reading Like a Writer*, asserts, 'Close reading helped me figure out, as I hoped it did for my students, a way to approach a difficult aspect of writing.'[17] Writerly reading is not an end in itself but, rather, a part of the problem-solving process for the writer. We read closely not to copy great writers but to become more aware of options in our own work, whether it be moving our plots forward or manipulating rhymes in our sonnets.

Though our attention to close reading may be one reason why Creative Writing is housed most often in the English department, writerly reading is not reading merely for plot, theme or historical relevance. Writerly reading is reading not so much for what the text means as it is reading especially for how it means. When reading like a writer, a student considers what choices the writer has at any given point and what the results of decisions are. This approach to reading increases awareness of writing as a process and of choices that are continually made – and re-made – to shape the prose or poetry.

Writerly reading also furthers an understanding, even empathy, for the other. Instead of asking does this character relate to me or claiming that is how it really happened, the student explores the author's perspective as well as how the author can represent yet another other in the story, poem or creative nonfiction essay. Writerly reading, paradoxically, gives the writer greater insight into his or her own options by getting out of his or her own self or perspective.

In addition to developing writerly reading skills, Creative Writing students, of course, hone a variety of writing skills. Because we must admit that most undergraduates will not go on to publish creative work, we should recognize that these language skills are transferable and, therefore, widely useful to students. Our students practice options for structuring sentences and choosing words. They learn to work within and manipulate boundaries such as formal constraints or length limits in which they must prioritize, balancing and rebalancing breadth and depth. Student writers also practice revision, learning to test their writing, question first intentions, and experiment. All this practice prepares students for any future writing by developing their skills and also their awareness of any writer's choices.

Craft – writing skills – is the aspect of our field that best fits academia, in part because craft is, to some extent, observable and measurable. As Mary Cantrell states in 'Teaching and Evaluation: Why Bother?': instead of grading individual drafts, 'we can ask students to supply other evidence of learning, evidence that is both easier to assess and easier for the students to have assessed'.[18] Cantrell suggests such tasks as quizzes on writerly concepts, essays analysing published or classmates' work, and revision that addresses concerns raised in workshop conversation.[19] Numerous writing guidebooks commonly used in Creative Writing courses focus on craft, in part because this aspect of Creative Writing is easier to articulate but also because it is crucial to the practice of the field. Craft is our toolbox; craft is how we do what we do.

Cantrell rightly admits that this sort of evaluation – and grades that draw from it – 'do not indicate whether a student will succeed in future endeavors, nor do they seem to prevent students from achieving the goals they have set'.[20] Evaluation, nonetheless, provides students, instructors, and institutions with evidence that students have acquired writing skills and also allows Creative Writing to fit into the academic environment that almost always requires grading of student work and accrediting based on outcomes.[21] Craft, then, is our most clearly delineated contribution to our students' education and, therefore, to our institutions' missions. If we relinquish all else to craft and evaluation, however, we may succumb to selling out by checking off metaphor, image, point of view and other elements of student writing on a formulaic rubric.

To avoid selling out, we must not forget the creative in Creative Writing. The workshop, an overarching pedagogical approach in which students share and discuss their creative pieces, has long been criticized:

> One of the wintry criticisms of writing workshops is that they produce such homogeneity within a false democracy of tender critical standards, notions of worthiness of subject and tone in writing, and back-slapping As poetry is what gets lost in translation, there is an argument that variety, ingenuity, individuality, and originality are what gets lost in writing workshops. That need not be the case.[22]

In my experience and according to research into what fosters creativity, just the opposite of homogeneity is likely the case. For example, Nancy Andreasen, currently a professor of psychology and formerly a professor of Renaissance literature, concludes, that, while artistic creation requires individual effort, 'It is more difficult for the creative brain to prosper in isolation.'[23] In other words, while the act of writing requires solitude, interaction with others and exposure to a variety of ideas fosters creativity. Andreasen explains further, 'creative people are likely to be more productive and more original if surrounded by other creative people. This too produces an environment in which the creative brain is stimulated to form novel connections and novel ideas.'[24] So, a community of creative people increases innovative thinking in its individual members. Instead of trying to write more like each other, creative writers in a workshop engage with the ideas and writing of others in ways that make their own work more original. Moreover, while a vicious writing workshop is unnecessary and probably detrimental, 'creative people are individualistic and confident. They may thrive best when pitted against one another.'[25]

Mentoring or apprenticeship, according to Andreasen as well as AWP, is also a catalyst for creativity. In the case of writing, those accomplished faculty in AWP's hallmarks serve this important role. Wallace Stegner articulates this mentoring role, in part: a teacher 'doesn't have to invent this young writer, he only has to help train him'.[26] Stegner goes on to condemn the writing teachers who produce cliques filled with clones. Instead, he calls for the following qualities: 'sympathy, empathy, a capacity to enter into another mind without dominating it'.[27] John Irving, in a television interview, used terms more akin to apprenticeship to describe his mentor, Kurt Vonnegut: a mentor saves a young writer time in figuring things out.[28]

This open exchange of ideas for innovation and this mentoring for guidance may well benefit from interdisciplinarity, and Creative Writing may well be inherently interdisciplinary. Creativity is related to divergent thinking: 'creative people can free themselves from conventional thought patterns and follow new pathways to unusual or distantly associated answers'.[29] Those three featured undergraduate programs recognized interdisciplinarity: Knox requires coursework in other creative arts, most of Oberlin's Creative Writing students complete a second major, and Sarah Lawrence encourages professors to bring varied texts and fields together in courses and encourages students to work with different professors in different fields. Once one acquires preparation – which can involve a long stage of knowledge gathering and practice – then changes in perspective allow creative people to make innovative connections.[30] In the case of Creative Writing, attention to craft provides focused preparation necessary for achievement in the field, but interdisciplinarity – wide reading, varied experiences, and curiosity – may allow for creativity to enliven craft. As Robert Frost put it, 'the object in writing poetry is to make all poems sound as different as possible from each other, and the resources for that of vowels, consonants, punctuation, syntax, words, sentences, meter are not enough. We need the help of context – meaning – subject matter.'[31] The hammer needs to make contact, and the nail is designed to pierce; our tools must shape something. In other words, craft provides us with the resources and fundamental skills of our discipline, but we also need subject matter and meaning to do Creative Writing.

Let me illustrate the interplay among writerly reading craft and creativity. A student in my introductory course a few years ago wrote a poem about her aunt, who had recently been diagnosed with breast cancer. The draft the student brought to the workshop was heartfelt, and she thought she had said what she wanted to say. But the poem was riddled with abstractions, clichés and adjectives. She responded to the workshop discussion by reworking the poem with different abstractions, clichés and adjectives. During her final conference with me, however, I challenged her: what if it were not about your aunt? what if the poem did not state your feelings? what if Barbie got breast cancer? how would she cope? This was not what the student wanted to hear, but I reminded her of the Denise Duhamel poem we had read, pointed to the sections of our textbook *The Poet's Companion* that dealt with images and metaphor, and suggested researching cancer for the basic knowledge and terminology she did not know. Importantly, I asked her to trust me and to know that she would get credit for the attempt even if it failed. As I expected, the student succeeded, noting that she had ended up saying more truthfully how she felt about her aunt and about cancer by letting the imagined Barbie speak and had also written a better poem than she thought she could. That is my goal especially for undergraduates: to build an environment with the conditions necessary – writerly reading, craft and creativity among them – for students to surprise themselves.

No single formula exists for Creative Writing programs in the United States. Moreover, it seems unlikely that a student's surprise – or her exceeding of her own expectations – can be measured directly, even if teachers observe it time and time again. That said, Creative Writing has bought into the academy and adapted itself to many of the necessary procedures and practices of the institutions that house us. We are responsible to some extent, individually and on the whole, to the institutions that support us and should probably work harder to delineate what we do, how we do it and why it matters.[32] Far from selling out, though, Creative Writing has reinvigorated English departments across the country and continues to make significant contributions to students' lives and to the culture at large. Creative writers housed in these departments continue to produce exciting poetry, fiction and nonfiction. Where writerly reading, craft and creativity co-mingle, we all reap rewards.

Notes

1. David Fenza, 'About AWP: The Growth of Creative Writing Programs,' Association of Writers and Writing Programs website, www.awpwriter.org/aboutawp/index.htm (accessed 28 February 2012).
2. *The AWP Official Guide to Writing Programs*, Association of Writers and Writing Programs website, www.awpwriter.org/programsearch/index.php (accessed 28 February 2012).
3. Margaret Schramm, et al., 'The Undergraduate English Major,' *ADE Bulletin* (Spring/Fall 2003): 68–91. Schramm, p. 72.
4. Schramm, p. 74. State mandates that students planning high-school teaching careers major in subjects outside education have likely bolstered numbers of literature majors nationwide.
5. Schramm, p. 72.
6. Schramm, p. 75.
7. Jane Ciabattari, 'A Revolution of Sensibility,' *Poets & Writers* (Jan./Feb. 2005): 69–72.
8. Ciabattari, p. 70.
9. Ciabattari, p. 71.
10. Ciabattari, p. 72.
11. Ciabattari, p. 70, p. 72.
12. Ciabattari, p. 72.
13. Ciabattari, p. 69.
14. *The AWP Director's Handbook*, Association of Writers and Writing Programs website, www.awpwriter.org/membership/dh_4.htm (accessed 28 February 2012). AWP delineates its hallmarks further and some items support Ciabattari's analysis of Knox, Oberlin and Sarah Lawrence. For instance, AWP recommends that intermediate and advanced Creative Writing courses are restricted to 12–18 students, with an optimum workshop size of twelve. The extra-curricular opportunities in these three programs is also in keeping with AWP's recommendations for such things as student-run literary journals to publish student work, internships, ability to participate in public readings, and access to visiting writers.
15. My coverage of the AWP hallmarks or of aspects of the field of Creative Writing is not comprehensive but, I hope, are representative. Self-knowledge and

self-expression, for instance, are aspects of Creative Writing covered by Hans Ostrom in, 'Hidden Purposes of Undergraduate Creative Writing: Power, Self, and Knowledge,' elsewhere in this collection. Also in this collection, Maureen Freely offers another take on US Creative Writing programs by comparing them with those in the United Kingdom in 'No Factories Please – We're Writers.'

16. *The AWP Director's Handbook*, Association of Writers and Writing Programs website, www.awpwriter.org/membership/dh_4.htm (accessed 28 February 2012).
17. Francine Prose, *Reading Like a Writer: A Guide for People Who Love Books and for Those Who Want to Write Them* (New York: HarperCollins, 2006), p. 12.
18. Mary Cantrell, 'Teaching and Evaluation: Why Bother?' *Power and Identity in the Creative Writing Classroom*, Ed. Anna Leahy (Clevedon: Multilingual Matters, 2005), p. 71.
19. Cantrell, p. 71.
20. Cantrell, p. 74.
21. Of recent interest is the report from US Secretary of Education Margaret Spellings available at www.ed.gov/about/bdscomm/list/hiedfuture (accessed 28 December 2012). Here, Spellings outlines the shortcomings of higher education in the United States and calls for increasing educational quality and innovation, starting with greater accountability focused on outcomes and performance rather than input and reputation. One concern about Spellings's recommendations is the possibility of a one-size-fits-all national assessment program that squelches variety and fails to capture the value of some fields, particularly the arts. Another concern is the report's emphasis on science and relative neglect of the humanities.
22. David Morley, *The Cambridge Introduction to Creative Writing* (New York: Cambridge University Press, 2007), p. 118.
23. Nancy C. Andreasen, *The Creating Brain: The Neuroscience of Genius* (New York: Dana Press, 2005), p. 128.
24. Andreasen, p. 129, italics mine.
25. Andreasen, p. 129.
26. Wallace Stegner, *On Teaching and Writing Fiction* (New York: Penguin, 2002), p. 52.
27. Stegner, p. 52.
28. John Irving, 'Interview,' *The Daily Show with Jon Stewart* (Comedy Central, 17 August 2005).
29. Ulrich Kraft, 'Unleashing Creativity,' *Scientific American Mind*, 16, 1, (2005): 16–23.
30. Kraft, pp. 22–3.
31. Robert Frost, *Robert Frost: Poetry & Prose* (New York: Holt, Rinehart and Winston, 1972), p. 393.
32. See, for example, the following texts: Anna Leahy, Ed., *Power and Identity in the Creative Writing Classroom* (Clevedon: Multilingual Matters, 2005); Steven Earnshaw, Ed., *The Handbook of Creative Writing* (Edinburgh, UK: Edinburgh University Press, 2007); Kelly Ritter and Stephanie Vanderslice, Eds., *Can It Really Be Taught?* (New York: Heinemann Boynton/Cook 2007).

9
Hidden Purposes of Undergraduate Creative Writing: Power, Self and Knowledge

Hans Ostrom

In the United States, one fierce critic of undergraduate Creative Writing taught it for several decades: the late Karl Shapiro (1913–2000), winner of the Pulitzer Prize for Poetry in 1945 and professor of Creative Writing at Johns Hopkins University, the University of Chicago, the University of Nebraska and the University of California at Davis. He was among the post-World War II generation of writers who joined the academy and developed Creative Writing as a distinct species of English Studies, but as late as 1993, Shapiro was still criticizing the subject: 'I only wish that Creative Writing would not be confused with education, that it would not try to compete with language and literature training as an equal.' Shapiro defended his own participation thusly:

> For someone who has made a comfortable living all his adult life teaching Creative Writing it would seem irrational and wrong-headed to oppose it. If CW (Creative Writing) is no more than what lawyers call a good faith effort to help writers and poets have a job, that would be enough to justify it. Why shouldn't poets have a job, even if they only have to lean on their shovels?[1]

I disagree with some elements of Shapiro's critique. Still, it invites us to make positive statements about the purposes of Creative Writing. Indeed, many have already stated these purposes.[2] We may not rank these identically, but we get to them with similar moves: we come to Creative Writing believing it can and should be taught; we come as teachers and as writers who learned from teachers; we come with an unsentimental love that is reticent to over-state questions of innate 'genius' and 'talent' but that is ready to emphasize the improvisatory *work* of writing. Although our pedagogies may have evolved beyond just 'the workshop', we have not lost sight of the 'work' part.[3]

We often see Creative Writing as a modern equivalent of classical imitation, which was part of Quintillian's educational program.[4] We see it as one more way to teach writing, a way that invites students to write about what is important to them but also to write for real audiences. And we see it as a potentially 'liberatory' (Paulo Freire's term) form of English studies, one in which students may use writing to represent and confront issues of power, identity, social friction and oppression.[5]

It is this last topic I want to explore more fully – how Creative Writing is potentially liberatory. My working-claim is that although literacy, imitation, the study of craft and experiencing literature as a writing reader are worthy elements of Creative Writing, the subject has more or less hidden purposes that are just as real and worthy. Creative Writing allows students a distinctive way of occupying a space that Michel Foucault, located among power, self and knowledge.[6]

Power

A colleague in Communication Studies has developed a historically grounded course on the rhetoric of nineteenth and twentieth century civil-rights movements in the US. To some degree, the course is about 'the rhetoric of race'. When I hear him describe the course, he often emphasizes how he is not interested in students' 'emoting' (his word) – that he and his course are not interested in how students 'felt' about issues of race, racism and civil rights. His course centres on rigorous, historically based analysis, which 'emoting', presumably, might hinder. Emotion has the power to erode academic rigour, he worries. Emotion and the study of history, apparently, do not mix well. Emotion is forceful enough to require prohibition.

Some questions: How is it even possible, let alone desirable, to remove emotion from the topics of race-relations, the rhetoric of race and civil rights? What is inherently inappropriate about *any* kind of 'emoting' in an academic setting? Might all students reasonably claim that keeping the option of 'emoting' open is their privilege if not their right, within a reasonable academic structure? And finally, to what extent does the prohibition itself reveal considerable emoting in the form of fear? Mostly, however, I am fascinated by how much *power* my colleague believes emotion possesses.

Creative Writing is inextricably connected with students' emoting. Both those who teach and those who do not teach Creative Writing are, like my colleague in Communication, often troubled by emotion's presence in Creative Writing. Creative Writing teachers can, of course, try to resist or control emotion by how they establish workshop environments and protocols for peer-review. They can also focus on the alleged unemotional study of 'craft'. They can insist that writing is really only a matter of playing with words, is a linguistic game in which one need not and should not be emotionally invested. They can admonish students not to be 'sentimental' in their writing. Finally, they can insist that a Creative Writing course must not become a therapy session or a support group.

How emotion functions in Creative Writing and how to frame debates about emotion are important topics. For 'emotion' – variously defined, valued or devalued – possesses social and discursive power. Foucault's work suggests that if Creative Writing and 'emotion' possess such power and cause such consternation, then they are obviously worthwhile, if for no other reason than that they invite one to analyse the nature of academic institutions, curricula, writing, English Studies, constructions of 'analysis' and 'reason', and so on. One move Foucault often makes is to ask whether those who wish to control something are actually creating it as they try to control it.

Emotion experienced and remembered is obviously inextricably part of Creative Writing. Emotion's power can be problematic because it is connected to the power of feeling, the fear – in academia and elsewhere – of feeling, and the function of the concept of 'emotion' in our discursive practices and in the ways we configure ourselves as teachers and academics.

Self

In spite of everything Modernism, Post-structuralism and Post-Modernism have done to 'the self', including obliterating it, I know I often fall back on an old-fashioned view of self and self-expression. Perhaps you do, too. The American poet and teacher Richard Hugo approached the topic fatalistically.[7] He said that we all had our obsessions – things and even words we could not help but think about; that these were part of who we are, our selves; and that they would come out in our poetry, no matter what.

At other times, however, and in specific ways, my Creative Writing classes demonstrate how complicated the issues of self and self-expression are. I want briefly to discuss one of these ways, and in so doing I will also touch on the subject of 'failure' in Creative Writing.

A recent student, J., wrote a long story featuring three main elements: the story of two childhood friends in Chicago, the story of one of these friends visiting the rural South, and the story of this same friend getting killed by a white racist mob. J., who is African American, has taken several classes from me, and I know how passionate she is about questions of racism and how widely read she is. We did not like the particular shape of her long story, and one observation seemed to make sense to her. I thought the piece contained at least three separate stories and the writing itself revealed that she was deriving the most pleasure from telling the story of childhood friends in a black neighbourhood in Chicago. J. agreed and seemed relieved to be given license, as it were, to write something not explicitly about race-relations.

The semester ended before she could revise the longer story or fully turn it into separate stories, so technically, the longer piece could be counted as a 'failure'. Yet our discussions comprised a success, partly because J. was able to reconsider her 'self' – what Foucault might call her 'author-function' – and to recognize that she had placed a significant burden on herself, whereby she felt obligated to write explicitly socially-conscious fiction.

The idea of writing what is pleasurable to write had not fully occurred to her before we talked about how much she seemed to enjoy writing the neighbourhood story. In concrete ways, then, J. reexamined her 'self' in relation to how her fiction takes shape, what her fiction is obligated – and not obligated – to do at different times, and how she viewed herself as a writer.

Another recent student, E., seemed to want to write nothing more than 'genre-fiction' – specifically, vampire stories. I tried to help make these stories more original, by disrupting some of the genre's familiar conventions, but because she was so immersed in these (she had been reading vampire narratives for a long time) E. resisted.

In class she often told anecdotes about her personal life, which included an unusual upbringing in Texas. Little of this material made it into her fiction, however, until she wrote her final story, which was a restrained, third-person piece in which the main character is simply called 'she' or 'the girl', but which clearly drew on E.'s experiences in Texas. To both of us, this story was written with great power, and I believe E. saw a productive detour around vampire-fiction. She was able to liberate herself from the comfortable but limiting writer's position of 'the one in the class who writes those vampire stories'.

Other students successfully redefine their writing-selves away from the personal, toward socially conscious, more overtly political writing. For instance, I recall one student with strong, sophisticated religious beliefs; he was reticent to base his fiction on them because he believed neither I nor his classmates would take well to such fiction. When he revealed this, I argued that he should certainly write about what interested him, and he produced fine stories involving religious and ethical questions. In a sense his move was toward the personal, but in another, it was away from the merely personal toward big societal and spiritual questions.

Knowledge

We may underestimate the extent to which Creative Writing is a way of knowing – of making knowledge. While students can write about anything, none of us knows what sort of knowledge they will create in advance. This uncertainty – this expansive field of possibilities – is enormously powerful. Creative Writing is uniquely positioned in undergraduate studies to allow students this sort of discovery and to allow them to assimilate everything and anything they have learned.

Creative Writing also blends old and new. Every time I teach, I encounter new topics, situations, and language – everything that is new about this new generation. Also, literary forms, conventions and language change constantly. Nonetheless, students still participate in ancient traditions of narrative, image-making and sound-making. They are practicing old ways of knowing – story and song.

How do students *make knowledge* in Creative Writing, albeit differently from the way they make knowledge in other academic disciplines? This may be an important question for us to ponder. I do not have room to ponder the question further in this chapter, so I will leave that particular space open, hoping you will fill it with your answers about Creative Writing and knowledge.

In addition to both the customary and relatively new, the real and alleged purposes of Creative Writing, therefore, some intriguing, mysterious purposes connected to power, self and knowledge are among the gifts the subject holds for us and our students.

Notes

1. Karl Shapiro, 'Notes on Raising a Poet,' *Seriously Meeting Karl Shapiro*, Ed. Sue B. Walker (Mobile, AL: Negative Capability Press, 1993), pp. 109–30; Karl Shapiro, 'University' [poem], *New and Selected Poems, 1940–1986* (Chicago: University of Chicago Press, 1987), p. 19; Karl Shapiro, *V-Letter and Other Poems* (New York: Reynal and Hitchcock, 1944).

2. Wendy Bishop, *Released Into Language: Options for Teaching Creative Writing* (Urbana, IL: National Council of Teachers of English, 1990); Wendy Bishop, 'Crossing the Lines: On Creative Composition and Composing Creative Writing,' *Writing on the Edge* 4, 2 (Spring 1993): 117–33; Wendy Bishop, *The Elements of Alternate Style* (Portsmouth, NH: Boynton/Cook, 1997); Wendy Bishop, 'Places to Stand: The Reflective Writer-Teacher-Writer in Composition,' *College Composition and Communication* 51, 1 (September 1999): 9–31; Wendy Bishop, *Thirteen Ways of Looking for a Poem: A Guide to Writing Poetry* (New York: Longman, 2000); Wendy Bishop and Hans Ostrom, Eds., *Colors of a Different Horse: Rethinking Creative Writing Theory and Pedagogy* (Urbana, IL: National Council of Teachers of English, 1994); Wendy Bishop and Hans Ostrom, Eds., *Genre and Writing: Issues, Arguments, Alternatives* (Portsmouth, NH: Boynton/Cook, 1997); Wendy Bishop and Hans Ostrom, Eds., *The Subject Is Story* (Portsmouth, NH: Boynton/Cook, Heinemann, 2003); Patrick Bizzaro, *Responding to Student Poems: Applications of Critical Theory* (Urbana, IL: National Council of Teachers of English, 1993); Richard Hugo, *The Triggering Town: Lectures and Essays on Poetry and Writing* (New York: W.W. Norton, 1979); Hans Ostrom, 'Undergraduate Creative Writing: The Unexamined Subject,' *Writing on the Edge* 1, 1 (Fall 1989): 55–65; Hans Ostrom, 'Countee Cullen: How Teaching Rewrites the Genre of "Writer,"' *Genre and Writing: Issues, Arguments and Alternatives*, Eds. Bishop and Ostrom, (Portsmouth, NH: Boynton-Cook, 1997); Hans Ostrom, '"Carom Shots": Reconceptualizing Imitation and Its Uses in Creative Writing Courses,' *Teaching Writing Creatively*, Ed. David Starkey (Portsmouth, NH: Heinemann/Boynton-Cook, 1998), pp. 164–72; David Starkey, Ed., *Teaching Writing Creatively* (Portsmouth, NH: Boynton-Cook, 1998).

3. Anne Bernays and Pamel Painter, *What If?: Writing Exercises for Fiction Writers* (New York: HarperCollins, 1990); Patrick Bizzaro, *Responding to Student Poems: Applications of Critical Theory* (Urbana, IL: National Council of Teachers of English,

1993); Hans Ostrom, Wendy Bishop and Katharine Haake, *Metro: Journeys in Writing Creatively* (New York: Longman, 2000); David Starkey, Ed., *Teaching Writing Creatively* (Portsmouth, NH: Boynton-Cook, 1998).

4. Hans Ostrom, '"Carom Shots", pp. 164–72; David Starkey, Ed., *Teaching Writing Creatively*.

5. Paulo Freire, *Pedagogy of the Oppressed*, Trans. Myra Bergman Ramos (New York: Continuum, 1981).

6. Michel Foucault, *The Archaeology of Knowledge*, Trans. A.M. Sheridan Smith (New York: Pantheon, 1972); Michel Foucault, *The History of Sexuality, Volume I: An Introduction*, Trans. Robert Hurley (New York: Vintage, 1980); Michel Foucault, *Power/Knowledge: Selected Interviews and Other Writings 1972–1977*, Ed. Colin Gordon, Trans. Colin Gordon, Leo Marshall, John Mepham and Kate Soper (New York: Pantheon, 1988).

7. Richard Hugo, *The Triggering Town: Lectures and Essays on Poetry and Writing* (New York: W.W. Norton, 1979).

10
No Factories, Please – We're Writers

Maureen Freely

Good writers make better readers. Good readers make better writers. These were the ideas that gave birth to the Warwick Writing Programme; many years on, they are still our guiding principles. I am writing this essay to propose a third: if they are to give their best to their students, teachers of writing must be able to move (and move with ease) between academic and literary cultures. Though they may be willing and even happy to conform to university regulations, they can never forget the ways in which those regulations stifle free expression and impede the workings of the imagination. They know from their own travels between the two cultures that there is more than one way of doing things: this insight informs every aspect of their work.

So it should not come as a surprise to know that every Creative Writing programme in Britain is in some important way different from all others. Most Creative Writing tutors in Britain made their mark in the literary world long before they found their way into universities. Having been formed by that world, they have gone on to create programmes that reflect its values. For example, we at Warwick feel that market forces have undermined the publishing industry, making it very difficult for editors who care about good writing to nurture or encourage literary authors who fail to make the bestseller list. So we have designed a programme that aims to fill that gap. We see ourselves as editors, working with young writers and sustaining them until they are strong enough to venture into the jungle. We encourage them to develop their own voices, nurture their own judgement, follow their own passions, take risks, find the courage to go their own way. Yes, there are certain things all writers must master. But unless we can pass on this expert knowledge in a reasonably free and easy way, we are no better than the market-driven publishing factories we claim to so abhor.

There is a strong belief amongst British Creative Writing teachers that factory tuition is the norm in the US, where Creative Writing programmes have been in place for many decades. For the vast majority of Creative Writing teachers in the US are themselves graduates of such programmes. Though none can expect to get very far up the ladder without a few contracts from leading mainstream publishers, many will beef up their CVs by publishing in university presses that exist (at least according to their detractors) to ease an ever-growing pool of not-quite-good-enough writers into cushy jobs. Once established in these cushy jobs, they will go on to publish their not-quite-good-enough friends, thereby nurturing of culture of mediocrity and a dreary stockpile of safe, standardized, university-friendly writing.

There is no doubt that a lot of this goes on, though the story is a bit more complicated than that. Having taught in the US, I would say that Creative Writing programmes serve as safe havens not just for fledgling writers but for their already published teachers; they are little worlds in which good writing matters and the laws of the market are not sacrosanct. Most of the best US writers – the writers we in Britain read with the greatest awe – have associations of some kind with the Creative Writing network. These people do not just foster originality and risk-taking in the classroom; as marketplace successes, they teach the market that it does not always have to dumb down to sell books. Most of these authors also work hard to help launch new and young writers. So you could argue that the US Creative Writing network is what keeps literary culture alive.

This is not yet the case here in Britain, though I live in hope. In the meantime, there is much to be gained from a closer and less prejudiced look at the US model. The first thing to know is that there is even more variety of provision in the US than there is here. The programmes in elite private universities bear little resemblance to programmes in state universities and community colleges. While some programmes are over determined, others offer no structure whatsoever. But in several important ways, they all challenge the factory mentality a lot better than we do.

This is a large assertion and I cannot begin to do justice to it in this small space. So let me keep things simple by pointing out a few significant differences between the Warwick Writing Programme and the two US programmes in which I worked during the eighties. Both US programmes were located in state universities; both institutions conformed to the standard US liberal arts model that people here rarely understand, because it is so very different from what we accept as normal in Britain. So perhaps I should explain that US students wishing to enter liberal arts programmes do not apply to a specific course but to the university. They are vetted and interviewed not by academics but by a university department that performs no other function. During a student's four years at university (and unless she is attending a community college, it is almost always four years) she will be expected to do a specified number of courses outside the subject she eventually chooses as her major. If a she has a concentration in the humanities, she will take some courses in the natural and social sciences. Though

Creative Writing programmes are usually located in English departments, many of their students will be temporary migrants from other disciplines.

In state universities, the range of ages and abilities in each classroom is enormous. At the University of Texas, where I taught in the early 1980s, many of my students were bilingual and produced work in both languages. At the Florida International University, where I worked in the mid-1980s, I taught a class in which one of my students could barely speak English and another student had five Ph.D.s. The former was in her early twenties, the latter in her late seventies. In both universities there was a high proportion of part-time students. Many studied at night after putting eight hours into jobs they were hoping a degree might help them escape. Though they often had huge holes in their education, they had an enthusiasm and a respect for learning that made them a pleasure to teach. Because teaching loads for those of us with tenure track jobs was much, much lighter than it is here, we also had a lot more time to spend on them.

From time to time, we would discover a gifted student and convince him or her to carry on writing; occasionally, one of our graduates would go on to publish. Most of our successes came from backgrounds so modest that they would never have got a literary door to open without our help. This is one of the great virtues of the US system – it provides a way into literary culture for the poor, the marginalized and the unconnected. In the long run, it challenges and changes the middle class bias common to most literary cultures.

There was, however, much pressure to dumb things down. The most dramatic example was the '12-day rule' at the University of Texas: any undergraduate class that did not have twenty bums on seats on the twelfth day of a semester was liable to cancellation, with the putative teacher being deprived of that portion of her pay. This definitely encouraged us to keep our readings lists short and our learning outcomes modest. We had no second markers or externals breathing over our shoulders, and no exam boards where we might find our marking methods subjected to scrutiny. Grade inflation was such a time-honoured tradition that grades were next to meaningless. As deplorable as that might be, it did mean that my students did not lose sleep worrying about marks.

They knew that I would fail them if they did not work and give them a decent enough mark if they attended class and did the best writing they could. This meant that they could relax and apply their minds instead to the vastly more ambitious dreams that had brought them into my classroom. Though they and I knew these dreams to be largely impossible, they were still keen to try; good sports that they were, they were not easily discouraged. In any event, I kept my basic aims modest: I was happy if I gave them a taste for contemporary writing, and if I had managed to get them to write about their own experiences in their own voices, rather than accept the version of life peddled by mass culture as more truthful or important than their own.

At Warwick we aim much higher. There are more than thirty applications for every place on our joint degree (English Literature and Creative Writing). We have the privilege of spending three years with students who are bright and confident and bursting with new ideas that take them far beyond our walls. They run their own writing groups, direct and perform their own plays. They set up their own magazines, publishing houses and community arts programmes. They publish their own short story anthologies and win national poetry competitions. They do not all come from privileged backgrounds but by the time they leave, they certainly know their way around literary culture. Some go straight into it; some go on to do doctorates in the humanities; others choose careers in law, politics, development and education. Whatever they choose, they know enough about writing, and enough about the way *they* prefer to write, to know that they can return to it at any time they wish.

What they may not know is how hard it has been to create the conditions to make all this possible. For we on the teaching side are under constant pressure to design our courses and our careers to factory-like specifications, and we are chronically understaffed. Our colleagues in the English department (and indeed our colleagues throughout the university and the country) face all the same pressures we do. But the constraints are particularly painful in a programme where all teaching is practice-based.

Though our lessons are carefully structured, and though every course involves reading as well as writing, we put student writing at the centre of everything we do. We ask all students to write for class or in class every week. This means that every week I read and lead class discussions on the work of seventy-five undergraduates. I do this by making some classes twice as long as regulations say they need to be, and by devoting far more time to my students than my official coarse load suggests. I often wonder why I bother, but when I read the long projects my students do in their final year, when I see how far they have come during their time with us, I remember why. You cannot teach people how to write if you do not spend a great deal of time with them and their writing. If you do give them the time they deserve, they can achieve great things.

But to find the time – to ring fence the space that makes our programme what it is – we come pretty close to pretending we have not done so. Let me put it like this: My colleagues and I could stop reading student work tomorrow and no one in the university hierarchy would notice, let alone complain. We could offer lectures on writing instead of looking at what they write. We could tell our students that we refuse to read anything but the assessed work they submit to us at the end of the year. We could keep our distance and devote our energies instead to the Research Assessment Exercise (REF). If we have refused to go this route, it is because it would make a nonsense of what we are here to do.

But to do what we are here to do, we must spend a huge amount of time conforming to standards that were designed for a very different kind of teaching. Take assessment. I have no problem with tough numerical assessment of academic work. But can we really say what makes a piece of imaginative writing merit a 67, and what exactly will bump it up to a 68? If we can make such a distinction, are we perhaps teaching our students to paint by numbers, instead of using their imaginations to go against the grain? And what of the machinery of mark-monitoring? Second markers, externals and exam boards exist to enforce standards. As important as they may be in our battle against grade inflation, standards standardize.

At Warwick we have always tried to turn university constraints into spurs for innovation. So when we see our students taking risks or attempting a form that we fear our externals may not appreciate, we warn them, of course. But we tell them that they should respect the university system of assessment, and that it is far fairer and more rigorous than the systems that will shape their careers as writers in the marketplace, we also say that they should not bend to the academic template any more than they should the commercial template: the point of writing is to be true to your own voice and your own way of seeing things. But this all happens behind closed doors, and (until today) in whispers.

We are lucky to be located in a department that has come to take teaching very seriously, and that is now actively encouraging innovation, and communication amongst innovators. We have students who are already confident high achievers when they join us. They are strong enough to dare to go against the grain, even if it means an exam board of strangers will see this as a reason to classify them as second-class scholars. Many of them do leave with firsts. Those who do will have distinguished themselves not just as writers but as scholars, for roughly two-thirds of their courses will have been in what we call 'straight English'. Whatever class degree they earn, they will have spent three years working intensively with teachers who take them seriously as writers, and who ask them to write every week. This is a rare sort of attention in the factories of British higher education today.

And who knows? Perhaps tomorrow the pressure from fee-paying parents and loan-weary students will be such that our managers will be forced to change direction. Perhaps they will decide that universities can no longer just see themselves as research-producing entities. Perhaps they will return us to older and more personalized forms of production. Perhaps they will turn their spotlights on their Creative Writing departments and find learning outcomes they wish to replicate elsewhere. Perhaps, or perhaps not. Whatever direction universities travel, I fear that the corporation metaphors, like the structures they reflect, will be hard to crack.

If the factory is here to stay, Creative Writing programmes will have to find a way to survive in it. If they are to give their best, they will also have to find ways to keep it from killing the imaginative spirit they exist to serve. If this is just about do-able today, it is because most Creative Writing tutors in Britain are hybrid creatures who move between two cultures, and who insist on the importance of doing so, even when those who run universities fail to see the point. But what will happen as these programmes mature? When most tutors are themselves products of other Creative Writing programmes, they may be less inclined to resist bureaucratic pressure. They may even fail to understand why they should. This is the real danger facing us. Or rather, this is the danger we have so far avoided discussing. We should, at the very least, begin to exchange notes. So here's my question: how do other Creative Writing tutors remain true to their literary values while also honouring university conventions? All answers on postcards, please – and in finely wrought prose.

Part IV
Postgraduate Creative Writing

Postgraduate Creative Writing gives students opportunities to develop creative works in depth. Many courses also offer opportunities to meet publishers agents and others involved in creative industries.

Steven Earnshaw's research questions the assumption that postgraduate Creative Writing consists of workshops and individual feedback alone. Rather, he argues why postgraduate programmes need to provide a 'complete environment', including opportunities to present and publish.

Jon Cook discusses implications of UK Universities being publicly accountable for what they do and why they do it in terms of Ph.Ds in Creative Writing. He concludes that Ph.Ds consider 1) research into content 2) research into form and 3) research into the relationship between the two.

Robin Hemley reflects on assumptions in the workshop model made famous through the University of Iowa insofar as students often only recall negative feedback from such workshops and are thus disabled in their writing. To address this, he suggests a low residency model in which students have one-to-one contact with a tutor over the year, only meeting collectively on occasions since this more closely resembles how professional writers work with editors and colleagues.

11
Teaching Creative Writing at Postgraduate Levels: the Sheffield Hallam Experience

Steven Earnshaw

This paper discusses the history and philosophy behind the MA in Writing at Sheffield Hallam University. Through this I tease out those elements and issues I believe are important to postgraduate Creative Writing teaching.[1]

Established in 1993 and one of the first postgraduate Creative Writing masters in the UK, the MA consists of a core module, 'What is Contemporary?' This includes first a main option, which represents the student's preferred genre and second, a subsidiary option, that is, a second genre. Options include novel, poetry, scriptwriting, short story, writing for children, the writer as teacher and literary editing. Teaching is delivered mainly through workshops, individual tutorials and feedback. At postgraduate level there is input from professionals outside academia (literary agents, publishers and professional writers). The course also offers several publishing outlets of its own. Requirements for acceptance onto the course are usually a first degree in English or a related subject, and a sample of Creative Writing showing potential to succeed at this level; 'non-standard' applications are also welcomed and considered. There has never been any desire to make the Hallam MA into a 'writing school'; the intention has always been to help those with talent become the best writers that they can be.

Part of the Hallam MA's distinctiveness is that it was set up on the back of an undergraduate degree in which Creative Writing was already a key element: the BA English Studies had (and still has) three strands – literature, language and Creative Writing – which are intended to inform each other. The literature strand stretches from the Renaissance to the present and has crucially always contained contemporary material – a one-time contentious issue throughout UK English departments. This integration of Creative Writing into the BA English Studies provided a good basis for developing the MA, which at that time had to fight its corner both within the University and within the broader context of Creative Writing within the academy. It means that the MA is not a 'stand-alone' unit, but part of a larger Creative Writing programme which now also includes Creative Writing Ph.Ds.

One difficulty for Creative Writing in academia, especially at postgraduate level, is how to judge its 'success' in order that it has academic parity. For example, Creative Writing on the undergraduate programme at Hallam was originally called 'writing skills' to make it acceptable in light of hostility at the institution towards introducing the term 'Creative Writing'. However, the fact that writing at Hallam was already tied closely to the English academic programme through the three strands approach certainly helped. In this way students are encouraged to be both writers and readers, at both undergraduate and postgraduate levels. Notions of 'publishability' and 'producibility' are also embedded into both levels and operate as an inbuilt quality control.

At postgraduate level especially, work is judged against academic and publishing/producing criteria. In effect, therefore, criteria for assessing Creative Writing on the MA are taken both from within and without the Academy. This is not without its problems, and with the expansion of Creative Writing into academia in the UK in recent years there will undoubtedly be an increase in a type of Creative Writing which is found acceptable within academia but which would not find an audience outside. Such a scenario has been one which creative writers themselves have feared, and has often fed into their mistrust of writing within the academy. The importance of keeping one eye on the market and insisting on published, publishing writers as teachers is therefore paramount. Without being market-driven, it is nevertheless important to know exactly what is happening in the publishing world and to avoid 'protecting' Creative Writing by giving it an academic micro-culture. Also, of course, to have 'publishable' and 'producible' as 'market' criteria presents difficulties when it might be felt that the standard of work being put into the public domain at any given time is not particularly high.

Introducing Creative Writing has also meant benefits for the academy. Less tangible, perhaps, but another significant context, is that the MA at Hallam was set up at a time when literary theory had become a fixed part of English Studies. In Creative Writing the appreciation of 'value' – crudely put: some texts are better than others – was maintained against the relativizing tendency of contemporary theory, a battle that is perhaps still prevalent, although not so overt. My own experience is that there is now a general reluctance on the part of students to assert some writing as superior to other writing, since it appears to them elitist and anti-democratic to judge in such a way. In other words, the conflict is no longer conducted within the sphere of literary theory but has become a more general relativist assumption that students bring to the workshop. It may be that some Creative Writing programmes find this perfectly acceptable, of course, although it is difficult to see how writers can be encouraged and helped to improve unless there are higher standards to aim at. It is still the case that there can be friction within the academy between 'straight' academics and those involved teaching Creative Writing, although it has to be said that such a division is rarely apparent to students themselves and the way that they perceive the status of Creative Writing within the academy.[2] Another inbuilt quality measure is that students must 'progress' through Certificate and Diploma stages before being able to submit for Masters. This has become increasingly important – no matter how much potential students show, there is nothing like the acid-test of producing work to discover the real capabilities of the writer. Although a pass is 40 per cent, anything under 50 per cent in the student's chosen genre will lead to a discussion as to how to proceed, and whether it is desirable. From bitter experience teaching staff have realized that it is far better to be absolutely honest and to dissuade a student from progression, where appropriate, than to limp on regardless.

The final submission is a book-length piece of work: a poetry collection, a completed script, a novel. This is accompanied by a critical commentary on the work itself. In progressing towards a piece of work that should be ready to venture into the world of publishing or production, with the numerous redrafts and discards that must take place to get there, a writing MA should come into its own. The one thing most difficult to assess from a sample of writing is the writer's ability to think architecturally and structurally. It happens that students can produce good writing in smallish amounts – that much is expected of anybody who succeeds in getting onto the course. The step up to producing *sustained* professional work is usually the most difficult adjustment for the student to make. And just as we would assess a novel or script on its overall coherence and structure, similarly short story and poetry collections need to demonstrate that they are not just a collection of the best random material written during the course, but that they again show something cohesive, demonstrate that they form a fully-realized artistic project. Working towards producing a finished, professional piece of work for the final submission is something that the MA in Writing can help students with in ways they would find difficult to obtain elsewhere. Constant rewriting in light of feedback is essential, a discipline that postgraduate courses should seek to help the would-be professional writer internalize.

A particular feature of Hallam's MA is a core critical module, 'What is Contemporary?' The philosophy behind this is that for students to have a genuine postgraduate learning experience they need to take a module which is common to all who take the MA, rather than simply participating in a series of workshops from their chosen genre. 'What is Contemporary?' offers the opportunity to develop a shared vocabulary that is not just an extension of that found in English critical studies, a vocabulary that can remain jargon-free whilst still being precise. The remit for what counts as 'contemporary' is therefore mainly to be decided by each cohort, hence the question-mark in the title. Nor is discussion confined to all things literary. The 'contemporary' is taken in the broadest cultural sense. Having said all that, students have sometimes questioned the module's value. If their main subject is novel, they might argue, why do they have to read and discuss poetry or film, or indulge the enthusiasms of other students (and staff), when they might be spending more time writing? Part of the process of the module is to help writers locate their work and themselves within contemporary culture. It is believed that to ask students to look beyond their own immediate sphere of interest directly helps them become better writers. Assessment consists of individual student presentations on their chosen topics which are then followed up in essays. Through this, students develop some respect for skills required in academia, and acquire those skills for themselves.

The number of publications to which MA students can directly contribute has gradually increased: an annual *Best of MA Writing*, mainly for internal consumption but increasingly a calling-card; *Matter*, which includes published writers as well as MA and Ph.D. students; *Proof*, an on-line magazine open to anyone; and the *Ictus*, an annual prize awarded to the best poet on the MA, the winner having a pamphlet of their work published by Mews Press (two of which have recently won the PBS Pamphlet Choice). Mews Press was initially established just for the *Ictus* but has recently taken on board *Matter*, and in 2005 published *Ten Hallam Poets*, an anthology of poetry from the best MA writers of the last ten years. Being able to publish in this manner is an important part of the MA in that it helps to promote the best writing and actually enhances the wider writing culture. Likewise, opportunities for public presentation of student work have opened up, with an end-of-year show in Sheffield and London, and a Hallam Poets Series.

The burgeoning of Creative Writing MAs throughout the UK has made things a little more pressured, but one of the advantages has been to spur on these recent developments, since students have come to expect such associated activities. It also means that we are constantly having to reflect and re-evaluate what we offer, how we assess, how we can improve and how we can further embed quality controls within the course. The outcome of this research is that teaching Creative Writing at postgraduate level is more than workshops and individual feedback alone, though these remain the bedrock: it is about creating the complete environment for writers that is both critical and supportive, about providing opportunities and stimulation that they would find difficult to come by outside the academy.

Notes

1. I would like to thank Professor E.A. Markham for providing much of the historical background for this piece.
2. Keith Green, 'Creative Writing, Language and Evaluation,' *Working Papers on the Web* 2 (November 2001), extra.shu.ac.uk/wpw/value/wpw.htm (accessed 28 February 2012).

12
Creative Writing and Ph.D. Research

Jon Cook

The emergence of Creative Writing as a significant presence in British higher education has coincided with major changes in universities themselves. Amongst these has been the requirement that universities should be publicly accountable in a new way. Universities no longer just do things like teaching and research. They have to accompany their activity with statements about what they do and why they do it. What is to count as research in any field is not exempt from these requirements. Their pressure, for good or ill, has been evident in debates about what is to count as research in Creative Writing and, therefore, about what it might mean to do a Ph.D. in the subject, if it is a subject.

This can create a fascinating and sometimes maddening pressure to be explicit about something called creativity. Universities have now become the stage for a time-honoured confrontation between the creative individual – free, spontaneous and unpredictable – and the requirements of an institution obliged to establish norms, objectives and predictable outcomes. There is a script at work here and it plays itself out compulsively. The connection between artistic work and a version of freedom has behind it a philosophical tradition that goes back to at least the time of Kant. But there is another side as well. Imaginative work has a long involvement with different institutions: the church, the court, the aristocratic patron, or the more anonymous forces of the law, the literary market place and the publishing industry. Literature is itself a modern institution of a particular kind, a point made by Derrida in a 1989 interview when he discussed his attraction to literature: 'the institution of literature in the West, in its relatively modern form, is linked to an authorization to say everything, and doubtless too to the coming about of the modern idea of democracy'. One aspect of this authorization to 'say everything' is that you did not need to explain what you were saying, let alone describe it as research, since that could be the task of a critic.

The movement of Creative Writing into universities may then demand an accountability of the writer that is at odds with at least one aspect of the modern institution of literature. There is no simple, brisk solution to this. At some level doing a Ph.D. in Creative Writing, for example, is going to encounter that lack of fit between prevailing ideas about what it means to do research in a university and what it is like to write a novel, or a collection of poems or a script. But there is a danger of creating mythical monsters here: on the one side the writer, all free spirit, imagination and intuitive force; on the other the university and its wearisome bureaucracies.

Is there a way out of the uncertainties that surround accounting for Creative Writing as a form of research? Various statements suggest that there is. The 2001 Research Assessment Exercise accepted research based upon 'the invention and generation of ideas, images, performances and artifacts including design, where these lead to new or substantially improved insights'.[1] This idea of research derives from the practice-based disciplines – art, design, music and drama – and Creative Writing can be placed in this spectrum. The funding bodies, whether for academics or Ph.D. students in the field, are in principle willing to fund work in these areas. But as is often the case with general statements of this kind there is an implied distinction and some unanswered questions that makes its efforts at clarification equivocal.

The distinction is between 'ideas, images and performances and artefacts' that do produce 'new and substantially improved insights' and those that do not. What is the kind of relevant evidence for this kind of insight? Is it contained in the work or does it have to be spelled out in an accompanying commentary? This question leads to another that is also left unanswered: insight into what? Embarking on a Ph.D. in Creative Writing, any writer might ask, given this account of research, what insight their work is supposed to produce. I want briefly to address this question here, initially by way of an imaginary anecdote.

A writer called George Eliot has submitted two novels, *Middlemarch* and *Daniel Deronda* – to an REF panel. Earlier in her career she had successfully submitted a collection of long stories, *Scenes from Clerical Life*, for the award of a Ph.D.[2] What kind of insight does this work provide? It is animated by a powerful ethical intention. The novel, in this writer's version of it, is a way of extending its readers' understanding and sympathy for the different shapes that human suffering can take such that the resources of story and character give a depth to our understanding of suffering that would not be reached by an abstract analysis of its causes and symptoms. The work realizes this intention by depicting a society that is often averse to this kind of sympathetic understanding. We walk about as the narrator puts it in one of her works, 'well wadded with stupidity'. This is work that has a strong critical edge, a sense of encounter and challenge with its readers. The writing deploys to powerful effect the rhetorical tropes of irony and pathos, and these tropes are integral to the ethical and philosophical project of the work. The language of these fictions echoes to understandings of human nature and history drawn from a wide range of philosophical, scientific and literary sources.

Where does a description like this leave the question of insight? Is what is expected something like 'insight into the human condition', a contribution, that is, to that reflection on the nature of the human that is distinctively carried on in the 'humanities'. So we could say that these works by George Eliot provide us with insights into how human beings act and behave, and how much of this action and behaviour is shaped by forces outside their control. To discover these insights requires acts of interpretation and criticism. And, of course, it is traditional by now to say that some or all of these insights are 'ideological'. They need to be questioned for their biases, their interests and their limitations.

I am not sure that this development of the notion of an insight quite captures what is at issue in the context of thinking about Creative Writing as research. What is missing is an understanding of how a particular instance of Creative Writing acts in relation to genre and form. How, for example, does a particular work change an understanding of what novels, or poems or script can do? What kind of intervention does it make in a particular context of practice?

These kinds of questions call for more clarification than can be given here. But there are at least two possible ways that they might be developed as research questions. One is to assess the intervention of a work in a prevailing literary economy. The work of Franco Moretti on the evolution of the novel, or Pascale Casanova's recently translated *The World Republic of Letters*, or James English's recent study of cultural prizes, *The Economy of Prestige* all provide insights into how what a literary work can do is intricately conditioned by a range of institutions and metropolitan centres that create hierarchies of literary value.[3] Literary prizes, for example – now awarded in unprecedented numbers – create those values by making judgements about what the best novel or poetry collection or short story might be. It is important to this process that judgements made are also always for some people, the *wrong* judgements. In James English's view that is exactly how prizes are meant to work. They confer value, and, in a few cases, sales, but they also provide the opportunity to assert that literary values have nothing to do with the award of prizes. In a recent review of English's book in the *New Yorker*, Louis Menand provides a succinct summary: 'we need literary prizes so that we can complain about how stupid they are'.

The second line is antithetical to the first. George Eliot, to take up the anecdote again, regarded writing as the practice of an art. She wrote in a letter that 'if Art does not enlarge men's sympathies, it does nothing morally' and this in a context that makes clear that she thinks the novel should be a form of art, and that it failed as art if it flattered the vanity of its readers. The realization of her ethical ambitions for the novel depended upon their success as works of art. If they were read as programmatic or didactic works they would fail, and, in her perception, failure was more likely than success. To achieve reconciliation between the ethical and the aesthetic was a demanding task. It was only if her novels moved readers in the way that works of art do that they would have the power to give a more than intellectual recognition of human suffering.

Of course these claims and identifications are matters of history too. They can be contextualized in terms of the history of concepts of art. They are part of a movement in the nineteenth and twentieth centuries to claim for the novel the status of a work of art. And they are part of a history of gendered identifications that made some women who wrote adopt male pseudonyms because they feared that their identification as women would condemn their work to the realms of the unserious.

Research into the history of the different ways that literature has been identified as an art – and the rejections of that identification – can form part of the research context for Creative Writing. And the obvious rejoinder to this proposal and its lines of development is to ask what the difference is between this kind of research and the research conducted under the headings of literary criticism or cultural history.

The difference need not be great or boldly obvious. No table has to be thumped. The proximity of research in Creative Writing to work in cultural history or literary criticism or philosophy or rhetoric is one its strengths. What makes the difference is the way these contexts are oriented towards a process of composition. If, for example, we concede that poetry is a form of verbal art this idea is not inhabited from the perspective of analysis and commentary alone, but from the perspective of a practice. The question, to rephrase it in terms of Roman Jakobson's formulation, becomes not simply what makes a verbal message into a work of art, but what makes this poem or collection of poems into works of art – how, that is, do they provide an insight into the emerging possibilities of an art form, or, possibly, into its cessation.[4] Research in Creative Writing becomes an enquiry into the artfulness of language, once its is acknowledged that language's mimetic powers are as much a part of its artfulness as are metaphor, irony or all those tropes that are yet to be created.

So far I have given a brief sketch of a research context for Creative Writing. This is intended to apply as much to writers engaged in a Ph.D. as to other kinds and levels of research activity. It shows ways in which the link between the creative and the critical component of a doctorate might be imagined. The research process is something different again. Analytically, it can be broken down into three components: research into a content, research into a form and research into the relation between them. In practice these three elements are always in play, always changing places with each other. Researching a subject may, in the case of an historical novel, overlap with established methods of research: archives need to be visited and sources consulted. But it will be something more than that, because the research activity will also be research into a language, in this case into the kind of language that will bring an historical moment to mimetic life or estrange or displace it. This research into language applies well beyond this particular example. It marks the point where research into content and research into form become connected. The writer works in the midst of dictation: all kinds of language could come onto the page; only some do and these in turn are subject to revision and shaping. The research into form is invariably an act of revision, working on drafts, rewriting. Research here proceeds by way of discovering what there is to be written, beyond any initial intention or conception. And these processes are necessarily connected to critical reading. Research into language, as it is sketchily proposed here, means researching what others have written in the relevant form or genre. It means borrowing, echoing and discriminating in a body of work. Writing about how a form is achieved, how, that is, form and content are related, can provide a useful focus for any critical commentary accompanying a piece of creative work. There is a tendency to think that this kind of writing should take an autobiographical or intimate turn. It need not and perhaps should not. The practice I am attempting to describe here reaches out into a culture that has sustained reflection on the issues briefly sketched here for more than 2000 years.

Notes

1. Research Assessment Exercise in United Kingdom (RAE), www.rae.ac.uk (accessed 28 February 2012).
2. George Eliot, *Daniel Deronda* (London: Penguin, 2004); *Middlemarch* (London: Penguin, 2003); *Scenes from Clerical Life* (London: Penguin, 2005).
3. Franco Moretti, *Signs Taken for Wonders: On the Sociology of Literary Forms* (London: Verso 2005). Pascale Casanova, *La Republica Mundial de las Letras* (Madrid: Anagrama, 2001). James English, *The Economy of Prestige* (Cambridge, MA: Harvard University Press, 2005).
4. Roman Jakobson, *Fundamentals of Language* (The Hague and Paris: Mouton, 1975).

13

A Critique of Postgraduate Workshops and a Case for Low-Residency MFAs

Robin Hemley

The original model for teaching Creative Writing was started in 1936 by Paul Engle at the University of Iowa where I am currently the Director of the Nonfiction Writing Program. Iowa is also my alma mater. I graduated from the Writers Workshop in 1982 in Fiction Writing, at a time when nonfiction was not considered *creative* in the same way as poetry and fiction. If Engle were starting the Writers workshop today, I am sure he would have included nonfiction in the mix. He was a visionary man, and after he founded the Workshop he went on to found the International Writing Program in which writers from around the world spend the Autumn semester at Iowa, and he facilitated the founding of the Translation Workshop at the University of Iowa.

He also pioneered the workshop method of teaching Creative Writing by which a group of students sit in a circle with their teacher and remark on student work, one story or poem or essay at a time. For years, it seemed the only model for teaching Creative Writing, and yet how useful is it really? In the hands of a skillful and diplomatic workshop leader, steering the discussion constructively, the workshop method can teach students how to critique and can help guide the student writer towards revision. Just as often as not, the student whose piece is being critiqued receives conflicting and confusing reactions from the class and the student leaves the workshop with a muddle of conflicting ideas, sometimes deflated and no longer able to see her work clearly. Sometimes, the only thing that sticks is a sense that the story or poem or essay failed in different ways for different readers. Most writers experience self doubts and even the most experienced writers sometimes selectively hear the negative in a workshop environment. At Iowa, there has always been a bit of a boot camp mentality towards this. Real Writers can take the heat. Yet, when I was a student, I saw talented writers so discouraged that I never heard another peep from them after graduation. In my own case, though I learned a great deal from the Workshop, I also have to admit that it took me about a year and a half after graduation before

I felt confident enough to write again without worrying how my peers and teachers would react to a piece.

When I started teaching at the University of North Carolina at Charlotte in the Autumn of 1986, I replicated the Workshop method because it was the only method I knew. I think I became pretty adept at steering the conversation, and I always dutifully met with students in conference. At UNC-Charlotte, there were as many as twenty-one students in a workshop, and this severely hampered the amount of time I was able to devote to each student in conference and in written comments. The workshop itself was easy, almost too easy. On some level, the Workshop method seems designed more for the teacher than the student. It allows the teacher, a practicing writer, the time and energy to devote to his own writing. How hard can it be to discuss two stories a week in a three-hour class that meets once a week in which most of the discussion is student generated? Of course, responsible teachers will fortify this method with individual conferences. During this time the teacher and student sort out all the confusion from the workshop and the teacher tries to guide the student toward revision, all the while glancing at the clock in anticipation of the next appointment. At worst, the student/teacher conference becomes a kind of literary field hospital with a kind of triage mentality. The most severely wounded are left to die and those with relatively small wounds are patched up and sent back to the front.

I should say right here that I have had many wonderful workshop experiences and students often benefit greatly from sitting in workshop with their peers, but sometimes it seems less like a method and more like a necessary evil.

When I first heard about low-residency writing programs, I thought they must be a scam. I envisioned a kind of summer writing conference with dilettantes who had a desire to be writers but not to write. I thought, boy, will I be on Easy Street when I'm well-known enough to teach in a low-residency program!

Happily, I couldn't have been more wrong.

Low-residency programs, when run competently and ethically, happen to generate an incredible amount of work for both teacher and student, but of a kind that is ultimately more rewarding than any other method I have encountered. The relationship of student to teacher is much more like that of the writer/editor relationship or apprentice/master relationship. Sure, a student can always get a bad 'master', but such mentors tend not to last long once they realize how much work is involved in the relationship.

The writer Bret Lott invited me to teach in the low-residency MFA Program at Vermont College in 1999. Vermont College is one of the oldest low-residency programs in the country. Low-residency programs began in the mid-1970s at Goddard College in Vermont, and then in a series of muddy and acrimonious feuds, the faculty split off and formed first the MFA Program at Warren Wilson in Swannanoa, North Carolina and then

Vermont College in Montpelier, Vermont. Goddard, somewhat unstable, maintained a shaky program throughout most of the last twenty-five years, and Bennington, also in Vermont, came along in 1994. For twenty years or so, these were practically the only low-residency programs in the world.

The idea was simple. Bring writers together for ten days twice a year to a common campus. During this time, the students and faculty give and listen to lectures, readings and panels and also participate in daily workshops. During the residency each student is assigned a mentor to work with after the residency. The student and mentor meet and devise a study plan for the next six months, including a reading list and a schedule for receiving packets of the student work. Generally, a student turns in five packets of work over six months while variously working on short critical papers, a larger critical thesis, a creative thesis, and/or a final lecture, all under the guidance of a succession of faculty mentors. These mentors have between four days and a week to respond to the student work, most often in the form of a letter. In my case, I respond with three to five single-spaced pages of comment on the work as well as margin notes. Each mentor works with five students or so a semester, and when a student is working on a memoir or a novel, the amount of time one is devoting to the student seems considerable.

And yet, it's the most rewarding teaching I have ever experienced, and I would venture to say that the large majority of my colleagues at Vermont College feel the same as me. A real bond develops between teacher and student during the course of exchanging letters, and the teacher becomes invested in the student's work in a way that is difficult if not virtually impossible when teaching a workshop of fifteen or so graduate students in a traditional workshop. Likewise, many of the students who attend the low-residency MFA programs are already professionals in other fields. In my time at Vermont, I have taught a financial reporter from *The New York Times* working on a group of gorgeous stories based on her childhood in rural Minnesota, a woman whose father was a sometimes pilot/sometimes con artist who moved his family to Saigon in the 1960s, a freelance writer from Hong Kong working on a novel about the former Portuguese colony of Macau, and many others from around the world. While we should not count success only in terms of publications, the graduates of Vermont College over the years have published collectively nearly five hundred books, and include a number of very well known prose writers and poets. The same can easily be said of Warren Wilson and Bennington, who comprise the Ivy League of low-residency programs in the US.

Unfortunately, the low residency model was discovered several years ago by administrators who knew a cash cow when they saw one. In the last several years, well over two dozen new low-residency programs have sprung up around the country. It is easy to see why. They have low overhead and high tuition. The worst of these programs are designed to have the least impact on the lives of both teacher and student while at the same time awarding a degree that will become increasingly meaningless over time. However, it is likely that students will eventually be able to distinguish between the programs that demonstrate *some* kind of results, jobs or publications by their alumni, and those that do not.

One administrator of a low-residency program told me he designed his program to avoid any 'heavy-lifting' on the part of the faculty. This seems to me the low-residency equivalent of the workshop teacher who sees her job as a kind of sinecure. The job is simply an elaborate bait and switch. The students think the teacher is there to teach them when in fact it is the students who are there to become collective patrons for the teacher's own writing. Do not get me wrong. I believe that writers who are also teachers need to protect the time for their own work. Just yesterday, a former student of mine called me up to discuss a job offer he had received. The school wanted him to teach a 4/4 load *and* teach in the summer *and* help start a new BFA for the school. From my position of employment, I could not advise him to refuse the job, but fortunately, he has some other job options, and I hope one of those will come through. He is too good a writer to destroy, and such jobs are simply coal mines for writers.

It seems to me that the low-residency model keeps both students and teachers in their best form. When administered properly, it is difficult for a low-residency teacher to become lazy in the way that an experienced workshop leader can if he or she chooses. In many of the low-residency programs, the faculty consists of a group of some of the most famous and respected writers in the country, many of whom teach nowhere else. A student studying with, say, Andrea Barrett at Warren Wilson, or Phillip Lopate at Bennington, or Mary Ruefle at Vermont will have that writer's full attention for six months while at many traditional MFA programs, the well-known writers are often away at any given moment doing readings or finishing books or else are so remote and preoccupied with their own work that students rarely have the opportunity to receive their undivided attention.

If Paul Engle were starting the Iowa Writers Workshop today, I wonder if he might envision it as a low-residency program. I wonder, too, if the rise of low-residency programs means the eventual decline of the traditional workshop. If one wants to make connections, a high-powered writing program such as Iowa or Columbia might be the answer. But if one wants to hone one's writing, perhaps a low-residency program, chosen wisely, might ultimately be the best choice.

Part V
Reflective Activities

At the heart of Creative Writing pedagogy is its focus on process as well as on the final creative product. For this reason, students learn and are assessed on how to reflect on decisions they make in producing the final creative work.

Robert Sheppard uses surveys and interviews with teaching staff and students on BAs, MAs and Ph.D.s across Higher Education Institutions in the UK to consider assumptions in a range of reflective activities in Creative Writing. He compares assumptions in assessment and functions of reflective activities and suggests future developments.

Stephanie Vanderslice argues how development of students as critics and reflective writers goes hand in hand with their development as creative writers. To explore this assumption she focuses on the following BA course assignments: reflective book reviews, written critiques of peers' work and critical introductions to peers' work, process narratives, cover letters and executive summaries.

Tony Curtis gives a personal reflection of his experiences from Wales to Vermont in the UK and USA. He describes his assumptions as a postgraduate student in the USA as well as his experiences setting up and teaching on a UK distance learning postgraduate degree course modelled on these earlier experiences.

14
Reflections on Reflection: Supplementary Discourses in Creative Writing Teaching in the UK

Robert Sheppard

The most interesting debates in Creative Writing pedagogy may centre on how we permit students to reflect upon their writings constructively (both for their future work and for their own general intellectual development), and what forms these supplementary or complementary discourses should take.

While I am far from a neutral observer – the modes I have called poetics get my vote – research I undertook for the English Subject Centre has given me a clear sense of what I think is happening in the UK at the moment.[1] Using a mixture of surveys and interviews with teaching staff across a range of Higher Education institutions, this research was carried out in 2002–3. Readers are invited to investigate the full report on-line to assess its methodology and specific data.[2]

There is divergence in what these supplementary discourses are called, although the most popular terms, 'commentary' and 'journal', could be described respectively as reader-centred and writer-centred. Other terms (such as 'reflection', 'self-assessment', 'critique') emphasize the importance of the analysis by students of writing produced or of the student's creative processes (or both).

Most students are required to produce supplementary discourses with their creative work, to reflect on individual pieces of writing but many are asked to reflect on their progress over a module, programme or year. (I will leave aside what are often called Reading as a Writer exercises which involve responding to, and learning from, other writers, which could include other students' work, of course.)

Using data drawn from my research, we find that most courses assess supplementary discourses, with just over a quarter awarding a separate grade to them. The weighting of this, in relation to marks awarded to creative work at undergraduate level, is most often 30:70, while 25:75 is most common at MA and Ph.D. level, although 50:50 is not unknown in a Ph.D. A minority of centres think that the concept of proportionality is inappropriate for courses on which supplementary discourses are assessed as part of a global, overall mark and is not assigned a separate percentage. Supplementary discourses are not always supported by formal marking criteria. This either suggests an unsystematic approach to its production, function and assessment, or could, more positively, demonstrate the encouragement of developmental, non-assessed journal or notebook work.

There is little uniformity over the length of any given reflection, although word length is not left to student discretion on most courses. The current undergraduate range of 500 words to 2500 reveals little, given that the exercises involved might range from a self-assessment on a short poem to a major act of manifesto-writing! At Ph.D. level the discourse ranges between 20,000 and 30,000 words. There is a sense that the quality – but not the function – of the discourse will vary according to level, the complexity of reflection increasing by level. These forms of writing are still emerging, and their practice (like much in undergraduate writing teaching) has filtered down from MA level to undergraduate levels.

There is broad agreement as to the function of supplementary discourses among tutors and students. The latter, however, tend to emphasize the function for their own self-development and seem less aware of the rhetorical possibilities of the discourses with relation to assessment. In a world obsessed with measurement (which proposes that you *can* fatten a pig by measuring it) this is reassuring.

For tutors, the importance of supplementary discourses for assessment is clear. They are regarded as a useful statement of the writers' intentions for a tutor's judgement as to appropriateness in terms of market, publication and/ or genre – as well as matching performance in terms of success and failure against stated aesthetic intentions. This, at its most positive and enabling, allows students to establish and state their own benchmarks for individual pieces of work.

Supplementary discourses are often seen as 'safety nets' in terms of the assessment procedures, so that intention can be rewarded if execution is inadequate or experimental. This immediately throws up the question of whether process and/or product is being tracked and rewarded. Some lecturers stress the recording of process to dispel residual illusions of inspirational theories of composition, but still favour assessing the account of product, for example. Depending on the nature of the supplementary discourses, students are able to track larger processes over a course or module, and to speculate about future work and the writing processes' connection to larger social and aesthetic forces and to theoretical concerns. Between undergraduate and masters' degree levels there is progression from the description of process to the consideration of a finished project in just these terms. Reflection becomes more autonomous at each level, rising to complete autonomy at Ph.D. level. Likewise poetics as a speculative discourse upon the philosophy of writing, or even as a manifesto, is found in its most developed forms at the higher levels, but given the cascade pattern of Creative Writing pedagogy I would expect this to 'filter down'.

Students' reflections clearly influence the awarding of the final grade. No tutor can *un*-read them, although some claim not to be influenced by them. Clearly if process (which might be visible partially through the drafting procedure) is assessed then the supplementary discourse will be important. It might make the process transparent to the assessing tutor as well as to the assessed student. It seems obvious to me that such a detailed account of creation also addresses issues of plagiarism, but this does not feature highly in tutors' recorded responses.

Tutors see the function of the discourse for students in a reciprocal way. They stress the importance of students explaining and evaluating retrospectively, but they also see a speculative function for the discourse, in that it might be part of the students' developmental progress, but there is some fear that the discourse is used by students to influence tutors by special pleading.

Students broadly agree with their tutors, although the vocabulary used to describe the discourse (and the vocabulary *in* the discourse) increases in sophistication with level. One surprising element is that only a minority realizes that the exercise is potentially rhetorical. For students who are trained to think about the audience of writing, they show little awareness that the discourse might influence the mark they receive by persuading a reader about the creative work, despite the tutors' fears about 'influence'.

MA students similarly show a lack of understanding about the rhetorical role of the discourse, and see it solely as student-centred, but then they have usually elected to join such courses primarily to improve their writing, rather than to gain an academic qualification. They are happier to explore issues of poetics, to examine questions of text and writerly technique and text in social and cultural contexts.

Ph.D. candidates mirror some of the perceptions of the writer-academics who run these fast developing and individual programmes nationally. They are more extrinsically motivated than other groups, aware that regulations should inform them of their responsibilities and the divisions between the 'creative' and 'critical' parts. Some see the discourse as a tracing of writing process (which creates problems in terms of presenting the work as 'original research'), but some see the relationship between the two in terms of a writerly poetics. Few see it as autonomously publishable or as absorbed into the creative work itself.

Leaving aside Reading as a Writer exercises, all writing tutors stress the relationship of the activity of reading to the practice of writing, but this is not to say that studying English Literature and practising writing share a reflective methodology. One questionable assumption about the nature of the supplementary discourse – even on programmes not formally linked to

English studies – is that its production consists of the exercise of the *same* critical skills employed by literary critics, the *same* skills taught by teachers of literature, and there is evidence that students themselves are confused about this. There is still perhaps a residual sense that the function of Creative Writing on English programmes is to teach literary appreciation by other means. Student writers are sometimes expected to read their own work as though they were reading it from the outside, or as if they were ordinary readers rather than its unique originator. It is arguably unhealthy (or impossible) for writers to achieve this. It is one thing to chart the creative process or the philosophy of composition – what I call poetics – but another to interpret one's own particular text for a reader. It is not clear what *use* this exercise is to a developing writer – it could even affect the creative process – whereas I see poetics as a thumbnail blueprint for further work. Discussions of craft and intention are not favoured in literary discussion, while they are common on writing programmes. As more students study Creative Writing within the context of English programmes, the effect on English Literature pedagogy should not be underestimated in that it will make 'text' a more malleable, processual concept.

A general question remains concerning the nature of this reflection and whether it is sufficiently distinct from the kinds of reflection students are asked to undertake elsewhere on their courses, which might include Personal Development Profiles (PDPs) for example (as well as even aspects such as course evaluation). While the developments of PDPs may assist the cause of reflection in general, in the context of Creative Writing they have the potential to confuse (although they could offer useful models to institutions, since Creative Writing is ahead of this particular game). If there are no other kinds of reflection available to the student, or if the institution or department is not committed to forms of student reflection, it is difficult to see how such habits of projective introspection as reflection or poetics may be inculcated successfully, without specific tuition. It is clear that reflective modes of writing, along with any other assessed practice, should be taught and that it might have specific needs as a form of reflection and speculation.

Innovations proposed around the country include attempts to develop aspects of recording writerly *process* as well as the final project. There have also been attempts to make the supplementary discourses more of a (literal) dialogue between tutor and student. The most far reaching suggestions propose an investigation of interdisciplinary modes of writing, beyond the traditional barriers between creative and critical writing, the hybridity often found in forms of poetics.

The standardization of the provision and assessment criteria for supplementary discourses is generally not approved of. There is, however, a trust in the robustness of both formal and informal exchanges within the subject community to develop such standards.

There are several developments that might be considered, firstly concerning whether process or product (or both) are the objects of self-reflective forms of supplementary discourse, and whether (or how) this differs by level. Forms of supplementary discourses that encourage 'dialogue' between tutors and students seem potentially the most useful advance possible, but also the most difficult to devise. Whether tutors consider adopting formal criteria and the separate awarding of a clearly defined mark to supplementary discourses or not, my research suggests that students should be made more aware of their function in assessment procedures, although this should not damage their developmental and speculative functions for them. Adventurous teams will be encouraged, I hope, to develop ways of combining critical and creative exercises in a hybrid discourse of its own – one of the manifestations of what I call poetics – or of the investigation of the relationship of Creative Writing with disciplines other than English Literature. Possibly this work will be carried on at Ph.D. level, at which the discourse – hybrid or supplementary – should be thought of as autonomously publishable. (This raises questions about the academic publishing prospects of such writings, an issue well beyond this piece.) In short, tutors across the discipline might benefit from sharing both the practice of developing supplementary discourses and of ways of teaching it as a specific discourse with demands of its own.

Notes

1. My account of poetics may be found in *The Necessity of Poetics* (Liverpool: Ship of Fools Liverpool, 2002) which also appears, in a slightly earlier version, on the *Pores* webzine, issue one: www.bbk.ac.uk/pores (accessed 28 February 2012). It will also appear as part of my full-length study of poetics in progress, provisionally entitled, *The Kinds of Poetry We Want.*
2. The full report, *Supplementary Discourses in Creative Writing Teaching in Higher Education*, which was written by myself with research assistance from Dr Scott Thurston, may be found in full on the English Subject Centre website, at: www.english.heacademy.ac.uk/find/search (accessed 28 February 2012).

15
The Lynchpin in the Workshop: Student Critique and Reflection

Stephanie Vanderslice

Studies of the writing protocols of successful student writers in the seventies and eighties revealed that fluent writers were metacognitively more aware of their own writing processes and their development as writers than their less-advanced counterparts.[1] Cognitive research, moreover, which studies writer's reflections on the writing process and how they engage with it, subsequently supports the relationship between the extent to which a writer considers her process and her fluency in developing as a writer.[2] In the Creative Writing classroom, instructors have seen this phenomena manifested again and again in their courses: the development of students as critics and reflective writers usually goes hand in hand with their development as creative writers.

Moreover, providing students with a shrewd critical sense with which to read their own work is probably one of the lasting benefits a Creative Writing program can confer on them, one they will continue to refine and develop long after they leave our classrooms. The more we encourage and provide opportunities for students to exercise their metacognitive faculties, then, the stronger writers they will become. This is especially true for undergraduates whose habits as writers are still being developed. This research will describe several course assignments designed to foster students'critical sensibilities, assignments that are often used not only to enhance student learning but also to assess it: reflective book reviews, executive summaries/ cover letters, critical introductions, written critiques of peer work and critical introductions to peers' work. Ultimately, it will not only argue for the critical dimension of the Creative Writing course, but also provide suggestions for achieving it.

Author studies

Recently, at a meeting of a community book club I belong to, I was asked what I thought of a popular novel. I allowed that while I had enjoyed it, I thought the end was rather trite and the plot conspired with itself a bit much. When my fellow club member exclaimed, 'Gosh, are there any books you actually *like*?' I realized that my personal reviews of books are often rather, how shall we say, *qualified*, because after many years of training as a writer, I read like one. This does not mean that I dislike a great number of books but that I am more apt to be more interested in the *marionette-wires* and how they function in a piece of writing than those who are just looking for a good read. In heightening students' powers of critique and enhancing their development as writers, we need to teach them to read the same way (and, if they are like me, to learn a bit more self-editing among the general public).

In this respect, one method often used to introduce students to the elements of critique is to remove the personal factor and first ask them to critique or review the work of a published author. This may be accomplished as a class – by workshopping a published piece before students begin to respond to one another's work, or by individual students studying particular authors or texts with the guidance of the workshop leader. In the latter case, students analyse published work not in the traditional literary sense but with an eye towards interrogating technique. For example, they may discuss such questions as, 'How does this poem's title function?' 'Is this novel character or plot-driven and what is its effect on the whole?' or 'How successful is the author's choice of point of view?' In addition, it can also be effective to encourage students to discuss how what they have learned critiquing a particular author or text will now inform their own work. Such assignments go a long way towards enhancing the subsequent depth and rigor of students' reflections on their own work and on that of their peers. Moreover, although they may enhance the critical sense of any developing writer, teaching students to read as writers may be particularly helpful to students in introductory courses who are often experiencing the workshop environment for the first time and need some guidance to get the most out of it.

The written critique

Students in my Creative Writing courses must submit a written critique for every piece we workshop over the semester – one copy for the student and one copy for me. I grade them, dropping the lowest two grades to allow for a learning curve. Because my mid-level Creative Writing courses can sometimes swell to over twenty students, this often means that students write over twenty critiques, not counting those which I require them to do of their own work (more on that later) or that of other published authors. In fact, in the thick of the semester, when students begin to realize the amount of work they have signed on for, some are likely to moan, 'What is this? A course in writing or in responding to writing?' By the semester's end, they understand my philosophy, however and have often seen it at work in their own burgeoning literary development: learning to reflect on and respond effectively to the written word is utterly intertwined with becoming a better writer.

Written critiques have practical purposes as well. They ensure that all student work gets proper attention (early in my career I learned that some students would freely admit that they had not actually read the piece in question, but go on to comment on it anyway!) and they prevent the band-wagon effect that can occur when a vocal minority anoints or condemns a work in question and the rest of the class hurries to fall in line. Moreover, in the same vein, they can also give quieter students a forum outside class discussion (some of my most talented writers and critics can barely be persuaded to utter a word in class) to present their views and may additionally give hesitant students more rehearsed remarks to use as crib notes. In this way, they naturally do wonders for raising the level of workshop discussion. But all practicalities aside, I learned that when I ask students to examine their peer's work closely and on paper, their own work improves dramatically.

Process narratives/cover letters/executive summaries . . . all manners of exegesis

The most significant piece of metacognitive reflection in the Creative Writing course, however, may be the process narrative, in which a student 'traces the generation, revision and development of a piece of writing over the time period when it was composed'.[3] There are any number of protocols that may be suggested to developing writers to encourage this kind of reflection – examining strengths, weaknesses, easy parts, 'hard' parts, techniques deployed from outside reading – but I always take care to ask my students also to outline what concerns them in their piece and how I might best address these concerns in my response. These questions give my own critiques a pointedness that can be of great assistance to them as writers – assuaging their fears (no, you handled the accident scene well, it was not too corny,) or confirming their first instincts (yes, that tribute to your mother does get a bit treacly in the third stanza).

Process narratives can take almost as many forms in a Creative Writing course as there are instructors to assign them. Some of the most common are those that accompany an individual work, but these can and often do also lead to expanded critical introductions to course portfolios, where they also lay the groundwork for teaching students to write the informed exegeses so commonly required of advanced students in graduate degree programs. These expanded exegeses can also do much to heighten metacognitive development by asking writers to look not only at their result in creating a particular piece, but also to 'evaluate a *changed* [emphasis mine] writing process or a draft sequence', by comparing their own work and charting their own development.[4] Finally, self-narratives and narratives about peers' work can be combined by asking students to reflect on the effectiveness of the critiques they received from me and from their peers and on those they wrote themselves. To this end, I ask students to include in their course portfolios a copy of the most helpful peer critique they received that semester, with an annotation describing why it was helpful, and a copy of the most helpful critique they believed they wrote that semester, with a similar annotation.

My belief in the power of reflective critique to enhance student's development as writers means that I weight this work heavily in my courses, indeed, often more heavily than the creative works themselves. I want students to understand that I take their development as 'writerly readers', in all senses of the word, quite seriously and it reflects in my grading system. Writing about their own work and that of their peers gives emerging authors practice in reading and analysing it, moving them one step closer to becoming their own best readers, to internalizing the critical practices of the 'workshop', so that they can ultimately transcend it.[5] It also invites them into a community of writers for whom examining one another's work with a close lens and talking as well as writing about it is common practice.

About ten years ago, Creative Writing theorist Hans Ostrom noted that the days when the Creative Writing workshop featured an 'economy of scarcity', where just one or two students might be singled out as stars, were numbered since such workshops were not particularly useful in sustaining writers in the long term. Instead, he called for an 'economy of abundance, in which every student is an explorer of language, literature, memory, the social construction of literary standards, authorship . . . meaning, and so forth, an economy in which student texts' are less "commodities" that need to be "priced" . . . and more a means of discovery.'[6] In response to this call, the metacognitive workshop can do much to teach students that the critical and creative process are actually two sides of the same coin and create the kind of economy that will not only accelerate our student's development as writers but also provide them with resources that will sustain them as they face the long, uncertain road that often greets them when they leave the ivory tower. At its heart, then, providing such critical training is at once the most the Creative Writing workshop *can* do and the very least it *must* do.

Notes

1. Janet Emig, *The Composing Process of Twelfth Graders* (Urbana, IL: National Council of Teachers of English, 1971); Linda Flower and John R. Hayes, 'A Cognitive-Process Theory of Writing,' *College Composition and Communication* 32 (1981): 365–87.
2. Ann Penrose and Barbara Sitko, Eds., *Hearing Ourselves Think: Cognitive Research in the College Writing Classroom* (New York: Oxford UP, 1993).

3. Wendy Bishop, *Released Into Language: Some Options for Teaching Creative Writing* (Portland, ME: Calendar Islands Publishers, 1998).
4. Stephanie Vanderslice, 'Rethinking Ways to Teach Young Writers: Response and Evaluation in the Creative Writing Course,' *Teacher Commentary on Student Papers*, Ed. Ode Ogede (Westport, CT: Bergin & Garvey, 2002), pp. 81–8.
5. Vanderslice, as above.
6. Hans Ostrom, 'Introduction: Of Radishes and Shadows, Theory and Pedagogy,' *Colors of a Different Horse: Rethinking Creative Writing Theory and Pedagogy*, Eds Wendy Bishop and Hans Ostrom (Urbana, IL: National Council of Teachers of English, 1994), pp. xi–xxiii.

16

From Wales to Vermont – A Round Trip – a Personal Reflection on Creative Writing in the USA and the UK

Tony Curtis

The principle of teaching the creative arts is central to our civilization. From Socrates and Plato, through Wordsworth and Coleridge, Owen and Sassoon, Pound and Eliot to Lowell and Plath, the intimate and constructive sharing of ideas and words, the incorporation of another writer's ideas and strategies, underpins many original texts. It is a lonely business being a writer: sometimes it has to be, but sometimes that sharing of texts in formative stages can be a shared burden.

In Tobias Woolf's novel, *Old School* the narrator explains that his private boys' school holds literature to be as central as the conventional American goals of team sports. Famous writers are guests of the school and for each visit a competition is held: the best piece of student writing wins for that person a personal meeting, a tutorial with Robert Frost or Ernest Hemingway.

I am not exaggerating the importance to us of these trophy meetings. We cared. And I cared as much as anyone, because I not only read writers, I read *about* writers. I knew that Maupassant, whose stories I loved, had been taken up when young by Flaubert and Turgenev: Faulkner by Sherwood Anderson, Hemingway by Fitzgerald and Pound and Gertrude Stein. All these writers were welcomed by other writers. It seemed to follow that you needed such a welcome, yet before this could happen you somehow, anyhow, had to *meet* the writer who was to welcome you. My idea of how this worked was not low or even practical. I never thought about making connections. My aspirations were mystical. I wanted the laying on of hands that had written living stories and poems, hands that had touched the hands of other writers. I wanted to be anointed.[1]

The American model is still that: one works to gain a place at an institution which holds a reputation through its faculty. They must be published writers with as many prizes and awards as possible. When you have completed your masters you carry their names and that association into your own career. As you will hear, I worked for my masters at Goddard in Vermont with Stephen Dobyns and Thomas Lux.

In 1979 I began two years of the MFA degree at Goddard College, Vermont. I was the only British writer and it took me a couple of residencies to grasp that the first few days of the week-long stay at that wooded campus close to Plainfield, Vermont had better include schmoosing the tutor you would most like to work with over the following semester. Goddard was a star-studded academy which had developed out of an idealistic open-access undergraduate college aiming to attract second-chance inner city students to the idyllic pine-tree slopes of one of America's smallest, most beautiful states. It had particular strengths in drama, a department in which David Mamet had both studied and taught, and photography, as well as in writing. On the faculty were Louise Gluck, Ellen Bryant Voigt, Robert Hass, Michael Ryan, Thomas Lux, Geoffrey Woolf (brother of Tobias) and Donald Hall. Guests in my time included Raymond Carver, Richard Ford and Galway Kinnell. My cohort of students included husband and wife, Mark and Ruth Doty, who published jointly under the name of 'M.R. Doty'. The principle in America has always been that the faculty attracts the students, because they are published and are award-winning. Goddard was very prestigious, very fashionable, and students travelled from all over North America, some covering more miles than I had from Wales. Entry was strictly by submission of a folio of work. I had published two books and had won an Eric Gregory Award in 1972 and the Welsh Arts Council's Young Poet's Prize in 1974.

A year after I graduated, because of administrative problems and as a consequence of its success, the Goddard College MFA ceased to operate in its original form and it split into two MFA courses, based now at the University of Vermont and in Warren Wilson College in North Carolina.

I returned to Wales and worked to introduce undergraduate writing options to our English students at the Polytechnic of Wales. After ten years these were very well established as free-standing modules and double modules in a diet of English offerings and the MA in Writing was offered in 1993, in what had become the University of Glamorgan. Some five years later this became the M.Phil. in Writing, a more prestigious research degree. Both degrees were predicated on my Goddard experience: two years distance-learning. Candidates have four weekend residencies in each academic year on campus, with a week-long stay in the first summer at the Ty Newydd centre in North Wales. There are eight writers in each cohort and eight tutors. From the beginning, I was keen to involve tutors, both part-time and full-time who were accomplished writers; these have included Helen Dunmore, Sian James, Gillian Clarke, Philip Gross, Catherine Merriman, Sheenagh Pugh, Chris Meredith, Matthew Francis and Stephen Knight.

The principle of distance-learning was crucial to our postgraduate development: I argued, and still would argue, that a weekly workshop based course anywhere outside London can exhaust too quickly the stream of good quality candidates. Also, students working at a genuine M.Phil., research level do not need to be seen weekly. The working practice of trans-Atlantic tutoring which I experienced in the late seventies by airmail has been enhanced greatly by the new technology. E-mail and affordable phoning and text-messaging mean that one's tutor is, literally, always to hand. Candidates can work with their individual tutor between residencies on the writing they agree to share with their cohort at that weekend in Glamorgan. Recent developments at Lancaster, directed by a former Glamorgan alumnus, would indicate that this is a model for future courses.

Since the 2002 Research Assessment Exercise (REF), the principle funding mechanism for funding in Britain, universities in the UK have been encouraged to develop Creative Writing as a discipline taught by practising and, essentially, publishing writers. If one's novel, travel book or collection of poetry is ranked alongside published books of literary criticism, then the creation of new posts will be assured for published, particularly prolific and award-winning, writers. In fact, the new discipline of Creative Writing has, during the 1990s, been just as rapidly expanded on the basis of undergraduate demand. Some universities in their hurried urge to be part of the new movement have created courses before appointing suitable staff: some academics with Literature backgrounds have found themselves leading and teaching such courses with no creative background or skills of their own, and this is a concern.

Of course, the expansion of Creative Writing at UK universities has meant that many writers of real achievement have been able to supplement their very meagre earnings as poets or literary fiction writers with a .5 or .3 post in a local university. This has been of considerable mutual benefit. The students work with a 'real writer', the university secures a proportion of that writer's published work for their REF submission, and the writer keeps free paper in his or her printer and the wolf from the door.

Writing in a 1952 radio broadcast on Edgar Lee Masters, Dylan Thomas reflected on his American campus experiences:

> In poetry workshops, by the way, would-be poets are supposed to study the craft under some distinguished practitioner. Perhaps the original idea was to provide for apprentice poets what a master's studio once did for apprentice painters. But the master painter used to paint all the time, and his apprentices assisted him and were busy under his direction. A master-poet, if he exists, is supposed, in these literary warrens, to spend nearly all his time dealing with, and encouraging, the imitations, safe experiments, doodlings and batchings of his students, and to do his own stuff on the side. What a pity he does not have the apprentice poets to help him with the duller bits of his own work. There is a future in this, however ghastly.[2]

In this Dylan was as witty as one would expect and more prescient than one might expect. Whilst the model of the painter and his studio may be used to justify the longer tradition of the creative studio or workshop, the principle of subservient collaborative work on a masterpiece will not inform the work of the novelist or poet, I think.

Creative Writing in the USA still has the University of Iowa performing the same iconic function as UEA in the UK.[3] Iowa's masters course was the criterion by which most others were judged for many years. Like most courses, Iowa's program had its roots in the vision and energy of one person: like Edwin Piper, who was teaching undergraduate and graduate classes, and began to teach verse-making classes, in the manner of George Cook's 'verse-making' classes in the late nineteenth century at that institution. Often Creative Writing classes met off-campus in private houses. This is echoed by the UEA pub tutorials with Bradbury and McEwan. The program itself came into existence, in part, as a reaction to the perceived stuffiness of the Ivy League schools. Schools like Princeton, Yale and Harvard would not accept the role of Creative Writing, perhaps lacked the freedom to experiment of a state school in the mid-West, a school which had no international reputation to risk. It was as early as 1922 that Iowa allowed creative work to count for credit towards a graduate degree, though classes in 'verse making' had occurred as early as 1897. In the wake of the Second World War, under Paul Engel (director for a quarter of a century), and again following the Korean War, mature men returned to the States and to higher education sponsored by the GI Bill. That income allowed Iowa to stage a series of notable guest writers, notably Robert Frost and Robert Penn Warren; later, Robert Lowell and John Berryman taught full courses at what had become known as 'the Workshop'.

Since the 1960s Iowa's courses have grown in size and reputation so that now only 3 per cent of applicants for its writing program of approximately one hundred places can gain entry. In addition, there are over three hundred other Creative Writing programs in the USA. Of course, the question of where such a Writing degree can lead is a vexed one: the weight of applications for Creative Writing positions in the States is very great. Obviously, most graduates of even the postgraduate schools have little chance of themselves entering a university as a Creative Writing teacher. In fact, they have probably no more chance of securing such a job than of actually getting themselves a publisher.

Clearly, there are some positive aspects to the American system, including a number of models, I would argue, for development in UK universities. Take, for example, Indiana University in Bloomington, Indiana.[4] They have a pedigree which stretches back to the 1940s, with Frost, Penn Warren and John Crowe Ransom as faculty members. They now run a three-year MFA, taking just twelve students each year. The fees are, typically, high by UK standards, though this will, I suspect, not be the case for much longer, as we move almost completely over to an American open access, fee-paying system. Also, typically, MFA postgrads may expect to offset a considerable percentage of their fees by teaching undergraduate classes at the lower first and second year, freshman and sophomore, levels.

In this respect our system in the UK has not developed; if we are to introduce commercial levels of fees, then we need also to adopt the American model of facilitating employment for a wide range of students, both on campus and in the wider community. American universities, even the less fashionable state colleges, have bursary and prize offerings for students of achievement and particular promise. We may see the beginnings of such awards presently being used by the Russell Group (British Ivy League) of universities and others to attract the cream of the crop – the straight-As applicants. With Cambridge reportedly turning down as many as five thousand such applicants in a year, there will be many such 'high fliers' to bid for by the other older institutions. With devaluation of the A grade, it may well be that UK departments of Creative Writing, even at undergraduate level, should move to make offers on a combination of academic results and a portfolio of original writing.

The Master of Fine Arts degree has traditionally validated writers as being suitable to teach at the university in the USA; it has always been the career-track, terminal degree in this discipline, rather than the Ph.D. However, even Iowa has felt the pressure to offer the doctorate as a default. In Britain the MA has become a taught top-up to the BA, leaving the Ph.D. as the only route to a career in higher education. We have never had the MFA as a possibility; I regret that, for the Ph.D. does not seem like the most appropriate signifier of literary excellence; it connotes a long, academically-referenced thesis with an entirely distinct approach, register and voice.

Many of the serious postgraduate Creative Writing courses have regular visits by agents. Agents are increasingly drawn to postgraduate writing courses in the UK and several have special or more formal relationships with those courses. For example, at UEA the agents Curtis Brown offer an annual prize. The courses with proven success are, in essence, performing much of the role previously the sole preserve of agents. A candidate's book manuscript will have been developed, edited, into a polished piece; while no course could possibly claim a direct route to a publisher or publishing success, it is clear that the tutoring, mentoring and workshop analyses of manuscripts in progress can prove invaluable to the writer. Agents have quickly come to realize that, as have publishers. Though it is also true that the author's blurb may neglect to mention the alma mater of their new author; the postgraduate writers course may be the one that dare not speak its name; it remains a valued myth that new authors are 'discovered' and 'launched' only by publishers.

As in the USA, the discipline is now evolving and promoting its strength and influence from within its own systems in Britain. It has always been difficult for writers to make a reasonable living, particularly in the UK and particularly if one is a serious, literary writer, but that has changed substantially over the last ten years. Published poets and novelists with one or two books behind them, may now see university teaching, part-time probably, as crucial not only to the way in which they survive as writers, but also how they develop as writers. Postgraduate students and university colleagues can provide an informed and supportive context to the solitary business of being a writer.

I would argue that in the UK we have reached parity with the scope of Creative Writing teaching in the USA. Many people are now within commuting distance of a course – there are almost a hundred now. Distance-learning courses are growing, including those that are predominantly on-line, e.g. Manchester Metropolitan University. With the advent of video tutorials in the palm of one's hand, web publishing, blogging and electronic workshops the future is complex, energized and assured.

In this proliferation of Creative Writing postgraduate courses there is the risk of a considerable variation in the standards of teaching and assessment. Education in the new millennium Britain is likely to be as market-driven as other sectors. The best-taught and organized courses will establish reputations and a pecking order will emerge. Poorly researched journalists' articles still invariably focus on UEA and little else; they often ignore the fact that there is a wider choice now of equal worth and more flexibility.

Writers of the highest calibre are now associated with courses, either as part-time lecturers, visiting professors and fellows or as regular guests. One of our Glamorgan alumni, Tamar Yoseloff Lindsay, has been appointed as the first writer in residence at Magdalene College, Cambridge. The Magdalene position is designed to encourage undergraduate writing as well as liaising with community groups. Oxford is now offering a MSt. in Creative Writing through their Continuing Education Department, a course set up by another Glamorgan alumnus Jennifer Lewis. When Oxbridge colleges are joining the Creative Writing movement, when an MA in Creative Non-Fiction is offered at Imperial College, London, it is clear that the discipline has become rooted and is thriving throughout the sector. Other Glamorgan alumni teach at the Universities of Kent, Coventry, Lancaster and Sussex; those from Lancaster at Chichester and Sheffield Hallam; those from UEA at Kent, Warwick and elsewhere, while Tricia Wastvedt, Orange long-listed novelist and alumnus from Bath Spa, now teaches at that university, as do MA graduates Mimi Thebo and Lucy English. Clearly, there is a web of associations and influences; despite the concerns of some that a sort of literary cloning will result, the Creative Writing expansion is inevitable and, on the whole, a force for the good of literature in the UK. It seems unlikely that there will be any system for controlling the quality of experience for students on writing courses in British universities. Centres of excellence have emerged and will continue to be established, by virtue of the quality and reputations of their teachers and the success of their graduates. Though a necessarily small percentage of graduates will publish and become established writers, many others will go on to work in the creative arts in the wider community; and all will become stronger, more committed readers.

Notes

1. Tobias Woolf, *The Old School* (London: Bloomsbury, 2004), p. 7.
2. Dylan Thomas, *Dylan Thomas: The Broadcasts*, Ralph Maud, Ed. (London: Dent & Sons), p. 255.
3. University of Iowa, www.uiowa.edu/~iww (accessed 28 February 2012).
4. University of Indiana, www.indiana.edu/~mfawrite (accessed 28 February 2012).

Part VI
Critical Theory

Traditionally, Creative Writing and forms of critical theory have been at odds with each other. However, increasingly they are seen as complementary activities and are often taught side by side.

Katharine Haake explores how critical theory can help students in two ways 1) by empowering them to talk about and understand writing itself and 2) by locating creative texts in wider cultural and historical contexts. Arguing against thinking that opposes critical and creative, Haake concludes that Creative Writing may be ideally situated to integrate stands of English Studies insofar as it is 'a nexus of both reading and writing'.

Rob Pope also argues against separating critical from Creative Writing. He uses the term, 'Criticial-Creative Rewriting' to explore a hybrid pedagogy in which students use critical skills to analyse an existing creative text as well as critical skills to change that text, making it 'their own' and also writing a reflective commentary on the process. He describes two courses as examples and concludes that this hybrid pedagogy results in ways of bridging gaps that persist between Creative Writing and English Studies.

Kim Lasky explores tensions between critics and Creative Writing using her Ph.D. thesis as a case study. This includes not just the creative work but also a poetics. She then discusses the challenge of negotiating between positions of critic and writer and argues that assessment needs to allow for innovation.

17

Thinking Systematically About What We Do

Katharine Haake

Thirty years have passed since I entered my master's program in Creative Writing mindful of my father's observation that perhaps we were training a few too many writers in this country. By the time I matriculated in my doctoral program five years later, I had mastered what I had learned as an MA student but had yet to understand how poorly who I was as a writer – and writing itself – was served by how I had been trained. Although writing was my life and had been so for half a decade, it still made me feel a bit like a child performing for the friends of her parents. As a doctoral, I discovered theory, especially feminist theory, and though I found it difficult and strange, it gave me a way of understanding how thoroughly I had given my writing over to an inchoate idea of what I thought it was supposed to be. Theory did two things for me that it can still do for our students:

1. it provided a way to talk about and understand both writing itself – how it happened, what it was – and the texts it produced;
2. it helped locate this work in its cultural and historical context, especially with regard to the various institutions that governed and controlled it.

I was like a child discovering autonomy, independence, self. I was already thirty years old.

Although I did not know it then, the few rudimentary questions I had managed to pick up – what is language, what is narrative, what is writing – enabled me, however crudely, to embark on what a quarter of a century later I would call with Wendy Bishop 'thinking systematically' about writing.[1] Thinking systematically was a kind of code for theory because Creative Writing students even now approach its work with ambivalence and dread. And who can really blame them? Students, in general, come to writing with an urge, like an itch, to 'express themselves', and the challenge, from the very beginning, is to begin to convince them to transfer allegiance from what Richard Hugo calls their 'triggering subjects' to the disciplined practice

131

of language that is what writing is, along with what Toni Morrison calls, 'an effort of the will to discover'.[2]

Any teacher/writer worth her salt already knows this – that writing, when it is really writing, takes us beyond what we already know and is itself a process of discovering both what we are going to say and how we are going to say it. We know this, because writing, when it is really writing – what Barthes calls an 'intransitive act', or Calvino, 'combinatorial play' – is *both* the discipline that we can teach as daily praxis and craft, *and* the disappearance of the self into language acting that is writing and discovery together.[3] And the challenge for the teacher is always to acknowledge the two sides of what we do as the single seamless operation my old friend and teacher, Francois Camoin, used to call writing without thinking.[4] That was a trick, of course, a sly pedagogical sleight of hand, because Francois knew his Barthes but he also knew his students and their potential alienation between theory and writing, and when push came to shove, he would come down on the side of writing every time.

Creative writers inside the academy – students and teachers alike – have been choosing sides now for a least a quarter century. From the beginning, our affiliation with the romantic figure of the mostly male genius writer would organize our first text-centered workshops around the master mentor who dispensed gems of writerly wisdom and a few crackpot theories of his own. Students came together in these workshops to share writing and opinions on what 'worked' and what did not without much critical awareness beyond individual taste and more or less in agreement that their collective aim was to produce literary writing of publishable quality, as if that were a fixed thing, with its own inherent value. As the years went on and Creative Writing programs proliferated across America, this workshop-centered pedagogy remained standard, though by the late 1980s a nattering of discontent had begun to emerge, concurrent with our growing awareness that undergraduate students had very different reasons for coming to the writing class than their graduate counterparts and very different needs, once there.

Hence, the nattering, driven in part by a well-intentioned critique of the general parsimoniousness with which the discipline defines what counts as creativity and writing and who gets to do it. But if we were not training writers in our Creative Writing classes, what exactly were we doing?

Like many others, I used to think it had to be an either/or. My own early experiences in the workshop had not been without their successes, but yet the single most important lesson of my writing life came from *Moby Dick*, from which I had determined that I was neither smart enough nor talented enough to be a writer. Sixteen at the time, I quit writing altogether, until some five years later I discovered I could study it in school. After all that silence, I was keen – almost desperate – for the business of craft, which is what they taught then and which gave me the illusion of both order and control. An able, obedient student, I performed to please and learned quickly what to do and how to do it – curve a graceful narrative arc, turn a tidy sentence, suppress a subtle subtext. In retrospect, it seems a good deal to have learned, but it would not be enough and would leave me, over and over, as Jonathan Culler described it, 'gaping before the monumental inscriptions' that were not less paralysing because they were mine.[5]

It seems simple-minded enough to suggest that theory can provide the lens or language that will help us close our mouths. But from Saussure's systems of language, to Barthes' idea of writeability and the lure of the text that does not yet exist, to Derrida's logic of supplementarity by which language and writing unfold, to Lacan's idea of the suture which (like all contradictorily coherent concepts) holds together by the force of a desire that is also writing, to Foucault's principles of limitation and exclusion that reveal the constraints by which writing moves through the world, to feminist principles that describe how women (or any other muted groups) come to know themselves, already alienated, inside a language that works to suppress them, that is precisely what theory does when it works best in the Creative Writing classroom.[6] And we should never be afraid to say so. The most productive questions for our purposes are large questions that enable us to shift – students and teachers together – even just a little, in relation to what it is we think we are doing when we are writing. As Rachel Blau DuPlessis said, also long ago, 'a poetics gives us permission to continue'.[7] Theory enables us to construct one.

David Richter's *Falling Into Theory* begins by opposing two fundamental frameworks for pedagogies in English studies: 1) Henlen Vendler's that 'what we have loved, others will love', and 2) Gerald Graff's that 'our ability to [write] well depends more than we think on our ability to *talk well* about what we [write]'.[8] Because I knew the paradoxical power by which what I loved (*Moby Dick*) had worked to silence me, and because theory had trained me to see and say so, I took a hard line with my students, using not just narratology to train them to 'talk well' about what they were writing, but also early post-structuralism to foreground questions of language and desire and how writing holds them together and moves through the world. These days, though, between love and intellect, I can not help but wonder why the Creative Writing cannot contain both.

For twenty years I have used theory to bring students to the point of letting go that is writing, which is always a little bit like grace, something that cannot occur without tremendous discipline and work, but also something that cannot be willed. When students discover writing, as distinguished from writing a text – a poem, or a story, or a bit of nonfiction, or a play – a *thing* – everything changes for them, opening out in new and amazing ways. Theory can bring us to this opening out. But the binary logic by which the discipline at large has argued the either/or of theory and writing leaves us in a state of opposition that forces us to choose and turns us, more often than not, into one or the other – writers or theorists. And isn't that an odd thing, when it is always the point where the two come together to inform and confound one another that is the most generative and transforming?

The hyper-specialization that has occurred throughout English studies over the past quarter century has left many creative writers the last generalists in their departments. Today, creative writing students comprise an increasingly larger percentage of overall English numbers – 30 per cent at my own large public institution, 50 per cent at our neighbor, USC. Perhaps what these students are intuiting is that it sometimes seems as if Creative Writing is the last remaining strand of English studies still fully grounded in all the old pleasures of literature – story, language, form, beauty. As such, perhaps we have come around full circle since Creative Writing made its first appearance in the early twentieth century Harvard curriculum as an educational experiment to revitalize literary study from the inside. If theory has a purpose for the writer, it has to help us understand and so frame what really happens when we sit down at our writing desks to work.

In 1949, F.O. Matthiessen, reflecting on the great gulf that continued to separate American literature from that of Europe, posed the question: 'How do Americans become part of that greater world? Not', he answers himself, 'by pretending to be something they are not, nor by being either proud or ashamed of their vast special fortune.'[9] Shifting the paradigm to ask how creative writers become part of English studies will help illuminate some of the internal contradictions that continue to vex us. The gap between 'poet' and 'professor', as Marjorie Perloff argued in 1987, is 'phony' to begin with, but resolving it requires, even now, that we remember who we really are.[10] Between the entrenched anti-intellectualism that infects a large number of us and the self-abnegation endemic in the rush to scholarship (and respectability) that has left a good number of the rest of us sounding weirdly more like theorists than writers, there has to be a fruitful middle ground – a suture. It is not such a stretch, after all, to construe Creative Writing as ideally situated to integrate all the strands of English studies as a nexus of both reading and writing – of literature and its vital practice.

In this, we are all a little bit of bricoleur – and maybe just in time. Because the world, too, has changed around us, and in this strange new time we may find ourselves in terrible need of the old imperatives and pleasures of reading and writing all over again. Bahktin once called the novel 'the only ever-developing genre . . . that takes place in a zone of contact with the present in all its open-endedness'.[11] Theory helps us imagine the ever-developing nature of our project even as it provides a logic within which we may proceed beyond the letting go of thinking meaning or will to discover that is, at least in part, what writing is. But it also enables us to locate that writing in the moment of history that happens to be ours. For this, we are indebted to the largest questions it raises and frames.

Notes

1. Wendy Bishop, Ed., *Elements of Alternate Style: Essays on Writing and Revision* (Portsmouth, NH: Boynton/Cook, 1997).
2. Richard Hugo, *The Triggering Town: Lectures and Essays on Poetry and Writing* (New York: Norton, 1979). Toni Morrison, 'Unspeakable Things Unspoken: The Afro-American Presence in American Literature,' *American Literature, American Culture*. Ed. Gordon Hunter (New York: Oxford UP, 1999), pp. 538–58.
3. Roland Barthes, 'The Death of the Author,' *Modern Criticism and Theory: A Reader*, Ed. David Lodge (New York: Longman, 1988), pp. 167–72. Italo Calvino, 'Cybernetics and Ghosts,' *The Uses of Literature: Essays*, Trans. Patrick Creagh (San Diego: Harcourt, 1986).
4. Francois Camoin, 'The Workshop and Its Discontents,' *Colors of a Different Horse: Rethinking Creative Writing Theory and Pedagogy*, Eds. Wendy Bishop and Hans Ostrom (Urbana, IL: NCTE, 1994), pp. 3–7.
5. Jonathan Culler, *Structuralist Poetics: Structuralism, Linguistics, and the Study of Literature* (Ithaca, NY: Cornell UP, 1975), p. 134.
6. Ferdinand de Saussure, *Course in General Linguistics*, Eds. Charles Bally and Albert Sechehaye, Trans., Wade Baskin (New York: McGraw, 1966). Roland Barthes, as above. Jacques Derrida, 'Structure, Sign and Play in the Discourse of the Human Sciences,' *Modern Criticism and Theory: A Reader*, Ed. David Lodge (New York: Longman, 1988), pp. 107–23. Jacques Lacan, *The Four Fundamental Concepts of Psycho-Analysis*, Ed. Jacques-Alain Miller, Trans. Alan Sheridan (New York: Norton, 1978).
7. Rachel Blau DuPlessis, *The Pink Guitar: Writing as Feminist Practice* (New York: Routledge, 1990).
8. David Richter, Ed., *Falling into Theory: Conflicting Views on Reading and Literature* (Boston: Bedford Books of St. Martin's Press, 1994), p. 27, p. 40.
9. F.O. Matthiessen, 'The Responsibilities of the Critic,' *American Literature, American Culture*, Ed. Gordon Hunter (New York: Oxford UP, 1999), pp. 303–12.
10. Marjorie Perloff, 'Theory and/in the Creative Writing Classroom,' *AWP Newsletter* (November/December, 1987): 1–4.
11. M.M. Bakhtin, 'Epic and Novel,' *Essentials of the Theory of Fiction*, Eds. Michael J. Hoffman and Patrick Murphy (Durham: Duke UP, 1988), pp. 48–69.

18

Re . . . creation, Critique, Catalysis: Critical-creative Rewriting in Theory and Practice

Rob Pope

> The highest Criticism, then, is more Creative . . . . and the primary aim of the critic is to see the object as in itself it really is not.
>
> (Oscar Wilde, *The Critic as Artist*, 1891)

Writing about existing literary texts and writing creatively are often discussed as though they are separate and even ambivalent activities, one being academic or critical writing and the other being creative writing. However, this chapter explores the following research question: are there ways we can engage with texts that are both critical and creative? I refer to such approaches as critical-creative rewriting, the principles of which can be summarized as follows: change the text and weigh the implications! What distinguishes this from more 'self-centred' approaches to Creative Writing is that you begin with someone else's text and turn it into another that is in some sense 'your own'. What distinguishes this from more self-consciously 'academic' approaches is that you produce a 'primary rewriting' not just a 'secondary reading'. Students also include a critical commentary with their rewrite. This makes the grounds of comparison and contrast explicit, and includes a review of the research that went into the process of composition and revision. Still, overall, it comes down to changing the text and weighing the implications.

Fresh methods and models

The general methods and models that inform critical-creative writing are elaborated elsewhere.[1] Here I offer a reformulation as three interlinked 'triangles'. This plots key terms which I then discuss using two courses as examples. Each triangle should be considered separately at first, as each represents a specific cluster of concepts and a particular dynamic. Attention may then shift to the emboldened terms at the apexes of all three triangles. These form a larger triangle that can be read as an overarching statement (see Figure 18.1).

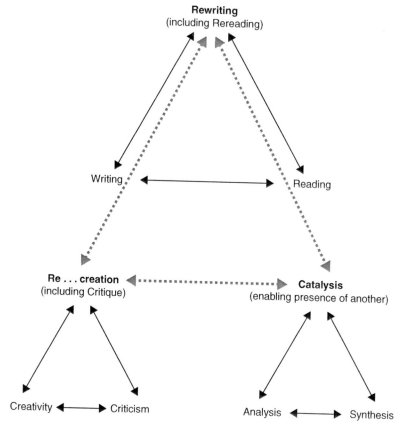

Figure 18.1 Rewriting, Re . . . creation, Catalysis

Rewriting / Re-reading (Triangle 1) is the crucial link between Reading and Writing. It confirms that these processes are complementary and continuous, not opposite and mutually exclusive: as with the 'chicken and egg' problem, there is little point in asking which comes first.

Re . . . creation (Triangle 2) designates how we create something from the original text, in medias res, and how we have the latest but never the first or last word. The suspension dots designate the gap between old and new; the text as found and as re-made, has to be renegotiated differently each and every time.[2] Critique is implicit throughout, in the way we meet the text in and on its own terms and then change and challenge them. This process may then be made explicit via critical commentary. Re . . . creation as Critique is, I would argue, a much richer and more empowering project than either Creativity or Criticism understood as notionally distinct activities.

Catalysis (Triangle 3) is proposed as the missing link that helps bind the processes of 'taking apart' (Analysis) and 'putting together' (Synthesis). Catalysis refers to all aspects of making and finding that depend upon the enabling and empowering presence of another. (The analogy is with chemical processes that require the presence of a 'catalyst' to get going or be sustained.) This catalysing 'other' may be distinguished as catalysts (things – a text or other object, a context or situation) and catalysers (persons – another writer or reader (dead or alive), a teacher or colleague, a parent, lover, friend, or enemy – including the idea or image of one of these). Often there's a mixture, not necessarily acting in concert, but all essential to the process.

There is insufficient space here to explain all interconnections of that 'larger triangle'. However, beginning with Triangle 1 Rewriting and Rereading, this entails:

- Radical overhaul of notions of 'Creativity' and 'Criticism' as nominally separate processes, and something like Re . . . creation as Critique as a more dynamic alternative (Triangle 2);
- Catalysis (Triangle 3) goes beyond the initially handy but quickly untenable oppositions between 'Analytical' ('critical', 'deconstructive'?) and 'Synthesizing' ('creative', 'reconstructive'?) activities; catalysis also recognises crucial roles played by all sorts of mediating and essentially transformative elements.

But I would not want to overplay the sense of 'wholeness' projected by these interlocked 'triangles'. My interest is more in the gaps they articulate (the '. . .' for example). Likewise, this model of rewriting also invites its own rewriting. 'Catalysis', for instance, may prompt someone else to devise a more elegant alternative. For then it will have done what it sets out to describe!

Courses using critical-creative rewriting

We now take a whistle-stop tour of two courses informed by critical-creative re-writing. First experiments were with Anglo-Saxon verse, with what a colleague (Alcuin Blamires) and I called 'critical-creative translation'. Students rendered thirty lines of Anglo-Saxon verse into whatever kind of translation they felt fit. They also supplied: (1) a preface indicating their overall rationale and intended readership; (2) an annotated text drawing attention to the main features of their version by comparison with the Old English; and (3) a commentary reviewing research, other translations consulted, and problems and possibilities encountered.

Take the first line of the poem known as 'The Seafarer', for example: 'Maeg ic be me sylfum soðgied wrecan'. One student translated this as 'I can fashion a true song of my self' while another made it 'All on my lonesome

I tell it as it is.' The former explained how the translation was slightly formal and archaic, but argued this was appropriate given the aim of a 'close' translation that also caught some of the alliterative savour (on 's') of the base text. The latter was the opening of a blues version and came with an audiotape and guitar accompaniment. While it made no bones about its status as a 'free translation', it also made a convincing case relating modern blues laments to Anglo-Saxon elegies. The former, out of strict deference to the original, was presented as 'Untitled, Anonymous'. The latter was called 'Oh me oh my – At sea again!' and designated, wittily and with a fine sense of fidelity to the blues, 'Words attrib. King; tune traditional'. Both students remade the poem and made their cases at much greater length. But this example gives the texture and tenor of this kind of work.

My second example is a course called 'Language through Literature', taught with a colleague from Applied Linguistics and English Language Teaching (Jane Spiro). It aims to get students to learn to play with English across all the main linguistic levels: from sound-structures and visual layout, through word-building and word-choice to phrase and sentence-structures and textual cohesion, and so on to genre and discourse. Students undertake linguistic analyses of literary texts and then use these as prompts to generate their own. For instance, we use poems by Hopkins for sound structure and word-building and by Cummings for layout and phrase structure.

The course consists of two parts, the first 'analytical' and the second 'synthetic'. (The 'catalysts' are the texts and the 'catalysers' are the teachers and other students.) In the first half we go through linguistic levels concentrating upon each in turn; this is basically an 'eight-step' approach to language, one that Jane has refined over the years.[3] In the second half we bring together all eight levels and encourage students to work over the full range. This we call 'dancing across the steps'. At this point, students take two texts already featured and generate another of their own that is somehow related to or prompted by both. That is, they produce a hybrid text of their own and, in the process, then play with all the verbal resources at their disposal. Students trial prototypes and get feedback on them in class; and when they submit finished versions, these include full linguistic analysis and critical comparison with the two base texts. Examples of texts generated in this way include: (i) versions of student life and visions of modern Oxford (where the course is taught) responding to both Hopkins's sonnet 'Duns Scotus's Oxford' and John Agard's part-Creole 'rant' against 'Mr Oxford Don'; and (ii) a two-handed 'insult game' done with another student using the style and structures of e.e. cummings on the one hand and Dylan Thomas on the other.

Our pedagogic practice is hybrid, too, using exercises and textual activities drawn from English Language Teaching and Applied Linguistics, Stylistics, Critical-creative Rewriting and Creative Writing. The differences between these last two are worth weighing. Firstly, whereas creative writing is often presented as a search for self-expression and the eventual finding of one's own voice, critical-creative rewriting is more a seriously playful exploration of self-through-others and the ceaseless remaking of a variety of voices. Secondly, critical-creative rewriting places as much emphasis upon evidence of reading, research and reflection as upon the production of a 'creative' text. Thirdly, emphasis upon writing as rewriting issues a direct challenge to many inadequate images of creative writers, especially those caught up the notion of 'creation from nothing'. Conversely, it reminds us that all creative writers draw on existing resources in making their own contributions. In the present terms, they offer kinds of re . . . creation, critique and catalysis.

Rewriting theory, rethinking subjects

Finally, critical-creative rewriting connects with some powerful theorizing and is a nifty vehicle for shuttling between 'critical theory' on the one side and 'creative practice' on the other. Students doing critical-creative rewriting often get so energized that they readily engage with most important issues in critical and cultural theory. To be sure, they remain properly sceptical of all the '-isms' and 'posts' of contemporary theory. But they do see the point of, and surprisingly often really get into, theorizing – with the emphasis on an ongoing reflection.

A beginning list of familiar theorists and topics that warrant revisiting in the light of critical-creative rewriting includes: (i) Bakhtin for observations that we always engage 'dialogically' with 'another's words in our own language' and that the challenge is to do so 'responsively' as well as 'responsibly'; (ii) Blanchot's, Ricoeur's and many others' conceptions of culture as a 'continuing conversation' and 'infinite exchange'; (iii) Barthes's celebration of 'text' as 'a tissue of quotations drawn from the innumerable centres of culture' and his still open invitation to celebrate 'the birth of the reader' at the expense of [an individualistic conception of] 'the author' (the report of whose 'death' has been widely misrepresented as well as much exaggerated); (iv) Genette's notion of intertextuality as a 'palimpsest' of the many and various writings and readings that have gone into and come out of texts; in terms of (American) Reader-Response Criticism and (German) Reception Aesthetics, these entail, respectively, various 'anxieties of influence' and 'horizons of expectation;'(v) Derrida's arguments for 'writing under erasure', 'counter-signing' and a whole host of other 'marginal' techniques of glossing and critique; and so on.

There are probably many more names and topics to add to or substitute for this list. However, what should be clear from this research outcome is how critical-creative re-writing bridges what commonly pass as distinct and potentially exclusive processes: criticism/creativity, theory/practice, analysis/synthesis and reading/writing. Critical-creative rewriting thus offers a way of 'getting over' the gaps that persist between 'Creative Writing' and

'English Literature'.[4] Such categories and labels may be where we nominally start from, but they are assuredly not where we are going. Indeed, whatever the signs on doors and departmental letterheads, many of us are already making quite different imaginative and textual spaces altogether.

Notes

1. Rob Pope, *Textual Intervention: Critical and Creative Strategies for Literary Studies* (London and New York: Routledge, 1995); Rob Pope, *The English Studies Book*, 2nd edn. (London and New York: Routledge, 2002); Rob Pope, 'Rewriting Texts, Reconstructing the Subject: Work as Play on the Critical-Creative Interface,' *Teaching Literature: A Companion*, Eds Tanya Agathocleous and Ann Dean (New York and London: Palgrave Macmillan, 2003), pp. 105–24; Rob Pope, *Creativity: Theory, History, Practice* (London and New York: Routledge, 2005); Rob Pope, 'Critical-creative Rewriting,' *Teaching Creative Writing*, Ed. Graeme Harper (London: Continuum, 2006).
2. This concept is fully explained in Rob Pope, 2005, as above, pp. 84–9.
3. Jane Spiro, *Creative Poetry Writing* (Oxford: Oxford University Press, 2004).
4. A beginning bibliography for critical-creative rewriting includes the following texts. The emphasis here is upon practical work informed by developments in Poetics, Rhetoric, Composition, and the Teaching and Learning of English as a Foreign or Second Language; also upon the changing shape and nature of university English Studies.

Bibliography

Avery, S., Bryan, C. and Wisker, G., Eds., *Innovations in Teaching English and Textual Studies* (London: Staff and Educational Development Association, 1999).
Bartholomae, David and Petrosky, Anthony, Eds., *Ways of Reading: An Anthology for Writers*, 5th edn. (New York: St. Martin's Press, 1999).
Bassnett, Susan and Grundy, Peter, *Language Through Literature: Creative Language Teaching Through Literature* (London: Longman, 1993).
Bennett, Andrew and Royle, Nicholas, 'Creative Writing,' *An Introduction to Literature, Criticism and Theory*, 3rd edn. (New York: Longman, 2004), pp. 85–92.
Burton, Deirdre, 'Through a glass darkly – through dark glasses,' *Language and Literature: An Introductory Reader in Stylistics*, Ed. Ron Carter (London: Allen & Unwin, 1982), pp. 195–216.
Carter, Ronald, *Language and Creativity: The Art of Common Talk* (London and New York: Routledge, 2004).
Carter, Ronald and McRae, John, Eds., *Language, Literature and the Learner: Creative Classroom Practice* (London: Longman, 1996).
Cook, Jon, 'Creative Writing as a Research Method,' *Research Methods for English Studies*, Ed. Gabriele Griffin (Edinburgh: Edinburgh University Press, 2005), pp. 195–212.
Corcoran, Bill, Hayhoe, Mike, and Pradl, Gordon, Eds., *Knowledge in the Making: Challenging the Text in the Classroom* (Portsmouth, NH: Boynton/Cook, Heinemann, 1994).

Downing, David, Hurlbert, C., Mathieu, P., Eds., *Beyond English Inc.* (Portsmouth NH: Heinemann Boynton Cook, 2002).

Doyle, Brian, *English and Englishness* (London: Methuen, 1989).

Evans, Colin, Ed., *Developing University English Teaching* (Lampeter: Edwin Mellen Press, 1995).

Fricker, Harald and Zymner, Rüdiger, *Einübung in die Literaturwissenschaft: Parodieren geht über Studieren* (Zürich: Schöningh, 1993).

Goodman, Sharon and O'Halloran, Kieran, Eds., *The Art of English: Literary Creativity* (Buckingham: The Open University Press, 2006).

Knights, Ben, *From Reader to Reader* (Brighton: Harvester Wheatsheaf, 1993).

Knights, Ben and Thurgar-Dawson, *Active Reading: Transformative Writing in Literary Cultures* (London: Continuum, 2006).

Maybin, Janet and Swann, Joan, Eds., *The Art of English: Everyday Creativity* (Buckingham: The Open University, 2006).

McRae, John, *Wordsplay* (Basingstoke: Macmillan – now Palgrave Macmillan, 1992).

Milne, Drew, Ed., *Modern Critical Thought: An Anthology of Theorists Writing on Theorists* (London: Blackwell, 2003).

Morgan, Wendy, *A Poststructuralist English Classroom: The Example of Ned Kelly* (Melbourne: Victoria Association for the Teaching of English 1992).

Nash, Walter, *An Uncommon Tongue: The Uses and Resources of English* (London: Routledge, 1992).

Nash, Walter and Stacey, David, *Creating Texts: An Introduction to the Study of Composition* (London and New York: Longman, 1997).

O'Toole, Shaun, *Transforming Texts* (London: Routledge, 2003).

Scholes, Robert, *Textual Power: Literary Theory and the Teaching of English* (New Haven, CT: Yale University Press, 1998).

Scholes, Robert, *The Rise and Fall of English: Reconstructing English as a Discipline* (New Haven, CT: Yale University Press, 1998).

Scholes, Robert, Comley, Nancy and Ulmer, Gregory, *Text Book: An Introduction to Literary Language*, 2nd edn. (New York: St. Martin's Press, 1995).

Thomson, Jack, Ed., *Reconstructing Literature Teaching* (Norwood, SA: Australian Association for the Teaching of English, 1992).

Wandor, Michelene, 'Creative Writing and Pedagogy 1: Self Expression? Whose Self and What Expression,' *New Writing: The International Journal for the Practice and Theory of Creative Writing* 1, 2 (2004): 112–23.

19

Couplings, Matings, Hybridizations: What Writers Can Gain from Critical Theory

Kim Lasky

Creative Writing and Critical Theory are in their closest relation ever in Universities, as more institutions offer Creative Writing degrees, MA or MFA programmes, and opportunities for postgraduate research. More writers are choosing to produce work in an environment that brings them into close dialogue with literary criticism, and Creative Writing programmes increasingly emphasize the combination of critical and creative writing, requiring writers to occupy a dual position as both writer and critic. This is an exciting development, but one that is not without its challenges as the traditionally demarcated positions of the writer and critic, and of primary and secondary texts, shift and often clash. Such positions have become destabilized as poetry, fiction and scripts are produced within a pedagogic environment historically concerned with the 'secondary' reading of such work through Critical Theory, and the creative process is subjected to conscious critical judgement as it happens, rather than after the event. This raises issues for writers and assessors at all levels in Higher Education.

Interactions between the writer and critic are always prone to tension, some writers dismissing theory as a limiting fixed frame imposed upon their work by a third party, academic in the pejorative sense of the word as in being of merely speculative interest, far removed from practice. In my experience many students entering the university environment fear that too much awareness of theory will paralyse or stifle their ability to plunge freely into their writing, that fragile happening that Hélène Cixous calls 'writing blind', inflicting them with what Carole Satyamurti calls 'premature evaluation'.[1] Every writer knows the dangers of being too concerned with audience in the early stages of composition.

This tension between practice and theory, then, seems to be one of time. Just as the writer needs distinct times in which to create and edit, there is an expectation that the writing of the work and its critical reading will take place at clearly demarcated times. This reveals itself in the etymology of *practice* in the Greek *prassein*, to do, and *theory* in Greek, a sight, from *theōrein* to gaze upon. Producing work in an environment concerned with the judgement of that work after the event of writing (this *being* in a climate of *being seen*) can throw these distinct temporalities into sharp relief for a writer, which can be an unsettling experience, particularly when Critical Theory actively destabilizes the idea of a writer's 'self', for example by critiquing notions of authorial voice. All this might at first glance appear dangerously undermining. As Denise Riley recognizes, 'It is a further benign cruelty to encourage . . . students of Creative Writing to "find their own voices", especially when, under the same institutional roof, a pedagogy of criticism may be drilling them in the intertextuality of literature, where everything's quotation.'[2] However, Riley's work stands as a positive example of how these tensions might be addressed from inside the composition, the poem becoming a dialogue exploring such interpellation in the active performativity of its heteroglossia.[3] This kind of willing immersion inside the exchange between writing and criticism opens up a space from which the writer can engage more deeply with composition in all its complexity, simultaneously influencing theoretical understanding from a unique position inside the process.

The writer willing to feed on these dichotomies, to play in and within them, has much to gain from engagement with theory, which can become a store-house of material in just the same way as other literary, philosophical and political texts can be. It is a much quoted truism that being a good writer starts with being a good reader, and theory can be part of that rich mix. The study of literature and theory alongside the production of creative writing allows a writer to set creative work within a tradition, a context of influence, which can facilitate a broader awareness of aims, methods and responsibilities. After all, the tenets of critical approaches such as deconstruction, and psychoanalytical, post-colonialist, Marxist and feminist theories have evolved in tandem with thinking in philosophy, psychology, socio-political, economic and linguistic studies, alongside cultural developments that have made our lives what they are today. The rise of theory in English Studies has taken place against a climate of the civil and women's rights movements and political protests of the 1960s, changing demographics that have seen more women and ethnic minorities enter academia, and developments in science that have destabilized notions of a fixed, knowable universe in favour of chaos theory; all of which have shifted our perceptions about the stability of structures of knowledge, authority and power, leading us to become all the more aware of the productive tensions at work as we attempt to understand and express experience – not least how language plays with and within these dynamics. This is not just the world that we think in, in abstract terms, it is the world we live in – it *is* what we know and how we know it.

Perhaps the biggest challenge for writers is negotiating the shifting, overlapping positions of writer and critic. This means balancing the benefits of an awareness of Critical Theory as a source of knowledge, against the demands of applying this theory to work-in-progress. This requires constant negotiation between positions, between those shifting temporalities, in order to produce original artistic work integrated into papers, dissertations and theses that satisfy criteria for academic assessment. It was this shifting of positions, this productive tension between writing and criticism, that I wanted to explore in the process of writing my own thesis for the D.Phil. in Creative and Critical Writing.

My thesis explores how some contemporary poets are challenging traditional demarcations between the activities of 'poetry' and 'criticism', bringing the two into dialogue in works that play reflectively within the tensions of this relation. Crucial to this is my own enactment of this hybridity in practice throughout the thesis. In looking at the work of Charles Bernstein and Rachel Blau DuPlessis, for example, I set my own writing in dialogue with theirs. Charles Bernstein sets out to challenge the 'frame-lock' of rigid critical systems within the academy, breaking down perceived generic boundaries between the poem and the critical essay, a relation he figures as a kind of marriage. My critical reading of his long poem-essay 'Optimism and Critical Excess (Process)' is interspersed with a poem exploring the dailiness of tensions within marriage as different ways of seeing collide in the askings and failings of language. This space is interrupted by glosses on the theme of weddings that arise from within the critical and creative thinking through which the piece was written – drawing upon sources as diverse as Marcel Duchamp's 'A Bride Stripped Bare by her Bachelors, Even' and theories about the performative utterance 'I do'. This has been delivered as a conference paper, merging the spaces of poetic and academic performance. In exploring Rachel Blau DuPlessis's use of midrash as a generative form of exegesis, I respond to her poem 'Quiptych', part of the long sequence, *Drafts*, with my own poem, 'Triptych', which is concerned with the triad relation between writer, text and reader, exploring literary, scientific and mythic notions of 'three' in terms of feminine experience. This poem is then folded into a critical reading of DuPlessis' poem, becoming part of the ongoing dialogue of this three-way relation, a conversation between the 'critical' and the 'creative' that demonstrates how the voices of these conventionally demarcated activities are actually overlapping, merging, continually meeting in this palimpsest space.[4] Throughout these readings and writings I draw upon the work of theorists including Julia Kristeva, Judith Butler, Jacques Derrida and Mikhail Bakhtin, and I come to share poet-critic Lyn Hejinian's view of theory, 'Theorizing is, in fact, the very opposite of theorem-stating. It is a matter of vulnerable, inquisitive, worldly living, and it is one very closely bound to the poetic process.'[5] Discoveries I make inside this process are explored in two reflective 'Poetics' sections to offer another perspective, another shift of position from which to assess the dynamics of this relation. By now, it is impossible to say for sure when theory ends and practice begins, or when practice ends and theory begins.

More and more I recognize these acts as folded intimately into one another, theory becoming less about gazing upon a thing already created, but an active element within that creation, a vital part of *being*, of actively *seeing*. Gertrude Stein emerges as a foundational influence in much of this innovative work, and her realization that 'two ways of writing are not more than one way' is a celebration of the potential for this fruitful exchange between Creative Writing and theory, between what we already know and what we might learn in the process of writing.[6]

As with any innovation, there have been challenges. Being immersed inside these competing tensions has not always been easy. But it *has* always been informative, alive, happening – which, for me, is the vitality creative research should harness. It has convinced me of the benefits a writer gains from engaging with theory, as well as the deeper understanding that practice-based research can offer the university within English departments and beyond. Inevitably, in work that moves away from traditional academic form, there are also challenges in terms of assessment, and this is an ongoing concern for those formulating assessment criteria in Creative Writing.

In terms of theses, dissertations or portfolios of work, a brief preface can come into its own here, acting as a statement of the terms upon which the work has been produced, which should be formulated over time in consultation with a supervisor. This can act as an anchoring device for assessors, a means of guiding the reader through the work and highlighting its intentions without becoming a simple paraphrase of them, or a judgement of success or failure, which always threatens to fall into narcissistic anxiety. There are a host of potential textual interventions, using Critical Theory creatively, that can be used in teaching Creative Writing from undergraduate to postgraduate level.[7] These might include using poetic form or narrative techniques in critical essays, writing a work of fiction that places a character in conversation with exponents of various schools of Critical Theory, or creating a dramatic dialogue engaging with the work of another writer alongside competing critical readings of that work. Reflections upon a writer's own process from within such experimental work might be recorded in a journal, charting the moments of confusion as well as the moments of startling insight, which would allow for another perspective on this learning. Students might also be encouraged to find their own ways of exploring this exchange, looking for guidance to works in which other writers do just this, for example, Lyn Hejinian's essay, 'Language and "Paradise"', is written as an exegesis or 'an extension of the trajectory' of her long poem *The Guard*.[8]

If writers are to engage fully with this spirit of experiment, assessors at all levels must recognize that this cannot only be about the end result; that all criteria for 'success' must consider the process itself and the corresponding growth in awareness. The exercise of writing a short story exploring the tenets of deconstruction may not produce the best literature ever written, but the knowledge the writer gains might well underpin their next innovative, thought-provoking work. We need to be able to fail if we are to create and learn, and this is particularly vital at undergraduate level, where writers will often be encountering the theory/practice relation for the first time. Deborah Wynne's case study, 'Teaching Theory and the Use of the Reading Diary', details how her undergraduate students use reading diaries to chart their engagement with feminist theory, allowing for responsive tailoring of material in seminar teaching, as well as weighting of assessment to recognize learning achieved during the course. This is an interesting example of adaptive teaching and assessment methods that might meet some challenges in Creative Writing in which students could be encouraged to respond to theory creatively as part of this learning process.[9] Hélène Cixous writes in a 'theoretical' essay that is itself infused with poetic language:

> I sense that in each book words with roots hidden beneath the text come and go and carry out some other book between the lines. And what words do between themselves, couplings, matings, hybridisations – is genius, an erotic and fertile genius.[10]

If Creative Writing teaching is to build upon this potential, writers must be encouraged to develop confidence in their own imaginative explorations of theory, and assessment must allow for innovation. Such widening of the horizons of both theory and practice will allow us to realize the benefits of the fertile exchanges between Creative Writing and Critical Theory.

Notes

1. Hélène Cixous, 'Writing Blind: Conversations with the Donkey,' Trans. Eric Prenowitz, *Stigmata: Escaping Texts* (London: Routledge, 1998), pp. 139–52. Carole Satyamurti, '"First time ever": writing the poem in potential space,' *Acquainted with the Night*, Eds. Carole Satyamurti and Hamish Canham (London: Karnac, 2003), p. 31.
2. Denise Riley, *The Words of Selves: Identification, Solidarity, Irony* (California: Stanford University Press, 2000), p. 61.
3. Denise Riley, as above, for example, in the chapter, 'Lyric Selves,' in which Riley explores the writing of two poems about Echo and Narcissus, pp. 93–112.
4. Charles Bernstein, 'Optimism and Critical Excess (Process),' *A Poetics* (Cambridge, MA: Harvard University Press, 1992). Rachel Blau DuPlessis, 'Draft 55: Quiptych,' *Drafts 39–57*, *The Best American Poems, 2004*, Ed. Lyn Hejinian (New York: Scribner); Rachel Blau DuPlessis, 'Pledge,' pp. 178–83, alongside her exploration of the process of writing this long poem in *Blue Studios: Poetry and its Cultural Work* (Tuscaloosa: University of Alabama Press, 2006), pp. 209–51.
5. Lyn Hejinian, *The Language of Inquiry* (Berkeley: University of California Press, 2000), p. 338.

6. Gertrude Stein, 'Henry James,' *Four in America* (New Haven, CT: Yale University Press, 1947), p. 123.
7. Rob Pope, *Textual Intervention: Critical and Creative Strategies for Literary Studies* (London: Routledge, 1995) explores a wide range of textual interventions that can inform literary studies. For experimental and playful interventions for writers see Bernadette Mayer's, 'Experiments,' Eds. Bruce Andrews and Charles Bernstein, *The L=A=N=G=U=A=G=E Book* (Carbondale: Southern Illinois UP, 1984), pp. 80–3.
8. Lyn Hejinian, 'Language and "Paradise,"' *The Language of Inquiry* (Berkeley: University of California Press, 2000), pp. 59–82 and 'The Guard,' *The Cold of Poetry* (Los Angeles: Sun and Moon, 1974, repr. 1994), pp. 11–37. The recent anthology, *American Woman Poets in the 21st Century*, is one example of the increasing tendency for works to appear alongside a writer's statement of poetics. See Claudia Rankine and Juliana Spahr, Eds., *American Woman Poets in the 21st Century: Where Lyric Meets Language* (Hartford, CT: Wesleyan University Press, 2002).
9. See the English Subject Centre website at www.english.heacademy.ac.uk/explore/publications/casestudies/assess/reading_diary.php (accessed 28 February 2012).
10. Hélène Cixous, as above, pp. 147–8.

Part VII
Assessment

Assessing Creative Writing fuelled debates in the past, but now various procedures are in place in one form or another to satisfy institutional requirements. Given this, there still seems to be more freedom for individual teachers in the USA to stipulate assessment terms in their own courses, while in the UK teachers increasingly tend to work with explicit marking criteria often agreed by others at Departmental level.

Especially in the UK, Creative Writing projects are often 'second marked' by another teacher to avoid discrepancy. If two markers disagree, a third is called in to arbitrate and so forth until a decision is reached. In extreme cases, this may involve external markers arbitrating if teachers working within the same institution fail to agree. Because institutions increasingly pursue objectivity in the UK, many institutions also have 'blind marking' in which one or more teachers assess anonymous students that they do not know and whose work they have not seen.

Working within such institutional conditions in the UK, Michael Symmons Roberts explores ways in which poetry can and cannot be assessed in Higher Education. In this context he argues why assessment should focus on technical concerns and craft but that this involves changing assumptions that poetry is about 'expressing something' to seeing it as 'making something'.

In the USA, Mary Cantrell begins by considering why assessment practices in Creative Writing are so often questioned by colleagues in other disciplines. Focusing on undergraduate entry level courses, she argues how assessment empowers students by ensuring they understand elements of craft. She explains how Creative Writing pedagogy centres on process as well as a finished written product. She also considers how assessment dispels misconceptions that have kept Creative Writing marginalized in the academic world.

In the USA, Stephen O'Connor takes a firm line against assessment. He makes a case by considering how qualities most valued in writing are beyond technical skills and agues against assessment that ranks student work and carries within its criteria assumptions of objectivity.

20

Assessment of Poetry in Higher Education Courses: What Are the Limits?

Michael Symmons Roberts

This paper is very much a poet's perspective, drawing on the reflections and experiences of other poets to explore the ways in which poetry can – and cannot – be assessed in universities.

I will begin with a bleak view shared by many poets, expressed in a recent interview by the poet August Kleinzhaler:

> The notion of teaching Creative Writing, teaching people to write poetry, is preposterous. You can't do it. It's like teaching someone to be kind or amusing or a wizard at languages. It's hard-wired.[1]

Kleinzhaler goes on to argue that the making of a poet requires a strange psychological set-up to trigger it, and a particular kind of personality to sustain it long enough to develop originality and expertise. For August Kleinzhaler, much teaching of poetry on Creative Writing courses is simply an encouragement of the students' self-esteem. If he is right, then this is another symptom of a deep-seated condition that afflicts poetry more than any other literary form – the assumption that writing a poem is not about 'making something', but 'expressing something'.[2] Put crudely (using terms that are now contentious in the poetry world) writing poetry is often viewed as closer to therapy than to craft. The process of teaching then becomes a kind of psychological mentoring, in which the student tries to discover what is his or hers to express as a poet, and the goal is to get it out of the heart and onto the page as powerfully as possible.[3]

This approach to teaching makes assessment of Creative Writing extremely difficult, because the writing is insufficiently distanced from the student. If writing poems is all about getting our deepest feelings out and onto the page, then what – or more to the point, who – is being assessed?

One counter-approach followed by some teachers of poetry is to build a strategy for assessment based on purely technical concerns. The poet Geoffrey Hill has argued that the term 'inspiration' should properly be applied to the final stage of a process, after much work, when the final

151

words are being put into place. He uses Yeats's image of 'the click like a closing box' when a poem is finished.[4] Kleinzhaler himself concedes that some elements of craft can be taught and assessed. These could include the following:

- skilled reading of poetry,
- knowledge of, and facility with different forms of metre, rhyme, syllabics and free verse,
- ability to self-edit and build a poem through successive drafts, making good technical decisions (rhythm, sound, line-breaks, stanza breaks) in the process,
- ability to write effective and recognizable (not necessarily humorous) parodies, demonstrating understanding of other poets' forms & music. This could include (as in Derek Walcott's teaching at Boston) learning poems by heart to internalize and understand their music.

The catch, of course, is that a student might fulfil those criteria to perfection, and still not produce a good poem. In fact, for many practising poets, there are crucial limits to technical self-consciousness. The most dangerous review to read of one's own work (whether couched in positive or negative terms) is a review that reveals the inner technical workings of the poems: '*this* is how her/his poems work'. The more insightful the technical analysis, the greater the risk to the poet: too much self-consciousness can kill the poetry.

Yet though many poets would resist making a detailed technical analysis of their own poems, any serious poet will have done this kind of technical apprenticeship in the past, on their own and other people's work. And this fascination with inner workings is a key part of what drives the 'making' of poems in the first place. Lavinia Greenlaw has described how, for her, 'the impulse to write a poem often comes from making sense of how things work. This might be a play of forces or a visual conundrum.' And she goes on to quote Elizabeth Bishop, who said of Marianne Moore that 'If she speaks of a chair, you can practically sit on it when she has finished.'[5]

Even if writing poetry is better described as a 'making' than an 'expressing', that does not mean it is reducible to purely technical considerations. It takes much more than that to make a piece of verse into a poem. The poet Kathleen Jamie has written:

> I believe this: just as much as sound and rhythm, what makes a poem is its relationship with truth. A poem is an approach toward a truth. Be it a discovered truth or a constructed one, a poem is an approach toward a truth. Truth is not exclusive to poetry, of course, but there is no poem which does not engage with truth.[6]

But can this truth seeking, this 'approach toward a truth' be taught or assessed? Well, as Kathleen Jamie points out, it does at least mean that the doors are open to anyone who wants to try to do this:

> I want to say that the place we enter when we are writing a poem is a moral place, and furthermore, a democratic place. Open to all, if writing a poem is an attempt to reach a truth, if poetry is a method of approaching truths, and each of us with a human soul and 'a tongue in oor heids' can make an approach toward a truth, poetry is inherently democratic. For sure, we make plenty of poor poetry – clumsy moves towards a banal truth – but that's okay. My father's house is an open house, and it has many mansions.

A good poem – a 'true' poem – must be technically accomplished in its use of language and form, acutely observed and thought through as Lavinia Greenlaw suggests, and approach 'truth' in the manner described by Kathleen Jamie, so how do you assess these things on Creative Writing courses? Assessing technical dexterity is not too difficult, but beyond that, the lines look rather blurred. There may well be ways of judging the acuteness of a poet's observation, but it gets much harder the further the poet moves away from naturalism and narrative. And how on earth can you assess a piece of writing for 'truthfulness' or 'truth seeking'? A teacher may well have a view on the 'truth' – or lack of it – in a student's work, but could they give it a summative assessment? If so, then what are the benchmarks? Lying poems fail; half-true poems get a 2nd, etcetera.

The Australian poet Les Murray has devised a model of 'real' poetry as 'wholespeak'.[7] This – in Murray's terms – involves a balance of three elements – the daylight conscious mind or reason, the dreaming unconscious mind and the body. In other words, a true poem should demonstrate a clear thread of conscious thought and control (the daylight mind), make connections and conjure images that take it beyond conscious thought (the dreaming mind), and muster a combination of sound and rhythm in such a way that a reader will react intuitively to it, as with music (the body). For Murray, a balance of these elements is what makes poetry 'wholespeak', as opposed to the 'narrowspeak' of most of the language that surrounds us.

For an individual poet, this model may well ring true. Too much daylight mind and the poem is a polemic, a diary entry or an argument; too much dreaming mind and the poem is a stream of consciousness; too much body (a rarer failing) and it is empty, nonsense verse. Most poems that fail can be seen as weak in one of these areas. But though it makes sense in the context of trying to make poems, Murray's model offers no tools of assessment to the teacher. I can not imagine awarding a student poem a good grade for dreaming mind and a mediocre grade for reason.

In reality, most Creative Writing courses focus their assessment of poetry on technical concerns and craft, and rightly so. Despite his assertion that writing poetry cannot be taught, August Kleinzhaler concedes that:

> You can teach them to read . . . to listen. You can encourage them in habits of mind, methods of execution. You can give them exercises to familiarise them with different ways of writing so that they have those arrows in their quiver. You can even suggest techniques whereby they can learn to edit themselves.[8]

Not only are these techniques teachable, they can also be assessed.

The heart of summative assessment (and of teaching) in poetry lies in technique: skill with, and understanding of formal and linguistic tools. Beyond that, assessment of elements such as 'originality', 'structure', and especially 'voice', seem more fitting for the role of a literary reviewer than an academic assessor. Discussion of these elements in workshops – particularly at MA level – can be instructive and constructive, but turning that into summative assessment is an imprecise science at best.

For MA and Ph.D. assessments, there are often more tools available than at BA level. The 'critical' component or commentary on the work can provide a means of measuring student achievement against expectation. This can extend beyond technical concerns into voice, originality and consistency of thought. But what is being assessed here? The poems? Or the relationship between the commentary and the poems? There is an analogy here with the introductions given to poems at poetry readings. Not many poets take the pure path and read the naked poems, but most are uneasy about lengthy introductions that discuss the impulse or event behind a poem, followed by a reading of the work itself. It becomes a kind of diptych, in which the prose and poetic versions of the same event shed light on each other and begin to replace the poem as a stand-alone work.

As discussed previously, too much critical self-awareness can undermine the creative process, but critical commentaries at MA and Ph.D. level run other risks too. The creative component (the poems themselves) can become compromised by a critical commentary that reveals faults or shortcomings in the poetry – 'if that's what you've intended then you've missed it by miles . . .' The best Creative Writing courses view the critical commentary largely as a record of process and ambition, reading and research rather than an exercise in turning the poems into critical prose.

Can anonymous assessment strengthen the process? It brings another – perhaps more objective – eye to that difficult area of assessment beyond the purely technical, but the same problems apply. Beyond craft, different readers value different qualities in voice and tone, and recognize different definitions of originality. I do not know any anthologist who has not been accused of including terrible poems and excluding the best. On these issues, an anonymous assessor faces the same challenges as any tutor.

In conclusion – from a poet's perspective – there is still much about the making of poetry (and poets) that cannot be taught, so how can it be assessed in Higher Education? A focus on technical aspects, and a critical reading of other poets can provide a way forward. This requires a shift in emphasis from poetry as 'expression' to poetry as 'making'. However, a poem can be well-made but empty and unoriginal. This is harder to assess with consistency and objectivity, but it should be possible – through guided reading, writing and workshopping – to create a critical community within a cohort of students to contribute to the process of assessment and to assist individual students in sharpening their self-critical skills.

Notes

1. Brian Henry and Andrew Zawacki, Eds., *The Verse Book of Interviews* (Seattle, WA: Wave Books, 2005).
2. Editor's Note: This view concurs with D.G. Myers's argument in the History section of this volume that Creative Writing is fundamentally defined by free expression and cannot therefore reform itself from within since it lacks a value system that moves beyond the subjective needs of individual expression. Paul Dawson argues a different view in *Creative Writing and the New Humanities* (New York: Routledge, 2005).
3. Editor's Note: In the Workshop section of this volume Michelene Wandors argues against this role.
4. John Haffenden, *Viewpoints: Poets in Conversation* (London: Faber, 1981).
5. W.N. Herbert and Matthew Hollis, Eds., *Strong Words* (Newcastle upon Tyne: Bloodaxe, 2000).
6. Kathleen Jamie, in W.N. Herbert and Matthew Hollis, as above.
7. Les Murray, *The Paperbark Tree: Selected Prose* (Manchester: Carcanet 1992).
8. John Haffenden, as above.

21

Assessment as Empowerment: Grading Entry-Level Creative Writing Students

Mary Cantrell

It happens at least once a year: someone asks me, usually in an awestruck voice, sometimes in an accusatory voice, how one *grades* Creative Writing. I teach at a community college, which offers only freshman- and sophomore-level courses, and the question always annoys me. Professors teaching other entry-level courses are not asked how they grade; no one is confused about how students studying mathematics or history or even piano are graded, the assumption being that in these courses, traditional assessments – exams, papers, presentations – accurately measure a student's learning. Why, then, are my grading practices questioned?

One answer is that Creative Writing as an academic discipline is relatively new, and its pedagogy is still evolving. As Anna Leahy mentions in her forward to *The Authority Project: Power and Identity in the Creative Writing Classroom*, 'college-level, Creative Writing teachers learn largely without field-specific teaching mentors, pedagogy guidebooks, or shared bodies of knowledge about what it means to lead a Creative Writing course'.[1] We have recently started to make explicit what we do, to demonstrate to our colleagues in other disciplines that our courses are intellectually demanding, that we share, as professionals in any discipline, a lexicon, an understanding of theory, and a dedication to scholarship. Nonetheless, many still view Creative Writing classes as unscholarly, and the cliché that writing cannot be taught persists.[2] Because one of the hallmarks of Creative Writing as a discipline is its emphasis on process over product, some of what students learn – persistence, the ability to improve, versatility, a willingness to absorb informed criticism – cannot be easily taught or tallied into percentages and letter grades. Furthermore, the focus on process and the professor's close readings and individual conferences with students creates a professor–student relationship unlike that in a lecture or even a seminar course. As both mentor to the aspiring student and final judge of the student's work, Creative Writing professors serve as nurturers as well as standard bearers, roles that may appear to (and sometimes do) conflict.

This emphasis on process and individual attention is also why, unlike our colleagues teaching composition, Creative Writing professors typically do not promote an external, anonymous evaluation of student work: we know that even the most knowledgeable and dedicated writers may not always produce great work in a semester, and we want to consider other evidence of learning. Most writing professors are themselves writers who understand that talent is elusive, that the qualities excellent writers possess – the drive, the ability to empathize, a sensitivity to language – are inspired and nurtured but probably are not 'taught' using traditional pedagogy. As John Gardner explains in *The Art of Fiction*, education provides 'both useful information and life-enhancing experience, one largely measurable, the other not'.[3] When treated merely as courses in useful information, he believes, such life-enhancing courses are taught poorly. In *Write Away: One Novelist's Approach to Fiction and the Writing Life*, Elizabeth George makes a similar point: 'there are two distinct but equally important halves to the writing process. One of these is related to art; the other is related to craft'.[4] George believes that, for those who teach Creative Writing, '[c]raft is the point'; it is 'the soil in which a budding writer can plant the seed of her idea in order to nurture it into a story'.[5] Because craft is not always the point, because we are also teaching those unquantifiable, life-enhancing experiences, Creative Writing professors may be reluctant to define a narrow set of course objectives and specific grading criteria, a reluctance that perpetuates the notion that Creative Writing cannot be graded.

At the undergraduate level, though, the 'useful information' that students should learn and that professors should grade can and should be made explicit. Students' abilities and goals differ significantly when they arrive in a beginning Creative Writing class, but most have seen our culture's romanticized representation of writers in films and on television, and their ambitions may be borne, in part, out of a desire to achieve fame and fortune. However, along with misguided notions of glory is almost always an appreciation for the way literature can move us. Given this, what all students need is knowledge of craft and exposure to literature. If they know anything about technique, it is usually superficial and sometimes incorrect. If they have read much literature, they have rarely been taught to identify literary devices or strategies, and they seldom have read contemporary works. Many even lack grammar and punctuation skills. In beginning Creative Writing classes, therefore, professors empower students by ensuring they understand elements of craft. They may quiz students over terminology, assign critical reading responses and essays, develop exercises in specific techniques, and assess how well the students' 'finished' work demonstrates a basic understanding of technique.

Such an approach to assessment does not ensure that only excellent writers emerge from the class, but it follows Bloom's taxonomy, which identifies knowledge, comprehension and application as the less difficult thinking skills that must be mastered in order to develop higher-level skills.[6] Jane Smiley, in *Thirteen Ways of Looking at a Novel*, offers a similar hierarchy for novelists. She describes 'a novel-writing pyramid of skills', with the bottom layers being mechanics and diction and 'the apex of the pyramid [being] the element most general and yet most difficult to attain: complexity'.[7] The goal for professors at any level should be to move students toward complexity and excellence in their works, but our goals are not the same as our grading criteria. No professor in any discipline can articulate quantifiable learning goals for everything she hopes students will learn; any professor at any level, however, can articulate some of what she expects students to learn and can devise a grading system that reflects the degree to which students have learned.

While it may be more difficult to grade Creative Writing than it is to grade a Biology exam or History paper, assessment in general is always difficult, often misguided, and sometimes even at odds with learning. Whether in the form of tests or other activities, articulating and assessing what students learn can seem reductive and contrary to our noblest goals as educators and champions of great literature. Assessment, though, is a matter of accountability: we must give grades, and to receive accreditation and funding, we must produce other evidence of student learning – 'measurable' objectives, learning outcomes, goals with results that can be 'demonstrated'. The evidence we supply to our accrediting institutions, much like the grades we assign, tells only part of what happens in our classes.

Telling part of what happens, though, can enlighten those who express doubts or consternation about Creative Writing as an academic discipline. The best workshops require students to learn certain terms, to develop critical thinking skills and to practice civil discourse; workshops also broaden students' appreciation of literature and test their determination to pursue their talent. For a student to comment intelligently on another's work, he or she must infer the writer's intentions, isolate elements of the poem or story and articulate clearly how they contribute to those intentions. Especially in entry-level courses, students read voraciously and write critical responses to published work. They also write prodigiously and revise extensively: dozens of poems for a poetry class, thirty to fifty pages of fiction in a fiction class. In many classes students submit a self-analysis along with their portfolio of finished poems or stories, a task that requires a thorough understanding of craft as it emerges (or fails to emerge) in their own creative pieces. In other words, Creative Writing courses require many of the critical thinking skills valued in other academic disciplines.

In all of our classes, we need to be explicit about our standards and to use assessment as a means of dispelling some of the misconceptions that have kept Creative Writing professors and students marginalized in the academic world. In entry-level courses especially, we need to dispel the notion that we are assessing the whole writer. Grades based on critical reading abilities, on class participation, on knowledge of craft and on the quantity as well as on the quality of work produced may result in high grades for mediocre writers, but at this level, grades need not indicate far-reaching abilities. An A in an introductory Creative Writing class does not signify that one will be a great writer any more than an A in a freshman Political Science class indicates one will become a senator, or an A in General Biology indicates one will develop a cure for cancer. Rather, high grades indicate the extent to which students learn concepts and practices that can complement and improve their innate talent. Privileging knowledge over talent, craft over art may, of course, send the wrong message to mediocre students. In recent years, editors and writers alike have complained about 'workshop stories' or 'workshop poems', the technically sound but emotionally bereft writing that emerges from many Creative Writing programs, but professors are not the gatekeepers of literary excellence. Our job is not to train writers the way law schools train lawyers; it is, rather, to empower them to be successful if they have the talent and ambition. Flannery O'Conner's famous statement that universities 'don't stifle enough' writers may be true, but is the world any worse for having too many would-be writers? As my poetry professor, Neal Bowers, used to say, it is not the same as having too many lawyers.

Writers are not born with the knowledge and skills needed to produce great literature, and successful writers can always point to an especially attentive teacher/reader whose lucid explanations and demanding expectations made a difference in their writing. Those who continue to believe that Creative Writing students are somehow beyond the pedestrian practice of grading, that what we Creative Writing professors do in our classroom is so complex and mysterious and profound that it cannot be explained in the form of course objectives or measurable outcomes seem to forget that Creative Writing courses exist as part of a continuum; our courses have prerequisites and course numbers, and exist within the academy. Like our colleagues in other disciplines, we assess how well students learn specific skills and concepts and hope that what they learn helps them succeed beyond our classes.

Notes

1. Anna Leahy, Ed., *The Authority Project: Power and Identity in the Creative Writing Classroom* (Clevedon: Multilingual Matters, 2005), p. 11.
2. Lynn Freed, 'Doing Time,' *Harper's* (July, 2005): 30–7.
3. John Gardner, *The Art of Fiction: Notes on Craft for Young Writers* (New York: Random/Vintage, 1991), p. 41.
4. Elizabeth George, *Write Away: One Novelist's Approach to Fiction and the Writing Life* (New York: HarperCollins/Perennial Currents, 2004), p. ix.
5. As above.
6. Benjamin Bloom, Ed., *Taxonomy of Educational Objectives: the Classification of Educational Goals. Handbook 1: Cognitive Domain* (New York: McKay, 1956).
7. Jane Smiley, *Thirteen Ways of Looking at a Novel* (New York: Knopf, 2005).

22
Ranking Student Writing as Bad Pedagogy and a Bogus Pretence of Objectivity

Stephen O'Connor

Academic tradition and individual wishful thinking incline many Creative Writing professors toward an exaggerated opinion of their own powers, especially in regard to ranking student talent and work. It would be one thing if the merits of writers and their writing could be evaluated merely by reference to a certain set of standards or skills, but artistic success is a far more complicated and mysterious entity than that.

What, after all, do we value most highly in literature? Not mere mastery of form. No writer has ever been given the Nobel Prize for the perfect execution of Alexandrines or for the harmonious linkage of plot and theme. While formal skill is certainly to be desired in writing, it is by no means a *sine qua non*. Whitman and Dostoevsky remain literary geniuses despite their occasional ungainliness and verbosity. Those qualities we value most in writing, and from which literature derives its cultural significance, can only be designated in the vaguest terms: voice, vision, originality, beauty, truth, wit, imaginative flexibility. We can talk to students about the importance of these qualities, but we cannot teach them. They emerge in writing through some complex interaction of the author's life experiences, innate abilities, character (vices as well as virtues) and – most mysteriously of all – between all of these factors and the zeitgeist. Any ten-step guide to the development of a compelling voice would be sheer chicanery, exceeded in absurdity only by assessment standards purporting to be precise, objective and universal designations of merit. 'If the work in question', says Professor Gradgrind, 'meets these three criteria, it may be deemed true. And it must meet all fourteen of these criteria or it is not funny.' For these practical reasons I am against assessment that has as its goal the ranking of student work.

What is more, literary talent develops at varying rates, sometimes in bursts, sometimes very slowly. Just because a student does not produce quality writing in my class does not mean he or she is not working hard, learning or talented. Sometimes it simply takes a long while for a lesson to sink in, often beginning writers have to overcome a degree of defensiveness or insecurity before they are ready to accept new ideas. I have seen apparently hopeless

160

students end up producing remarkable work years after they have left my class. And I have had students who seemed utterly brilliant in the special environment of academe become utterly lost in the world beyond. Over the years a few of my students have gone on to publish very well, and while I have never been surprised, it is also true that I would never have picked any one of them as the sole member of his or her class most likely to succeed. For better or for worse, the formulae for literary success are too complex and variable for my judgement of a student's potential to be much more than a hunch. Why then should I pretend that my judgement has any objectivity? And, even discounting the inexactitude of my judgement, does it make sense to give any two equally talented and hardworking students different grades merely because one of those students failed to manifest fully his or her talent during the relatively brief duration of my class?

I am more confident of my ability to judge individual compositions, but even here, I am most sure of the basics: grammar, sentence structure, and certain elements of plot, pacing and dialogue. When it comes to voice, vision or any of the other most essential aspects literary writing, honesty compels me to admit my judgements are heavily determined by taste, experience and my particular needs and defense mechanisms – which is to say that my judgements are no more objective than my hunches about a student's potential for success.

Imagine the dream – or nightmare! – creative writing class, one containing, say, Virginia Woolf, Ernest Hemingway, Toni Morrison, William Burroughs and Henry James. Suppose, for the sake of argument, I think Hemingway is by far the best writer in the class. Would any of the other students – or indeed, literature itself – be helped were I to design my assessment criteria so that the highest grades went to works containing noun-heavy, adverb-light sentences about traumatized tough guys in Spanish-speaking countries? Would there be anything objective or universal in my giving *For Whom the Bell Tolls* an A+, *Naked Lunch* an A-, *Beloved* a B-, *Mrs. Dalloway* a C and *The Golden Bowl* a D? It is, of course, easier to rank lesser talents than the members of this dream class, but even in regard to the worst student work – and more so for the best – there is an inescapable subjectivity in our evaluations that makes all pretence at universality and scientific precision bogus, and thus potentially unfair and detrimental to the development of talent.

Academic and award giving institutions often seek to minimize the role of individual prejudice by having works assessed by committee. While it is true that such a strategy can diminish the significance of any one person's judgement, it is also true that 'group-think' has the capacity to validate prejudices each of the judges may have been reluctant to act upon individually. And, of course, the imperatives of politicking and compromise on committees have a well-known tendency to elevate mediocrity. Another common strategy – evaluation of anonymous manuscripts – can certainly reduce the role played by personal regard for a student, but it does nothing to enhance objectivity in any other way, and thus, like assessment by committee, has the at least potentially destructive tendency to cloak subjective judgement in undeserved authority.

One obvious reason Creative Writing teachers are encouraged to grade or otherwise rank students is that universities award degrees, and thus are gatekeepers to certain professions and other institutions. While Biology, Mathematics and Psychology departments clearly do serve as gatekeepers, that simply is not the case for Creative Writing programs, even on the graduate level. At best an MFA satisfies a minimum bureaucratic require-ment for being hired to teach at a university. But even then, one's chief qualification for the job is one's publication record: what one has done *outside* academe rather than within. The real gatekeepers of the literary profession are editors, marketing executives, agents, reviewers and, at a great remove, the professors of English, who select books for their syllabi.

So, let us take stock: if the merits of a piece of writing cannot be determined by reference to a set of clearly definable standards, and if there is no way of eliminating the subjectivity of our judgements regarding the most important elements in literary work, and if the writing a student produces within the confines of a single course does not necessarily reflect that student's effort, talent or future success, and if, finally, Creative Writing programs do not even function as gatekeepers to their profession, does the ranking of student writing according to merit have any pedagogical or practical justification? Very little that I can see.

One of the most common justifications for grading or otherwise publicly assessing student performance is that it motivates students to work harder. I have to say that, in my twenty years teaching at university level, I have seen virtually no evidence supporting this claim. Most of the programs I have taught in only ask professors to give Creative Writing students a passing or a failing grade. Not only has motivation never been a problem in any of my classes, the students receiving letter grades have never seemed more hard working or engaged than any of the others. The reason for this is simple: no one is ever required to study Creative Writing. Students enroll in classes because they want to, or, in some cases, are *driven* to write – and for all the obvious reasons: writing really does help students make sense of this vast and confusing world; it really does allow them to give vent to their feelings, and, of course, writing can be a lot of fun. Under such happy circumstances, the supposed extra motivation provided by grades is simply unnecessary. And what is more, given that the main reason students some-time have trouble writing is their fear that they are talentless, it is hard to see how the threat of a bad or even a middling grade could do anything to relieve their anxiety. The one time I did see evidence of grades affecting student motivation was when I was a writer-in-residence at a college where grades were heavily emphasized. I had two students in my class who seemed to have no interest in writing and almost as little talent. When I confronted one of them he confessed that he and his friend had signed up for the course because they wanted to boost their grade point average and had heard that Creative Writing classes were an 'easy A' – which is to say that, at least in regard to these students, grading was actually detrimental to motivation. Had the class been pass-fail, neither would have enrolled in it.

The other common justification for grades is that they give students valuable feedback – a contention that, once again, I find highly dubious. Grades, exam-scores and other forms of ranking writing are simply not specific enough to help students see what they do really well or poorly, or what they need to do to improve. All that such ranking really shows students is how the ranking entity (a professor, a committee) sees them in relation to their peers. Students can, of course, learn a great deal by comparing their own work to that of their classmates – such comparison is the raison d'être of workshops and Creative Writing classes generally – but only when the comparison is specific, when the students can see exactly what their class-mates have done and how to duplicate or avoid it. The ranking of student work, not only does nothing to facilitate such productive cross-fertilization, it encourages the very worst form of comparison: competition. Some few students will, of course, feel anointed by good grades or by a contest victory, and thereafter may find it easier to write, but the vast majority will consider themselves branded by their mediocrity. Is this really the sort of pedagogical practice that will help most students develop to their maximum ability? Not in any way that I can see.

Consider the case of one of my former students, who is now a very highly regarded author and an inspiration to younger writers. While she was obviously prodigiously talented when she studied with me, she had not yet done her best work, and what is more, there were other students in that class who seemed equally imaginative and at the time, more technically accom-plished. Had I been forced to single out the best writer among that group, I would not have chosen this particular student. I can not say for certain what effect being labelled second rate might have had on her development, but it is difficult to imagine how it might have made her work harder or learn faster. The literary world is already savage enough on aspiring writers; why should institutions committed to nurturing young talent make life any more difficult than it already is by ranking students before they have fully developed – especially, once again, considering the inescapable biases and inefficiencies of any ranking system?

When I am required to give students grades other than 'pass' or 'fail' I do so exclusively on the basis of effort, as manifested by such factors as attend-ance, class participation and the timeliness of papers. I say 'attempt' because I came to realize many years ago that my opinion of students' writing has a subtle effect both on how they manifest their effort and on how I evaluate it. I am, for example, far more likely to call on a student whose work I respect, and such a student is far more likely to raise his or her hand and thus appear to be putting more effort into the class. Since I can not see any way actually to grade my classes according to my ideal standard, I inform my students of my human weakness at the start of every semester and assure them that my opinion of their writing will add no more than a plus or minus to their grade, which I believe is an accurate representation of what actually happens.

Now it is time to contradict myself. Having thoroughly established my objections to the public assessment of writing, I must confess that I do see one area in which the ranking of students is an inescapable necessity, and that happens to be the one area in which academic departments actually do serve as gatekeepers: the admission of students to advanced classes or graduate programmes. It is a simple fact that advanced writers learn faster when they are in classes with students at roughly their own level than when they are in classes with mere beginners (the reverse is not true, alas), and if such select classes are to exist, practical necessity requires that prospective students be sorted out according to ability. But just because this sort of assessment is inescapable does not make it any more objective, precise or universal, nor does it mean that ranking students serves any pedagogical purpose once a class has been established.

When I am in a classroom, I never see myself as a gatekeeper, but only as a coach or guide. My goal is to help young writers, at whatever level of ability or accomplishment, gain greater control over form without losing access to that shadowy, anarchic and wholly individual sector of the imagination that is the true source of art. In a real sense what I am trying to do is help at least my most ambitious students get past the *real* gatekeepers of literature, but my ultimate object is to help students accomplish the far more difficult task of writing works that might profoundly affect readers and enrich the culture.

The best way by far to help my students become better writers is simply to read their work carefully and address each piece's particular strengths and weaknesses. I give my classes assignments, lectures and readings intended to acquaint them with various techniques and styles of writing, but I set no specific performance goals – apart from requiring the generation of a certain number of pages. Not only do definable goals tend to limit class attention to merely technical matters (all that can be clearly defined), they are often unrelated to students' individual needs and abilities. Even the most rigorous screening method cannot guarantee that all students in the class are on the same level.

I have known many an undergraduate who can write as well as a typical graduate student, and I have had many, even quite talented graduate students who need to learn such basics as how to designate paragraphs and punctuate dialogue. Does it make any sense for me to abandon my especially advanced undergraduates because they have already exceeded the performance goals for their level? By the same token, does it make any sense to neglect a student who has been admitted to a graduate programme but turns out to have problems one would be distressed to find in an undergraduate? I think not.

While it is true that I tend to spend a great deal more time discussing basic matters of structure and language with undergraduates, the real business of teaching occurs almost exclusively on a one-to-one basis, and so is the same on any level. I use my capacity to judge – or assess – writing, not to rank, but to analyse students' work, and to draw their attention to areas where the actual writing seems least in accordance with their apparent ambitions. I make detailed marginal remarks on every paper, write two to four page, single-spaced endnotes explaining my overall reaction, and have thirty to sixty minute conferences with each student every time his or her work is submitted to the class for discussion or 'workshop'. Insofar as issues are cut and dried – regarding grammar, for instance – my remarks on papers and in class are cut and dried. But for the most part my goal is to help students understand that writing is always a matter of choice, and that there are always other choices that can be made. If I think a student has made a wrong choice, I identify it, explain the effect it has had on me and suggest other possibilities and the effects they might have.

Although academic convention and my professional experience give my judgements undeniable weight, I do my best to present them as personal responses rather than the enunciation of objective standards. I want students to be wholly responsible for their decisions – aesthetic and otherwise – because it is only by deciding on their own, and sometimes in agonies of uncertainty, that young writers hammer out their literary credo and develop the artistic authority that will enable them to become authors.

As much as I possibly can, I want to leave my students the freedom to follow their inspiration, as anarchic, obscure and even troubling as inspiration can often be. Professor Gradgrind's ten criteria for measuring originality in literary expression may satisfy his own anxieties about authority – as well as the academic bureaucracy's – but they do nothing whatsoever to foster genuine originality, vision, beauty, truth or any of the other qualities we value most in literature. This is because literature is, in its very essence, a pondering of the imponderable, our attempt as individuals and as a civilization to explore and comprehend the vast portion of existence that lies between and often contradicts established categories, ideas and standards. Literature is also an interaction, in solitude, of separate sensibilities: the author's and the reader's, an interaction as complex, mysterious and particular as that between any two lovers. We can no more tell our students how to succeed in this complex interaction than we can tell them how to be happy in love. All we can say is: 'This is what other people have done, this is what I think, and here are some things you might want to think about yourself. Otherwise, you're on your own. Give it all you've got, and let's see what happens.'

Part VIII
Uses of Information Technology

Information technology is increasingly used to enrich teaching. It functions as an area for resources such as collections of texts and talks by authors to a teaching tool itself as a part of campus-based or entirely online distance learning teaching.

John Nieves and Joseph Moxley explain how technology is a key to advancing Creative Writing in the twenty-first century by building its pedagogy of experimentation, and they introduce a range of technical tools to enhance quality of Creative Writing experiences in Higher Education.

Graham Mort explains how IT structures a distance learning MA in Creative Writing as well as a mentoring scheme with eight African countries. He reflects how it breaks down many barriers to education as well as how these experiences have informed use of virtual spaces on campus and also how it can unite campus and distance learning students.

23
New Tools for Timeless Work: Technological Advances in Creative Writing Pedagogy

John A. Nieves and Joseph Moxley

Creative Writing has always been at the forefront of experimentation. New ideas and practices keep the field vital and relevant, and Creative Writing teachers should maintain this tradition by taking advantage of new tools and pedagogical practices. Technology, which has changed more in the past three generations than in all prior generations combined, is the key to advancing Creative Writing in the twenty-first-century classroom. Weblogs, wikis, e-mail workshops, discussion boards, MOO communities and creative writing software are some of the new tools available. This paper introduces these tools and offers ways in which they may improve the quality of Creative Writing experiences in Higher Education.

Weblogs

Weblogs, or blogs, provide revolutionary new workshop possibilities. A blog is a public on-line document, usually password protected so that only intended users may add original content. However, once the content is added, it is in the public domain. Anyone who reads the work may comment, but not alter the original text. Some blogs that are easy to use are www.writingblogs.org, www.seo-blog.org, and www.blogger.com.[1] Both writingblogs and seo-blog allow the blog's administrator to create categories. These could be student names, thus creating a group blog. Group blogs foster strong ties between members. They give students opportunities to edit each other's work multiple times and to add new ideas whenever they arise. Everything on a blog site is archived, so it is equally possible to comment on a piece recently submitted and one submitted months ago. A blog can also be set up to e-mail users whenever someone adds new comments. The e-mail also specifies which entry the comment was made to, which prevents students wasting time constantly checking for new feedback.

Applications of such technology are stunning. It is not only possible to run a class-wide on-line workshop accessible twenty-four-hours-a-day, seven-days-a-week, but it is also possible to run a workshop with students from different universities around the world. Because anything posted on a blog is considered electronically published, there are very few copyright problems with this method. Likewise, because the blog is a public document, students can receive feedback, not just from their peers and instructors, but from the general public. This offers new perspectives about how potential readers outside of their field view students' work. This kind of experience is priceless when considering publication and even mass-marketing of students' creative works.

Wikis

According to Wikipedia, one of the best known wikis in the world, a wiki 'is a web application that allows users to add content and their own version of history, as on an Internet forum, but also allows anyone to edit the content'.[2] A wiki is a web site that allows collaboration in the truest sense of the word. It is possible to password protect a wiki so that only intended users can upgrade the content. Wikis save and catalog older versions of themselves so that it is possible to review the creative process. One of the best and easiest to use free wiki providers is found at www.projectforum.com/pf/wiki.html.[3]

A wiki has a wide array of possible pedagogical applications. A wiki can be used to create a collaborative work, such as a short story, novel or epic poem, which an entire class can add to and revise over the course of a semester. A wiki also provides an environment to practice editing and revising one's own work while being able to consult all previous versions. Updates on a wiki can either be authored or anonymous. This relieves some of the most common tensions of active peer review. A wiki can also be used for collaboratively authored books when the co-authors live too far from each other for actual meetings to be financially feasible.

E-mail workshops

E-mail workshops offer some of the same advantages as weblogs and wikis; however there are some integral differences. If each student is instructed to pass each draft to only one specific other student, regardless of whose draft is being reviewed, a round-robin-type workshop can be created. By instructing students to send all work as attachments, reviewers can use the *track changes* function to suggest changes and make comments. When the author's own draft has been to every student, it will be returned with all suggestions visible on one screen in multiple colours. This is useful because it allows authors to absorb criticism and feedback from many people at one time. If this same strategy were used on paper, the feedback would probably be illegible, cramped, or hopelessly distant from the physical part of each work that specific criticisms deal with.

Another possible application for the e-mail workshop is to create a class list service. This allows students to distribute drafts privately and instantaneously to peers any hour of the day. Because each response can be privately made to the author, this is a far more discreet method of criticism than weblogs or wikis. Creative writers often either need or crave instantaneous feedback. In classes that meet infrequently, such as once a week, works may languish in a creative limbo, not because authors have run out of ideas, but because they want to ask a question before continuing. E-mail workshops solve this problem. Any student in class, or the professor, can offer feedback as soon as they see the e-mailed document. While it is inevitable that some people will not answer, sending work to everyone increases the probability of receiving a meaningful reply.

Discussion boards

Discussion boards, which are online forums that document ongoing conversations, have very different application possibilities from weblogs, wikis and e-mail workshops. Conversation on discussion boards consists of threads that any member can add. They function similarly to a weblog in that sense, but are not intrinsically public documents. Teaching programs like Blackboard and WebCT contain blank discussion boards for every course.[4] Unlike any of the other tools described, a discussion board organizes all threads of a discussion like an outline. It is possible to see the subject heading of each thread and its order in the discussion with a quick glance. While discussion boards are more limited than other tools for actual workshopping, they are far better for discussion of ideas.

One pedagogical application for them allows students open forum to discuss assignments and obtain clarification on comments made by classroom peers. Because it is possible to see the subject of each conversation and each thread within a conversation, students need not wade through material they are not concerned with, as they would on a blog or a wiki. This allows students to focus attention on areas where they feel they need clarification or assistance. Most teaching programs automatically include the instructor in the membership of any discussion board, so this tool can also foster better student–teacher relations by allowing the instructor to address issues class-wide in the discussion forum and then answer questions that students have in subordinate threads. This streamlines the amount of time it takes to explain a new assignment or goal, hence, leaving more class time for workshop sessions and personalized feedback.

MOO communities

A MUD Object Oriented (MOO) community is an on-line virtual society in which a real person assumes an alternate persona and does everything possible to, not only authenticate and enrich that persona, but to become completely immersed in it.[5] The quest for rich and believable characters is one shared by fiction writers, narrative poets, dramatists, screen writers and, sometimes, even authors of short verse and songwriters. In a community in which perfect strangers constantly interact with a character the author created, it is possible to test every aspect of that character. Other community members may even ask pointed questions or force the character into virtual situations that call for actions and reactions outside of the plotline that the character was created for. This kind of character development and exposure to outside stimuli can foster the creation of characters with great depth, believability and a strong sense of personality.

While testing characters is by far the easiest application of a MUD Object Oriented (MOO) community, testing plot is also possible. Since a MOO community is a virtual environment, it is possible either to suggest plot threads and gauge the reactions of other community members, or to summarize plot as events that the character took part in while away from the community, then gauge interest and believability based on feedback received. While this kind of testing is more problematic than character testing due to the possibility that someone may steal an original plot thread and use it as their own, it also helps the author, as a precautionary measure, practice only telling the audience what is necessary to advance the plot and nothing more. This can help an author practice 'showing' rather than 'telling' and can help writers master both suspenseful writing and minimalist technique.

Creative writing software

A large body of new software is also emerging. These products include many programs for fiction, screenwriting, drama and non-fiction writing. The programs do more than just organize; they edit, give publication tips and often come attached to an on-line workshop that will provide live feedback to the student. Some of these programs even create storyboards for scripts. These applications are ideal for independent studies and lower level classes because they offer guidance through some of the more basic creative writing issues. While they are no substitute for an actual workshop, they may be useful for streamlining live workshops by eliminating some of the more common errors that classroom time is constantly and repetitively wasted correcting. The following programs have garnered some acclaim in the writing community: NewNovelist, Story Weaver, Power Writer, Storybase, Movie Magic Screenwriter, and Dramatica Pro. For reviews of new and accessible creative writing software, visit creative-writing-software-review. toptenreviews.com.[6]

Conclusion

Technological advance is inevitable, and in this new millennium, Creative Writing teachers have more pedagogical options than ever before. It is imperative to understand the new tools available before deciding whether or not to implement them. Therefore, it is the responsibility of Creative Writing faculty to sample new technology and assess its worth in each individual classroom. This is not a task that faculty should shy away from, but one that should be cherished as an opportunity to leave an indelible and progressive mark on a new generation of writers.

Notes

1. Some examples of easy to use blogs: www.writingblogs.org, www.seo-blog.org, and www.blogger.com (accessed 28 February 2012).
2. www.en.wikipedia.org/wiki/Main_Page (accessed 28 February 2012).
3. A free and easy to use wiki provider is www.projectforum.com (accessed 28 February 2012).
4. Information on Blackboard and WebCt can be found here: www.blackboard.com (accessed 28 February 2012).
5. Information on MUD Object Oriented (MOO) communities can be found here: www.well.ac.uk/wellclas/moo/MOOtools.htm (accessed 28 February 2012).
6. Reviews of new and accessible creative writing software can be found here: creative-writing-software-review.toptenreviews.com (accessed 28 February 2012).

24

Lancaster University's Creative Writing MA by Distance Learning

Graham Mort

The distance learning MA (DLMA) in Creative Writing at Lancaster University was established in 1999 and is a two-year, part-time option mediated through blended research and practice. It relates closely to its full-time, campus-based antecedent and terminates in an identical examination portfolio: 30,000 words of creative writing plus a self-critical reflective essay of 3,000 words. Entry to the course is based upon possession of a first degree in any discipline and a strong sample of creative writing.

Our primary assumption is that students are both committed and writing freely upon entry; our methodology is to bring together students working in poetry, fiction or scriptwriting as a study group directed by academic tutors who are practising writers. We do not teach literary genre or modules based on literary forms or techniques. The forge of literary production lies in the writing workshops where new work is critiqued then re-drafted. Our emphasis is upon composition, critical reading, reflection on the creative process and revision. Our view is that each new piece of writing invents unique developmental problems in relation to the student's creative intention. Those problems are addressed through a student-centred pedagogic process involving close textual engagement, supportive criticism and intensive writing practice.

In each biennial intake, the DLMA admits eighteen students to a virtual community where all communication is online vie email and our virtual learning environment (VLE). Information about the course, its procedures and assessment practices is available to students through a Postgraduate Handbook that is mounted on our postgraduate portal as an online resource.[1]

Tuition consists of twice-termly personal eLearning tutorials and a once-termly online writing conference. Over a two-year period, students undertake twelve tutorials (preceded by a diagnostic tutorial which addresses a proposed programme of work) and six online conferences. In the final term of the first year we also run a summer school where students meet their tutors and engage in a week of intensive face-to-face workshops, tutorials and readings.

Our students are still mainly from the UK, but are increasingly drawn to Lancaster via our website, finding us by subject searches rather than a desire for specific location. Given that they can attend our mandatory summer school, students can participate from anywhere in the world. For each intake we receive over fifty applications and choose eighteen students. Our teaching methodology is relatively cost-effective and reaches across a number of significant barriers: age, domestic commitments, geographical remoteness, illness or disability. Ease of access to learning seems the most obvious benefit of an MA studied through distance learning, but it also brings the benefits of a culturally diverse student constituency to the process.

The virtual academy is not infinite, but it creates a more inclusive demographic, allowing students from within and beyond the UK and EC to come together as a community of aspirant writers. Our MA groups have included students from the UK, Sweden, the USA, Japan, Singapore and Italy, including those managing mental health problems and coping with physical disabilities that would make attending a campus very difficult. Their ages range from 26–60 years. The benefits of this heterogeneous group (many of them experts in their own fields) is an experiential richness. This establishes a broad constituency of student writers exploring different styles, genres and thematic approaches, whilst also embodying a range of readers with individual histories, insights and experience to bring to bear on the emergent writing. So, the catholicity of distance learning recruitment mobilizes a wide range of human resources in the learning experience.

The DLMA is administered from Lancaster, but taught by off-campus tutors – a team of published professional writers who are experts in distance learning. The use of this flexible resource within our established academic framework allows us to deploy a 'virtual' department where personnel do not depend upon physical space and resources. They can work from home, fitting tuition into their personal writing schedules, pursuing their own development alongside that of their students in a reflexive way. This effectively doubles our limited departmental resources, giving us much more flexibility in matching tutors to students in terms of genre, gender, subject matter and technical approach.

In their writing tutorials, students submit 5,000 words of creative writing to their tutor accompanied by an 'assignment commentary' of around 1,000 words. The commentary promotes reflection, focusing on special difficulties or achievements in the writing, directing the attention of the tutor to where the student needs it most. Acting as an informed reader and expert practitioner, the tutor returns a detailed report on the creative work. This responds to the commentary, focuses closely on the texture of the writing, considers wider issues of structure or viewpoint, suggests strategies for revision and also refers to creative, pedagogic or other literature that might further the student's development. The student is encouraged to print out and store all assignments and essential correspondence in a Writing

Journal – this becomes the record of an original piece of research, jointly developed by both tutor and student that can be reviewed at any point in the course.

The Lancaster-based course convenor reads the reports of tutors and advises them on their tutorial approach. This is effective quality control, but it also creates an archive of pedagogic practice that is used in the training and induction of new tutors. A distinct advantage of distance learning programmes is the establishment of a comprehensive record of tutorial exchanges between tutors and students: an interesting contrast to the ephemeral nature of face-to-face tuition. The written process also allows a tutor to be strategic, dealing with problems incrementally in order to sustain the student's confidence.

Online conferences are organized into groups of six students led by one tutor. They are facilitated by the University's virtual learning environment and consist of conference facilities plus an Internet café where students can meet informally. Each student posts an assignment up to 3,000 words for the conference and responds critically to every other posting in around 600 words. The tutor acts as *agent provocateur*, stimulating critical discussion and cross-talk within a strict protocol. Again, the key process is to test new writing against a sympathetic, informed, but critical readership.

Our basic methodology is simple: electronic media are used to facilitate the easy exchange of writing. But the advantages of IT extend beyond mere exchange. The key advantage of distance learning involves its very use of distance: the spatial and temporal gap between reader and writer. Writing and reading skills are deployed at all levels in the process as pedagogic and creative processes converge. All literature inhabits a virtual domain, where typographically encrypted information stimulates an imaginative response from a reader we never meet. Distance learning in Creative Writing accurately replicates this relationship between readers, writers and text, but assigns interchangeable roles to the actors who alternate between writing and reading creatively and critically. This process is – crucially – underpinned by the tutor's own ongoing writing practice.

The advantage of electronic exchange lies in its very virtuality. Electronic drafts remain fluid, provisionally suspended in electronic solution: language, form and intention are emulsified, precipitated, then emulsified again by the critical intervention of tutors and peers in a reflexive process that persists until the final draft. Distance is re-defined as more symbolic than actual, since temporal and spatial distance is dissolved in a process that is formal in its protocols and structures, yet intimate in its responsiveness, speed and flexibility. Body language is removed from the tutorial process, just as literature removes it from orature to develop a newly expressive written form. Distance learning students deploy writing skills in a seamless creative/reflexive discourse, developing creative and critical expression simultaneously.

Virtual learning also carries the advantage of allowing skilled practitioners to intervene in their students' work – a difficult process in face-to-face workshops. The tutor can import the student's electronic text into their report and work on it through re-drafting or through annotating and recording changes. This is invaluable in *showing* rather than *telling* a student what might be technically or emotionally effective. It has a range of practical applications, including editing text that is descriptively over-laden, resetting line endings in a poem, identifying verbal patterns or repetitions, re-setting dialogue, adding sensory richness, conveying point of view and depicting consciousness. Such techniques empower the tutor as a creative practitioner rather than merely deploying them as a critical commentator, giving them a hands-on approach to teaching such as that deployed by musicians, sculptors, painters or dancers. An essentially performative element is added to pedagogic process.

The reflexive methodology of the DLMA found an extension in *Crossing Borders* (2001–6), a Lancaster University/ British Council mentoring project funded by the Council. Operating in eight Anglophone countries across sub-Saharan Africa, we enrolled over 300 African writers and a team of twenty-five UK-based mentors to mentor them. The British Council offices in each country acted as electronic postboxes, enabling work to be exchanged efficiently. The scheme was hugely successful in its reach and effectiveness and has revealed a significant new inflection of the assignment commentary. The reflective discourse in which creative work is enveloped has become a space where cultural and linguistic difference can be mediated. In work received from Africa in English for a UK or global audience, cultural and historical references, language styles and customs are all issues to be tested – even negotiated – in anticipation of a readership.

This pan-African network has stimulated a need for resources that could only practically be supplied via the Internet. Accordingly, we have created a *Crossing Borders* website with discussion boards, news and educational facilities.[2] The *Writers on Writing* section features a gallery of creative pieces by established writers accompanied by a reflective essay on the genesis, cultural provenance, technique and intention of each piece. This heterogeneous resource responds to our multi-cultural constituency and remains developmentally fluid, unlike print-based textbooks. A new virtual magazine was also launched to showcase the work of young Africans. This includes creative work, editorials and articles on professional development supplied by publishers, agents and editors.

The success of *Crossing Borders* suggests the possibility of developing a fully-fledged DLMA in the African context. The barriers to this process are fiscal rather than methodological. But overseas developments and the popularity of the DLMA have also stimulated our thinking about the use of virtual space on campus. We are now developing new systems of support through our virtual learning networks. The deployment of electronic social space, online conferences, research training and web-based publication offer enriched resources for both distance learning and campus-based students, showcasing creative work, enabling critical discourse and developing editorial and publishing skills. This will effectively unite our actual and virtual constituencies, creating a wider sense of community and a rich and stimulating learning environment. Our postgraduate learning communities have been transformed into transcultural networks through eLearning. The implications and opportunities of this phenomenon are now being explored through the establishment of an eLearning Ph.D. programme, the extension of our virtual learning and research environments, and the founding of our Centre for Transcultural Writing and Research.[3]

Notes

1. www.transculturalwriting.com/vre/index.php?title=Main_Page   (accessed 28 February 2012).
2. www.radiophonics.britishcouncil.org (accessed 28 February 2012).
3. www.transculturalwriting.com (accessed 28 February 2012).

Further Reading

Addonizio, Kim and Laux, Dorianne, *The Poet's Companion* (New York: Norton, 1997).

Aldridge, John W., 'The New American Assembly-Line Fiction,' *American Scholar* 59 (1990): 17–38.

Aldridge, John W., *Classics and Contemporaries* (Minneapolis: Augsburg Fortress Publishers, 1992).

Andreasen, Nancy C., *The Creating Brain: The Neuroscience of Genius* (New York: Dana Press, 2005).

Arts and Humanities Research Council (AHRC), www.ahrc.ac.uk (accessed 28 February 2012).

Avery, S., Bryan, C. and Wisker, G., Eds., *Innovations in Teaching English and Textual Studies* (London: Staff and Educational Development Association, 1999).

AWP *(Association of Writers and Writing Programs in United States), AWP Director's Handbook*, www.awpwriter.org/membership/dh_4.htm (accessed 28 February 2012).

AWP Official Guide to Writing Programs (Paradise, CA: Associated Writing Programs, Dustbooks, Annual), 2008.

AWP Official Guide to Writing Programs, www.awpwriter.org Type 'guide' in AWP search area (accessed 28 February 2012).

Babbitt, Irving, 'On Being Creative,' *On Being Creative and Other Essays* (Boston: Houghton Mifflin, 1932).

Babbitt, Irving, *Rousseau and Romanticism* (Austin: University of Texas Press, 1979).

Bakhtin, M.M., 'Epic and Novel,' *Essentials of the Theory of Fiction*, Ed. Michael J. Hoffman and Patrick Murphy (Durham: Duke UP, 1988), pp. 48–69.

Bartholomae, David and Petrosky, Anthony, Eds., *Ways of Reading: An Anthology for Writers*, 5th edn (New York: St. Martin's Press, 1999).

Bassnett, Susan and Grundy, Peter, *Language through Literature: Creative Language Teaching through Literature* (London: Longman, 1993).

Bawer, Bruce, 'Dave Smith's "Creative Writing",' *New Criterion* 4 (December, 1985): 27–33.

Beach, Christopher, 'Careers in Creativity: The Poetry Academy in the 1990s,' *Western Humanities Review 50*, Spring (1996): 15.

Bennett, Andrew and Royle, Nicholas, 'Creative Writing,' *An Introduction to Literature, Criticism and Theory* (Harlow: Longman, 2004), pp. 85–92.

Bernays, Anne and Painter, Pamela, Eds., *What If?: Writing Exercises for Fiction Writers* (New York: Harper Collins, 1990).

Bernstein, Charles, 'Optimism and Critical Excess (Process),'*A Poetics* (Cambridge, MA: Harvard University Press, 1992).

Bernstein, Charles, Ed., *Close Listening: Poetry and the Performed Word* (Oxford: Oxford University Press, 1998).

Bishop, Wendy, *Released Into Language: Options for Teaching Creative Writing* (Urbana, IL: National Council of Teachers of English, 1990).

Bishop, Wendy, 'Crossing the Lines: On Creative Composition and Composing Creative Writing,' *Writing on the Edge* 4, 2, (Spring 1993): 117–33.

Bishop, Wendy, 'Afterword – Colors of a Different Horse: On Learning to Like Teaching Creative Writing,' *Rethinking Creative Writing Theory and Pedagogy,*

Eds. Hans Ostrom and Wendy Bishop (Urbana, IL: National Council of Teachers of English, 1994), pp. 280–95.

Bishop, Wendy, *The Elements of Alternate Style* (Portsmouth, NH: Boynton/Cook, 1997).

Bishop, Wendy, 'Places to Stand: The Reflective Writer-Teacher-Writer in Composition,' *College Composition and Communication* 51, 1 (September 1999): 9–31.

Bishop, Wendy, *Thirteen Ways of Looking for a Poem: A Guide to Writing Poetry* (New York: Longman, 2000).

Bishop, Wendy and Ostrom, Hans, Eds., *Colors of a Different Horse: Rethinking Creative Writing Theory and Pedagogy* (Urbana, IL: National Council of Teachers of English, 1994).

Bishop, Wendy and Ostrom, Hans, Eds., *Genre and Writing: Issues, Arguments Alternatives* (Portsmouth, NH: Boynton/Cook, 1997).

Bishop, Wendy and Hans Ostrom, Eds., *The Subject Is Story*, (Portsmouth, New Hampshire: Boynton/Cook, 1997).

Bizzaro, Patrick, *Responding to Student Poems: Applications of Critical Theory* (Urbana, IL: National Council of Teachers of English, 1993).

Blackboard and WebCT Virtual Learning Environments, www.blackboard.com (accessed 28 February 2012).

Blogging Websites, writingblogs.org, seo-blog.org, www.blogger.com (accessed 28 February 2012).

Bloom, Benjamin, Ed., *Taxonomy of Educational Objectives: the Classification of Educational Goals. Handbook 1: Cognitive Domain* (New York: McKay, 1956).

Bourdieu, Pierre, *Distinction: A Social Critique of the Judgment of Taste*, Trans. Richard Nice (Cambridge, MA: Harvard University Press, 1984).

Broderick, Danny, NAWE Members' Archives, 1999, www.nawe.co.uk (accessed 28 February 2012).

Burton, Deirdre, 'Through a Glass Darkly – through Dark Glasses,' Ed. Ron Carter, *Language and Literature: An Introductory Reader in Stylistics* (London: Allen & Unwin, 1982), pp. 195–216.

Camoin, François, 'The Workshop and Its Discontents,' *Rethinking Creative Writing Theory and Pedagogy*, Eds. Hans Ostrom and Wendy Bishop (Urbana, IL: National Council of Teachers of English, 1994), pp. 3–7.

Cantrell, Mary, 'Teaching and Evaluation: Why Bother?' *Power and Identity in the Creative Writing Classroom*, Ed. Anna Leahy (Clevedon: Multilingual Matters, 2005).

Carter, Ronald, *Language and Creativity: The Art of Common Talk* (London and New York: Routledge, 2004).

Carter, Ronald and McRae, John, Eds., *Language, Literature and the Learner: Creative Classroom Practice* (London: Longman, 1996).

Casanova, Pascale, *La Republica Mundial de las Letras* (Madrid: Anagrama, 2001).

Ciabattari, Jane, 'A Revolution of Sensibility,' *Poets & Writers* (Jan./Feb. 2005): 69–72.

Ciardi, John and Williams, Miller, Eds., *How a Poem Means* (Boston: Houghton Mifflin Co., 1975).

Cixous, Hélène, 'Writing Blind: Conversations with the Donkey,' Trans. Eric Prenowitz, *Stigmata: Escaping Texts* (London: Routledge, 1998), pp. 139–52.

Cook, Jon, 'A Brief History of Workshops,' *The Creative Writing Coursebook*, Eds. Julia Bell and Paul Magrs (New York: Macmillan – now Palgrave Macmillan, 2001), pp. 296–303.

Cook, Jon, 'Creative Writing as a Research Method,' *Research Methods for English Studies*, Ed. Gabriele Griffin (Edinburgh: Edinburgh University Press, 2005), pp. 195–212.

Corcoran, Bill, Hayhoe, Mike and Pradl, Gordon, Eds., *Knowledge in the Making: Challenging the Text in the Classroom* (Portsmouth, NH: Boynton/Cook, Heinemann, 1994).

Cowan, Andrew, 'Questions, Questions,' *Writing in Education* 41 (2007): 56–61.

Creative Writing Software Reviews, creative-writing-software-review.toptenreviews. com (accessed 28 February 2012).

Crossing Borders-African Writing, www.transculturalwriting.com/radiophonics (accessed 28 February 2012).

Culler, Jonathan, *Structuralist Poetics: Structuralism, Linguistics, and the Study of Literature* (Ithaca, NY: Cornell UP, 1975).

Dawson, Paul, *Creative Writing and the New Humanities* (London: Routledge), 2005.

Dooley, David, 'The Contemporary Workshop Aesthetic,' *Hudson Review* 43 (1990): 259–80.

Downing, David, Hurlbert, C., and Mathieu, P., Eds., *Beyond English Inc.* (Portsmouth NH: Heinemann Boynton/Cook, 2002).

Doyle, Brian, *English and Englishness* (London: Methuen, 1989).

DuPlessis, Rachel Blau, *The Pink Guitar: Writing as Feminist Practice* (New York: Routledge, 1990).

DuPlessis, Rachel Blau, 'Draft 55: Quiptych,' *The Best American Poems 2004*, Ed. Lyn Hejinian (New York: Scribner, 2004), pp. 75–9.

DuPlessis, Rachel Blau, 'Pledge,' *Blue Studios: Poetry and its Cultural Work* (Tuscaloosa: University of Alabama Press, 2006), pp. 209–51.

Earnshaw, Steven, Ed., *The Handbook of Creative Writing* (Edinburgh: Edinburgh University Press, 2007).

Easthope, Antony and Thompson, John O., Eds., *Contemporary Poetry Meets Modern Theory* (Hemel Hempstead: Harvester Wheatsheaf, 1991).

Elbow, Peter, 'Ranking, Evaluating, and Liking: Sorting Out Three Forms of Judgment,' *College English* 55.2 (Feb. 1993): 187–206.

Elbow, Peter and Belanoff, Pat, *A Community of Writers* (New York: McGraw-Hill, 1995).

Electronic Poetry Center, www.epc.buffalo.edu (accessed 28 February 2012).

Eliot, George, *Middlemarch* (London: Penguin, 2003).

Eliot, George, *Daniel Deronda* (London: Penguin, 2004).

Eliot, George, *Scenes from Clerical Life* (London: Penguin, 2005).

Emerson, R.W., 'The American Scholar' (1837), in *Selected Essays* (New York: Penguin Books: 1982).

Emig, Janet, *The Composing Process of Twelfth Graders* (Urbana, IL: National Council of Teachers of English, 1971).

English Subject Centre Survey of English Curriculums and Teaching in United Kingdom Education, Report Series Number 8, www.english.heacademy.ac.uk/ explore/publications/currsurvey.php (accessed 28 February 2012).

English Subject Centre Website, www.english.heacademy.ac.uk (accessed 28 February 2012).

English Subject Centre Magazine, *Wordplay*, www.english.heacademy.ac.uk/explore/ publications/magazine/index.php (accessed 28 February 2012).

English, James, *The Economy of Prestige* (Cambridge, MA: Harvard University Press, 2005).

Epstein, Joseph, 'Who Killed Poetry?' *Commentary* 86 (August 1988): 13–20.

Evans, Colin Evans, *English People: the Experience of Teaching and Learning English in British Universities* (Buckingham: Open University Press, 1993).

Evans, Colin, Ed., *Developing University English Teaching* (Lampeter: Edwin Mellen Press, 1995).

Everett, Nick, 'Creative Writing and English,' *Cambridge Quarterly* 35, 4, (2005): 231–42.

Fenza, D.W., 'Growth of Creative Writing Programs,' *The Writers's Chronicle*, www.awpwriter.org/aboutawp/index.htm (accessed 28 February 2012).

Fenza, D.W., 'Creative Writing and Its Discontents,' *The Writer's Chronicle* (Mar/April, 2000), www.awp.org/magazine/index.htm (accessed 28 February 2012).

Ferry, Anne, *The Title to the Poem* (Stanford, CA: Stanford University Press, 1996).

Fieldhouse, Roger, and Associates, *A History of Modern British Adult Education* (Leicester: NIACE, 1996), pp. vii–viii.

Flower, Linda and Hayes, John R., 'A Cognitive-Process Theory of Writing,' *College Composition and Communication* 32 (1981): 365–87.

Forster, E.M., *Aspects of the Novel* (New York: Harcourt, Brace & Company, 1956).

Foucault, Michel, *The Archaeology of Knowledge*, Trans. A.M. Sheridan Smith (New York: Pantheon, 1972).

Foucault, Michel, *The History of Sexuality, Volume I: An Introduction*, Trans. Robert Hurley (New York: Vintage, 1980).

Foucault, Michel, *Power/Knowledge: Selected Interviews and Other Writings 1972–1977*, Ed. Colin Gordon, Trans. Colin Gordon, Leo Marshall, John Mepham and Kate Soper (New York: Pantheon, 1988).

Framework for Higher Education Quality in United Kingdom, www.qaa.ac.uk/Publications/InformationAndGuidance/Pages/the-framework-for-higher-education-qualifications-in-England-Wales-and-Northern-Ireland.aspx (9 November 2011).

Freire, Paulo, *Pedagogy of the Oppressed*, Trans. Myra Bergman Ramos (Portsmouth, NH: Boynton/Cook, Heinemann, 2003).

Fricker, Harald and Zymner, Rüdiger, *Einübung in die Literaturwissenschaft: Parodieren geht über Studieren* (Zürich: Schöningh, 1993).

Frost, Robert, *Robert Frost: Poetry & Prose* (New York: Holt, Rinehart and Winston, 1972).

Gardner, John, *The Art of Fiction: Notes on Craft for Young Writers* (New York: Vintage, 1991).

Geok-lin Lim, Shirley, 'The Strangeness of Creative Writing: An Institutional Query,' *Pedagogy* 3 (Spring 2003): 157.

George, Elizabeth, *Write Away: One Novelist's Approach to Fiction and the Writing Life* (New York: HarperCollins/Perennial Currents, 2004).

Goldberg, Natalie, *Writing Down the Bones* (Boston: Shambhala, 1996).

Goodman, Sharon and O'Halloran, Kieran, Eds., *The Art of English: Literary Creativity* (Basingstoke: Palgrave Macmillan, 2006).

Goodman, William, 'Thinking About Readers,' *Daedalus* (Winter, 1983): 65–84.

Graham, Robert, The Iowa Writers' Workshop, February 2002, www.nawe.co.uk (accessed 28 February 2012).

Green, Keith, 'Creative Writing, Language and Evaluation,' *Working Papers on the Web* 2 (November 2001), extra.shu.ac.uk/wpw/value/wpw.htm (accessed 28 February 2012).

Grimes, Tom, Ed., *The Workshop: Seven Decades of the Iowa Writers' Workshop* (New York: Hyperion, 1999).

Gwynn, R.S., 'No Biz Like Po' Biz,' *Sewanee Review* 100 (1992): 311–23.

Haffenden, John, *Viewpoints: Poets in Conversation* (London: Faber & Faber, 1981).

Halsey, A.H., 'British Universities and Intellectual Life,' *Universities Quarterly* 12 (1957–1958): 148.

Harper, Graeme, Ed., *Teaching Creative Writing* (London: Continuum, 2006).

Harper, Graeme, and Kroll, Jeri, Eds., *Creative Writing Studies: Practice, Research and Pedagogy* (Clevedon: Multilingual Matters, 2008).

Harris, Mike, 'Are Writers Really There When They're Writing about Their Writing? And can we theorise about what they say they do? *Creative Writing Theory and Practice* 1, 1 (March 2009): 31–49.

Hejinian, Lyn, 'The Guard,' *The Cold of Poetry* (Los Angeles: Sun and Moon, 1974, reprinted 1994), pp. 11–37.

Hejinian, Lyn, *The Language of Inquiry* (Berkeley: University of California Press, 2000).

Hemple, Amy, 'Captain Fiction,' *Vanity Fair* (December 1984): 90–3, 126–8.

Henry, Brian and Zawacki, Andrew, *The Verse Book of Interviews* (Seattle, WA: Wave Books, 2005).

Herbert, W.N. and Hollis, Mathew, Eds., *Strong Words* (Northumberland: Bloodaxe, 2000).

Higher Education Academy in United Kingdom, www.heacademy.ac.uk (24 November 2011).

Higher Education Funding Council for England (HEFCE), hefce.ac.uk (accessed 28 February 2012).

Higher Education Statistics Agency in United Kingdom, www.hesa.ac.uk (accessed 28 February 2012).

Holland, Siobhan, *Creative Writing: A Good Practice Guide, Report Series No. 6*, English Subject Centre, February, 2003, www.english.heacademy.ac.uk/explore/resources/creative/guide.php (accessed 28 February 2012).

Howe, Susan, *My Emily Dickinson (1985)* (New York: New Directions, 2007).

Hugo, Richard, *The Triggering Town: Lectures and Essays on Poetry and Writing* (New York: W.W. Norton, 1979).

Irving, John, 'Interview,' *The Daily Show with Jon Stewart* (Comedy Central, 17 August, 2005).

Jakobson, Roman, *Fundamentals of Language* (The Hague and Paris: Mouton, 1975).

James, Gill, 'The Undergraduate Creative Writing Workshop,' *Creative Writing Theory and Practice* 1, 1 (March 2009): 50–66.

James, Henry, *The Art of the Novel: Critical Prefaces* (New York: Scribners, 1934).

Jarrell, Randall, *Poetry & the Age* (New York: The Ecco Press, 1953).

Johnson, Charles, 'Storytelling and the Alpha Narrative,' *Southern Review* 41 (Winter 2005): 151–9.

Kerridge, Richard, 'Creative Writing and Academic Accountability,' *New Writing* 1 (2004): 3–5.

Knights, Ben, *From Reader to Reader* (Hemel Hempstead: Harvester Wheatsheaf, 1993).

Knights, Ben and Thurgar-Dawson, Chris, *Active Reading* (London: Continuum, 2006).

Kraft, Ulrich, 'Unleashing Creativity,' *Scientific American Mind* 16, 1 (2005): 16–23.

Kuzma, Greg, 'The Catastrophe of Creative Writing,' *Poetry* 148 (1986): 342–54.

Leahy, Anna, Ed., *The Authority Project: Power and Identity in the Creative Writing Classroom* (Clevedon: Multilingual Matters, 2005).

Leavis, F.R., *English in Our Time and the University: The Clark Lectures* (Cambridge, UK: Cambridge University Press, 1979).

Levy, Andrew, *The Culture and Commerce of the American Short Story* (Cambridge, MA: Cambridge University Press, 1993).

Light, Geoffrey, 'From the Personal to the Public: Conceptions of Creative Writing in Higher Education,' *Higher Education* 43 (March 2002): 265–66.

Lowell, Robert, *Collected Poems* (New York: Farrar, Straus and Giroux, 2003).

Mansbridge, Albert, *The Trodden Road* (London: Dent, 1940).

Matthiessen, F.O., 'The Responsibilities of the Critic,' *American Literature, American Culture*, Ed., Gordon Hunter (New York: Oxford UP, 1999), pp. 303–12.

May, Steve, 'Teaching Creative Writing at Undergraduate Level: Why, how and does it work?' (Report on English Subject Centre sponsored research project, 2003), english.heacademu.ac.uk/explore/projects/archive/creative/creative3.php (accessed 28 February 2012).

May, Steve, *Doing Creative Writing* (London: Routledge, 2007).

Maybin, Janet and Swann, Joan, Eds., *The Art of English: Everyday Creativity* (Basingstoke: Palgrave Macmillan, 2006).

Mayer, Bernadette, 'Experiments,' Eds. Bruce Andrews and Charles Bernstein, *The L=A=N=G=U=A=G=E Book* (Carbondale, IL: Southern Illinois UP, 1984), pp. 80–3.

Mayer, Bernadette and Bernstein, Charles, *List of Poetic Experiments*, www.writing.upenn.edu/bernstein/experiments.html (accessed 28 February 2012).

Mayers, Tim, *Writing Craft: Composition, Creative Writing and the Future of English Studies* (Pittsburgh, PA: University of Pittsburgh Press, 2005).

McLoughlin, Nigel, *Database for Resources and Articles to the Theory of Pedagogy in Creative Writing*, www.english.heacademy.ac.uk/explore/projects/archive/creative/creative8.php (accessed 28 February 2012).

McRae, John, *Wordsplay* (Basingstoke: Macmillan – now Palgrave Macmillan, 1992).

Menand, Louis, quote from review in *New Yorker*, American Studies Audio Cassette (London: Highbridge Audio, October, 2002).

Middleton, Peter, *Distant Reading: Performance, Readership, and Consumption in Contemporary Poetry* (Tuscaloosa, AL: University of Alabama Press, 2005).

Miles, Robert, 'Creative Writing, Contemporary Theory and the English Curriculum,' *Teaching Creative Writing: Theory and Practice*, Eds. Moira Monteith and Robert Miles (Buckingham: Open University Press, 1992), pp. 34–44.

Miller, Perry, *The Raven and The Whale* (New York: Harcourt, Brace, and World, 1956).

Milne, Drew, Ed., *Modern Critical Thought: An Anthology of Theorists Writing on Theorists* (Oxford: Blackwell, 2003).

Mimpress, Rob, 'Rewriting the Individual: a Critical Study of the Creative Writing Workshop,' *Writing in Education*, NAWE Members' Archives, www.nawe.co.uk (No. 26, 2002), (accessed 28 February 2012).

Monteith, Moira and Miles, Robert, Eds, *Teaching Creative Writing: Theory and Practice*, (Buckingham: The Open University Press, 1992).

Moodle, moodle.org and en.wikipedia.org/wiki/Moodle (accessed 28 February 2012).

MOO Tools and Communities, Mootools.net and en.wikipedia.org/wiki/MooTools (accessed 28 February 2012).

Moretti, Franco, *Signs Taken for Wonders: On the Sociology of Literary Forms* (London: Verso, 2005).

Morgan, Wendy, *A Poststructuralist English Classroom: The Example of Ned Kelly* (Melbourne: Victoria Association for the Teaching of English, 1992).

Morley, David, *The Cambridge Introduction to Creative Writing* (New York: Cambridge University Press, 2007).

Morley, Dave and Worpole, Ken, Eds., *The Republic of Letters: Working Class Writing and Local Publishing* (London: Minority Press, 1982).

Morrison, Toni, 'Unspeakable Things Unspoken: The Afro-American Presence in American Literature,' *American Literature, American Culture*, Ed. Gordon Hunter (New York: Oxford UP, 1999), pp. 538–58.

Motte, Warren F., Ed., *Oulipo: A Primer of Potential Literature* (Lincoln, NE: University of Nebraska Press, 1986).

Moxley, Joseph, Ed., *Creative Writing in America: Theory and Pedagogy* (Urbana, IL National Council of Teachers of English, 1989).

Murray, Les, *The Paperbark Tree: Selected Prose* (Manchester: Carcanet Press, 1992).

Myers, D.G., *The Elephants Teach: Creative Writing since 1880* (New Jersey: Prentice Hall, 1996 and 2006).

Nash, Walter, *An Uncommon Tongue: The Uses and Resources of English* (London: Routledge, 1992).

Nash, Walter and Stacey, David, *Creating Texts: An Introduction to the Study of Composition* (London and New York: Longman, 1997).

National Council of Teachers of English (NCTE), www.ncte.org (accessed 28 February 2012).

O'Rourke, Rebecca, *Creative Writing: Education, Culture and Community* (Leicester: NIACE, 2005).

O'Toole, Shaun, *Transforming Texts* (London: Routledge, 2003).

Odier, Daniel, *The Job: Interviews with William Burroughs* (London: Cape, 1970).

Olson, Charles, *Collected Prose*, Eds. Donald Allen and Benjamin Friedlander (Berkeley, CA: University of California Press, 1997).

Oppen, George, 'Statement on Poetics,' *Sagetrieb* 3, 3 (Winter 1984): 25–7.

Ostrom, Hans, 'Undergraduate Creative Writing: The Unexamined Subject,' *Writing on the Edge*1, 1 (Fall 1989): 55–65.

Ostrom, Hans, 'Introduction: Of Radishes and Shadows, Theory and Pedagogy,' Eds. Wendy Bishop and Hans Ostrom, *Colours of a Different Horse: Rethinking Creative Writing Theory and Pedagogy* (Urbana, IL: National Council of Teachers of English,1994) pp. xi–xxxiii.

Ostrom, Hans, 'Countee Cullen: How Teaching Rewrites the Genre of Writer,' *Genres of Writing*, Eds. Wendy Bishop and Hans Ostrom (New York: Heinemann, 1997).

Ostrom, Hans, 'Carom Shots: Reconceptualizing Imitation and Its Uses in Creative Writing Courses,' *Teaching Writing Creatively*, Ed. David Starkey (Portsmouth, NH: Heinemann/Boynton-Cook, 1998), pp. 164–72.

Ostrom, Hans, Bishop, Wendy, and Haake, Katharine, *Metro: Journeys in Writing Creatively* (New York: Longman, 2000).

Padgett, Ron, *Creative Reading* (Urbana, IL: National Council of Teachers of English, 1997).

Peers, Robert, *Adult Education* (London: Routledge, 1959, 1972).

PENNSound, www.writing.upenn.edu/pennsound/ (accessed 28 February 2012).

Penrose, Ann. M and Sitko, Barbara, Eds., *Hearing Ourselves Think: Cognitive Research in the College Writing Classroom* (New York: Oxford UP, 1993).

Perloff, Marjorie, 'Theory and/in the Creative Writing Classroom,' *AWP Newsletter* (November/December, 1987): 1–4.

Peters, R.S., 'Education as Initiation,' *Theory of Education: Studies of Significant Innovation in Western Educational Thought*, Eds. J. Bowen and P.R. Hobson (Brisbane: John Wiley, 1990).

Poe, Edgar Allen, 'Review of Hawthorne – Twice Told Tales,' *Grahams Magazine* (May, 1842): 298–300.

Poe, Edgar Allen, 'The Philosophy of Composition,' *Grahams Magazine* (April, 1846): 163–7.

Pope, Rob, *Textual Intervention: Critical and Creative Strategies for Literary Studies* (London: Routledge, 1995).

Pope, Rob, *The English Studies Book*, 2nd edn. (London: Routledge, 2002).

Pope, Rob, 'Rewriting Texts, Reconstructing the Subject: Work as Play on the Critical-Creative Interface,' *Teaching Literature: A Companion*, Ed. Tanya Agathocleous and Ann Dean (New York and London: Palgrave Macmillan, 2003), pp. 105–24.

Pope, Rob, *Creativity: Theory, History, Practice* (London: Routledge, 2005).

Pope, Rob, 'Critical-Creative Rewriting,' *Teaching Creative Writing*, Ed. Graeme Harper (London: Continuum, 2006), pp. 130–46.

Prose, Francine, *Blue Angel* (New York: Harper Collins, 2000).

Prose, Francine, *Reading Like a Writer: A Guide for People Who Love Books and for Those Who Want to Write Them* (New York: Harper Collins, 2006).

Putnam, Hilary, *Meaning and the Moral Sciences* (London: Routledge & Kegan Paul, 1978).

QAA (Quality Assurance Association in United Kingdom), www.qaa.ac.uk (accessed 28 February 2012).

Radavich, David, 'Creative Writing in the Academy,' *Profession* (1999): 106–12.

Ramey, Lauri, 'Creative Writing and English Studies: Two Approaches to Literature,' www.english.heacademy.ac.uk/find/search (accessed 28 February 2012).

Rankine, Claudia and Spahr, Juliana, Eds., *American Woman Poets in the 21st Century: Where Lyric Meets Language* (Middletown, CT: Wesleyan University Press, 2002).

Ravitch, Diane, 'Would You Want to Study at a Bloomberg School?' *Wall Street Journal* (May 12, 2005): A16.

Research Assessment Exercise in United Kingdom (RAE), www.rae.ac.uk (accessed 28 February 2012).

Richter, David H., Ed., *Falling into Theory: Conflicting Views on Reading and Literature* (Boston: Bedford Books of St. Martin's Press, 1994).

Riding, Laura, *The Laura (Riding) Jackson Reader*, Ed. Elizabeth Friedmann (New York: Persea Books, 2005).

Riley, Denise, *The Words of Selves: Identification, Solidarity, Irony* (Palo Alto, CA: Stanford University Press, 2000).

Ritter, Kelly and Vanderslice, Stephanie, Eds., *Can It Really Be Taught?* (New York: Heinemann Boynton/Cook, 2007).

Robinson, Marilynne, *The Death of Adam: Essays on Modern Thought* (New York: Picador, 2005).

Rowbotham, Sheila, *Hidden from History: 300 Years of Women's Oppression and the Fight Against It* (London: Pluto Press, 1977).

Saltzman, Arthur, 'On Not Being Nice: Sentimentality and the Creative Writing Class,' *Midwest Quarterly* 44 (Spring 2003): 324.

Satyamurti, Carole, 'First time ever: writing the poem in potential space,' Eds. Carole Satyamurti and Hamish Canham, *Acquainted with the Night* (London: Karnac, 2003), p. 31.

Scholes, Robert, *Textual Power: Literary Theory and the Teaching of English* (New Haven, CT: Yale University Press, 1985).

Scholes, Robert, *The Rise and Fall of English: Reconstructing English as a Discipline* (New Haven: Yale University Press, 1998).

Scholes, Robert, Comley, Nancy and Ulmer, Gregory, *Text Book: An Introduction to Literary Language*, 2nd edn. (New York: St. Martin's Press, 1995).

Schon, Donald, *Educating the Reflective Practitioner* (San Francisco, CA: Jossey-Bass, 1987).

Schon, Donald, *The Reflective Practitioner: How Professionals Think in Action* (Aldershot: Ashgate Publishing, 2006).

Schramm, Margaret, et al., 'The Undergraduate English Major,' *ADE Bulletin* (Spring/Fall 2003): 68–91.

Shapiro, Karl, *V-Letter and Other Poems* (New York: Reynal and Hitchcock, 1944).

Shapiro, Karl, 'University' [poem], *New and Selected Poems, 1940–1986* (Chicago: Smith, and New York: Pantheon, 1972).

Shapiro, Karl, 'Notes on Raising a Poet,' *Seriously Meeting Karl Shapiro*, Ed., Sue B. Walker (Mobile, AL: Negative Capability Press, 1993), pp. 109–30.

Shelnutt, Eve, 'Notes from a Cell: Creative Writing Programs in Isolation,' *Creative Writing in America: Theory and Pedagogy*, Ed. Joseph M. Moxley (Urbana, IL: National Council of Teachers of English, 1989), pp. 3–24.

Sheppard, Rob, 'The Necessity of Poetics,' *Pores* 1 (October, 2001), www.pores.bbk.ac.uk (accessed 28 February 2012).

Sheppard, Rob, *The Necessity of Poetics* (Liverpool: Ship of Fools Liverpool, 2002).

Sheppard, Rob and Thurston, Scott, *Supplementary Discourses in Creative Writing Teaching in Higher Education* English Subject Centre Website, www.english.heacademy.ac.uk/find/search (accessed 28 February 2012).

Smiley, Jane, *Thirteen Ways of Looking at a Novel* (New York: Knopf, 2005).

Spahr, Juliana, *Spiderwasp or Literary Criticism?* (New York: Explosive Books, 1998).

Spahr, Juliana, Wallace, Mark, Prevallet, Kristin and Rehm, Pam, Eds., *A Poetics of Criticism* (Buffalo, NY: Leave Publications, 1994).

Spark, Debra, *Twenty Under Thirty: Best Stories by America's New Young Writers* (New York: Scribners, 1986).

Spellings, Margaret, *Report on Future of Higher Education in United States*, www.ed.gov/ (accessed 28 February 2012).

Spingarn, J.E., 'The New Criticism' (1910), *Creative Criticism and Other Essays* (New York: Harcourt Brace, 1931).

Spiro, Jane, *Creative Poetry Writing* (Oxford: Oxford University Press, 2004).

Starkey, David, Ed., *Teaching Writing Creatively* (Portsmouth, NH: Teachers of English, 1994).

Stegner, Wallace, *On Teaching and Writing Fiction* (New York: Penguin, 2002).

Stein, Gertrude, 'Henry James,' *Four in America* (New Haven, CT: Yale University Press, 1947).

Stevens, Wallace, 'Adagia,' *Opus Posthumous*. rev. edn. (London: Faber and Faber, 1990), pp. 184–202.

Stevens, Wallace, 'The Irrational Element in Poetry (1939),' *Opus Posthumous*. rev. edn. (London: Faber and Faber, 1990), pp. 224–33.

Stewart, Garrett, *Reading Voices: Literature and the Phonotext* (Berkeley: University of California Press, 1990) and www.ubuweb.com (accessed 28 February 2012).

Thomas, Dylan, *Dylan Thomas, The Broadcasts*, Ed. Ralph Maud (London: Dent & Sons, 1991).

Thomson, Jack, Ed., *Reconstructing Literature Teaching* (Norwood, SA: Australian Association for the Teaching of English, 1992).

Tighe, Carl, 'Creative Writing?' *Writing in Education* 40 (2006): 51–7.

Transcultural Writing, www.transculturalwriting.com (accessed 28 February 2012).

Ubu Web at www.ubuweb.com (accessed 28 February 2012).

University of Buckinghamshire, bucks.ac.uk (accessed 28 February 2012).

University of Gloucester, www.glos.ac.uk (accessed 28 February 2012).

University of Indiana, www.indiana.edu/~mfawrite/ (accessed 28 February 2012).

University of Iowa, www.uiowa.edu/~iww (accessed 28 February 2012).

Vanderslice, Stephanie, 'Rethinking Ways to Teach Young Writers: Response and Evaluation in the Creative Writing Course,' *Teacher Commentary on Student Papers*. Ed. Ode Ogede (Westport, CT: Bergin & Garvey, 2002), pp. 81–8.

Voss, Arthur, *The American Short Story: A Critical Survey* (Oklahoma: Oklahoma University Press, 1973).

Wandor, Michelene, 'Creative Writing and Pedagogy 1: Self Expression? Whose Self and What Expression?' *New Writing: The International Journal for the Practice and Theory of Creative Writing* 1, 2 (2004): 112–23.

Wandor, Michelene, *The Author is Not Dead, Merely Somewhere Else: Creative Writing Reconceived* (Basingstoke: Palgrave Macmillan, 2008).

Wilbers, Stephen, *The Iowa Writers' Workshop* (Iowa City: University of Iowa Press, 1980).

WIKIs, www.projectsforum.com (accessed 28 February 2012).

Wikipedia, www.en.wikipedia.org/wiki/Main_Page (accessed 28 February 2012).

Wood, Anthony, *Athenae Oxonienses: an Exact History of all the Writers and Bishops who have had their Education in the University of Oxford from 1500 to 1690* (Oxford: Ecclesiastical History Society, 1848).

Woolf, Tobias, *Old School* (London: Bloomsbury, 2004).

Useful websites

Arts and Humanities Research Council (AHRC) www.ahrc.ac.uk (accessed 28 February 2012).

Asia-Pacific Partnership of Writers, apwriters.org (accessed 28 February 2012).

Association of Writers and Writing Programs (AWP), www.awpwriter.org (accessed 28 February 2012).

Australian Association of Writing Programs (AAWP), www.aawp.org.au (accessed 28 February 2012).

Blackboard and WebCT Virtual Learning Environments, www.blackboard.com (accessed 28 February 2012).

Blogging Websites, writingblogs.org, seo-blog.org, www.blogger.com (accessed 28 February 2012).

Creative Writing Software Reviews, creative-writing-software-review.toptenreviews.com (accessed 28 February 2012).

Creative Writing Teaching and Research Benchmark Statements in UK, www.heacademy.ac.uk (Accessed 28 February 2012).

Crossing Borders-African Writing, transculturalwriting.com/radiophonics (accessed 28 February 2012).

Electronic Poetry Center, www/epc.buffalo.edu (accessed 28 February 2012).

English Subject Centre, www.english.heacademy.ac.uk This site contains information and resources on teaching English, both print and web-based (accessed 28 February 2012).

Higher Education Funding Council for England (HEFCE), hefce.ac.uk (accessed 28 February 2012).

Holland, Siobhan, *Creative Writing: A Good Practice Guide*, Report Series No. 6, English Subject Centre, February, 2003, www.english.heacademy.ac.uk/explore/resources/creative/guide.php (accessed 28 February 2012).

International Centre for Creative Writing Research, www.graemeharper.com/sites/international_centre/index.html (accessed 28 February 2012).

Literature Training www.nawe.co.uk/the-writers-compass.html (accessed 28 February 2012).

May, Steve, 'Teaching Creative Writing at Undergraduate Level: Why, how and does it work?' (Report on English Subject Centre sponsored research project, 2003), english.heacademu.ac.uk (accessed 28 February 2012).

McLoughlin, Nigel, *Database for Resources and Articles to the Theory of Pedagogy in Creative Writing*, www.english.heacademy.ac.uk (accessed 28 February 2012).

MOO Tools and Communities, www.Mootools.net and en.wikipedia.org/wiki/MooTools (accessed 28 February 2012).

National Association of Writers in Education (NAWE), www.nawe.co.uk, United Kingdom based (accessed 28 February 2012).

National Council of Teachers of English (NCTE), www.ncte.org (accessed 28 February 2012).

Research Assessment Exercise in United Kingdom (RAE), www.rae.ac.uk (accessed 28 February 2012).

Sheppard, Rob and Thurston, Scott, *Supplementary Discourses in Creative Writing Teaching in Higher Education*, English Subject Centre Website, www.english.heacademy.ac.uk (accessed 28 February 2012).

Transcultural Writing, www.transculturalwriting.com (accessed 28 February 2012).

Ubu Web at www.ubuweb.com (accessed 28 February 2012).

Wikipedia, www.en.wikipedia.org (accessed 28 February 2012).

WIKIs, www.projectforum.com/pf/wiki.html. This is a free and easy to use wiki provider (accessed 28 February 2012).

Creative writing pedagogy international journals

AAWP has an online peer-reviewed journal, *Text*, www.textjournal.com.au (accessed 28 February 2012).

AWP has a peer-reviewed journal, *The Writer's Chronicle*, details through www.awp-writer.org/magazine/index.htm (accessed 28 February 2012).

Creative Writing: Teaching Theory and Practice is a recent internationally peer-reviewed journal, details, www.cwteaching.com (accessed 28 February 2012).

NAWE has a peer-review journal, *Writing in Education*, details through www.nawe.co.uk (accessed 28 February 2012).

Index